Critical Theology

Questions of Truth and Method

Gareth Jones

PARAGON HOUSE
New York

First U.S. edition, 1995

Published in the United States by

Paragon House
370 Lexington Avenue
New York, NY 10017

First published in Great Britain by
POLITY PRESS LTD
65 Bridge Street, Cambridge CB2 1UR

ISBN 1–55778–729–8 hardcover
ISBN 1–55778–730–1 paperback

For Library of Congress Cataloging-in-Publication Data

The Library of Congress
Cataloging in Publication Division
Washington, DC 20540-4320
202-707-5000

... a critical theology, taking seriously the revelatory dimension of the gospel, could be our best safeguard against selling out completely to a 'religionless Christianity' which is no more distinguishable from secular humanism.

Hugh T. Kerr, Our Life in God's Light

Contents

Acknowledgements

It is a great pleasure to thank many people who have helped me over the last three years, and who have taken such an interest in my work that to fail to acknowledge their contribution would be a genuine sin of omission. Much of the preparatory reading for this book was done while I was Bampton Fellow at Keble College, Oxford, and although by no means all of that work found its way into the end product, I am very grateful to the Electors of the Fellowship, and to everyone at Keble College, for their support in the academic year 1990–1.

More pertinently, the book was written after I became lecturer in systematic theology at the University of Birmingham in 1991. I would like to thank all of my colleagues here for their convivial and stimulating support, and also the students of this University, who have heard various aspects of my thought in their different degree courses. Without a willing and critical audience I would not have been able to define as well as I hope I have what I mean by critical theology.

I also want to thank several people who have invited me to speak to various seminars and groups, both in Britain and overseas, and who have greatly assisted me in developing particular chapters of this text: George Lindbeck and Gerhard Sauter, for their invitations to lecture in Yale and Bonn respectively in 1990; Oliver O'Donovan, for the opportunity to speak at the political theology seminar in Oxford in 1991; Lewis Ayres, for inviting me to speak at his 'Reactions to Reason' seminar in Oxford, 1991; David Ford, for inviting me to address the systematic theology seminar in Cambridge, 1992; Barry Falk and Paul Joyce, colleagues both, for their invitations to my participation at the Birmingham Philosophy Society (1993) and Hermeneutics seminar (1992) respectively; and Marius Felderhof, for the chance to speak twice at the Open End in Birmingham, in 1992 and 1993. To all of these people, and those who attended the sessions, many thanks: I benefited greatly from your comments and observations.

A number of people have read either the complete manuscript or certain sections of it, and although I remain solely responsible for what is published, I would like to thank them for their ideas, questions and responses. In particular, I must acknowledge Helen Smith, Rowan and Jane Williams, Lewis Ayres, David Moss, Peta Dunstan, Ross Collins, Todd Breyfogle, Chris Rowland, Alison Griffin and Rachel Leather: though I have not always agreed with your views, I have learned a great deal from the way in which you have constructively addressed my work.

I should like to thank HarperCollins Publishers, Inc. for permission to quote from *The Crucified God* by Jurgen Moltmann, English translation copyright © 1974 by SCM Press Ltd and HarperCollins Inc.

I must also thank my editor, John Thompson, and everyone at Polity Press – and particularly my anonymous reader – for the sympathetic and efficient way in which they have responded to my questions and expedited the processing of this book. In my hitherto limited career I have had little experience of other publishers, but if any match Polity's combination of flair and commitment then they will indeed be an impressive establishment.

More domestically, I want to thank my father and mother who, each in their different ways, have kept me going over the last twenty months as I strove to complete this text. As throughout my life, they have not always understood the work with which I have been involved, but they have never questioned its importance to me. Without their help this book would not have been written.

Finally, but most importantly, I must thank Helen, who appeared out of (nearly) nowhere as I began to settle in Birmingham, and who has changed my own life even as she has managed her own – with wit, affection, care and friendship. I dedicate this book to Helen with love and gratitude; long may she keep me aware of the humility of which Socrates spoke, and which is so apposite to any writer or reader:

> If you are the same sort of person as myself, I will willingly go on questioning you; otherwise I will stop. If you ask what I mean, I am one of those people who are glad to have their own mistakes pointed out and glad to point out the mistakes of others, but who would just as soon have the first experience as the second; in fact I consider the first a greater gain, inasmuch as it is better to be relieved of very bad trouble oneself than to relieve another, and in my opinion no worse trouble can befall a man than to have a false belief about the subjects which we are now discussing (Plato, *Gorgias*).

Author's Note

I have employed the Harvard (author–date) system to reference quotations and citations, directing the reader to the bibliography for details of publication. The bibliography also includes several items which, though not specified in the body of the text, were of such importance for my thought that I could not fail to recognize them at that end point. I have also employed footnotes to mention issues which were not central to the thrust of my argument, but were otherwise significant.

Biblical quotations and citations are from/to the Revised Standard Version. There is no hidden agenda to my use of 'the Fourth Gospel' rather than 'the Gospel of John'.

Finally, I have used feminine pronouns throughout the text to identify 'the theologian' and 'the reader', and other such anonymous individuals. This is in line with my practice in *Bultmann: Towards a Critical Theology*, and is intended solely as a move towards more progressive academic language.

Introduction

But there are also many other things which Jesus did; were every one of them to be written, I suppose that the world itself could not contain the books that would be written (John 21:25)

What is 'critical theology'?

Critical theology is a theoretical argument concerning Christian talk about God in the contemporary world. As such, it is designed to achieve two aims. First, I want to identify a way of acknowledging the pluralism of modern society and culture – particularly the relationship between Christianity and other religions – whilst simultaneously reaffirming the central doctrines of the Christian faith. This I take to be the question of truth. Second, I want to find a way of moving from theoretical reflection upon transcendence and immanence to the practical concerns of talking about God in a specific context. This I take to be the question of method. *Critical Theology*, therefore, is a book about making certain traditional claims for the Christian faith in a situation which demands a new way of understanding and communicating those claims.

For these reasons, this book is intended for anyone who is thinking about the way in which theology as a discipline is functioning (or dysfunctioning) in the 1990s, and although my arguments are expressed in the terms and questions of western academic theological discourse, I have tried to write as openly and as straightforwardly as possible. The issues I am concerned with – how we understand religious language today, how talk about Jesus Christ makes sense of something greater than can be conceptualized in one story, how faith and theology address each other via increasingly diverse communication media, *what* exactly *can* be communicated with any confidence – are ones which challenge the widest possible audience: professional theologians and philosophers, clergy, and lay people. Although I have assumed a certain knowledge of theology in this century, the questions I address are ones to several different levels of discussion and appropriation. I write about arguments and ideas in order to stimulate debate rather than to achieve any degree of *closure*.

Why *critical* theology, however? I use this expression for three reasons. First, this book is a theoretical argument expressed as rationally as possible, and is therefore critical of the structure of Christian discourse about God. It is not intended to address specific, practical issues; rather, it is a conceptual framework within which such issues can subsequently be addressed more directly.[1] Second, my argument is modern rather than postmodern, and therefore acknowledges the critical presuppositions derived in modernity from Kant's work at the end of the eighteenth century. Consequently, although I want to address contemporary questions such as pluralism, I do so from this modern, critical viewpoint. Third, my theology is critical theology because it takes seriously God's eschatological revelation in Jesus Christ. This, like Barth, I take to be axiomatic for any genuinely Christian theology.

Critical *theology*, therefore, is definitely talk about God and so at root imaginative and speculative, an attempt to interpret and understand the Christian faith, its traditional doctrines and ideas, in a recognizable situation – western society. But anyone expecting to find in this book a comprehensive discussion of recent critical and social theory will be disappointed; although I acknowledge the importance of such research, this book is about how one might speak of the Christian God today, rather than an analysis of those developments and their significance for modern theology.[2] Similarly, anyone coming to this book presupposing a particular type of theology will be provoked and perhaps disappointed; my aim is to offer a new way of asking some old questions, and so requires a degree of openness on the part of the reader. I hope that this book offers the beginning of a new *theoria*, a new way of looking. It is not intended to answer the questions others might be asking, or to employ anyone else's language and vocabulary.

At the same time as offering something new, however, I want to argue that critical theology arises naturally and inevitably out of modern theology, which explains my book's basic structure. Part I is a series of readings of twentieth-century theologians designed to interpret certain questions central to my understanding of critical theology. These chapters are not intended to be comprehensive analyses of, for

[1] By making this distinction between theory and practice, I acknowledge immediately that I am working within a context and definition of traditional western, catholic systematic theology. It is not my concern to argue that other forms of theology – ones more immediately issue-based – are wrong, simply that this is my historical context, and my way of approaching theology.

[2] I am currently working on a book on theology and social theory for Polity Press, which is due for publication in 1997.

example, Barth's theology, or Rahner's, or Bonhoeffer's; rather, they address aspects of their work which are illuminating to my own argument. I am as aware as anyone of the difficulty of doing justice to their work in a series of short chapters; but as modern theology is my intellectual context, my themes need to be established in a discussion of these origins. Part I is intended to contextualize the ideas which I want to develop as critical theology, thereby establishing it within certain recognizable parameters.

Part II takes up and develops these *modern* themes in three constructive chapters, addressing what I take to be the three principal questions facing contemporary Christian theology (at least methodologically): first, how to relate Christian truth claims about God to a more general level of religious belief which makes room for the truth claims of other faiths; second, how to talk about Jesus Christ as God's act of revelation in a situation demanding new creative insights; third, how to address such an informed Christology to contemporary society. To conceptualize these issues, I develop the terminology of mystery, event and rhetoric in chapters 6–8. These terms shape everything I want to say about how Christian theology might function in contemporary society.

Mystery, event and rhetoric: initial definitions

In elaborating the concepts of mystery, event and rhetoric, it is simplest to begin with the notion of the Christ event. I define "Christ event" straightforwardly as the eschatological *meaning* of God's action in Jesus Christ – understood from incarnation to ascension[3] – interpreted in terms of its historical significance. The Christ *event*, consequently, is a Christological analogue: its purpose is to highlight the theological relevance of everything that faith claims occurred in and through Jesus of Nazareth, as inclusively as possible and without reducing that relevance to any single aspect of God's action in Christ (for example, its atoning significance). This analogical way of talking about Jesus Christ necessitates the interpretation and development of different images of that individual, because analogy works by reasoning from approximately parallel cases and therefore admits of no single interpretation.

[3] The significance of the doctrine of Christ's ascension, as the necessary counterpoint to the incarnation, is too often ignored by systematic theology (but see Carnley 1987, pp. 76–7). I am indebted to discussions with Ralph Norman on this particular question.

As the reader will see throughout this book, and particularly in chapter 7, this more progressive understanding of the Christ event, in which I acknowledge the inevitability of reconstructing an image of Jesus even as one indicates Christ's theological significance, dominates my entire argument; it is the neck of the hourglass through which every thought and concept must pass. This includes my other two signal concepts, 'mystery' and 'rhetoric'; for everything mysterious in Christian theology is revealed – and concealed – by Christ, and everything such theology wishes to address rhetorically to its social context must be shaped by Christ. Within this equation, however, there is room for further movement and definition.

I deploy the term 'mystery' as the first stage of my constructive argument because I want to establish everything I have to say as a Christian systematic theologian in the wider context of human religiosity, and hence in humanity's experience of being ultimately limited in and by this world. The point of mystery language, consequently, is not to obscure what might otherwise be a precise series of propositions, but rather to acknowledge that any explicit name one articulates for God – for example, 'Jesus Christ' – has to be contextualized in the far wider human activity of naming God in general. In one sense, of course, this relativizes Christian discourse; but it does so in order to preserve a vital point for both truth and method, namely that God cannot be conceptualized and thereby domesticated by any religion or theology. In holding to a stage of reflection upon mystery as religious symbol for God, to be interpreted analogically, chapter 6 maintains this axiom.

By deploying the term mystery I am appealing to the apophatic tradition in Christian thought, and I am influenced by its consideration in recent Roman Catholic theology (see Rahner 1966f). By distinguishing between mystery and event, however, I do not want to suggest that what Christ reveals is somehow different from Christ Himself; on the contrary, I want to maintain that mystery is event, from any Christian viewpoint. But the key idea here is viewpoint; for one of the most important aspects of the Christ event, though often overlooked, is that it does not reveal the mystery of God as *God*, but rather God *incarnate*. The incarnation, consequently, is both a liberating and yet a limiting event, with significant implications for how Christian theology speaks of grace as God's presence in the world (see chapter 7).

Christologically, this definition of mystery maintains what I take to be a correct understanding of the incarnation as both revelation and concealment, with two significant implications: first, that pluralism in Christology must be expected, because there is no one way of describing how the mystery of God is revealed in Jesus Christ (and no viewpoint from which such an absolute description could be regarded); and second, consequently, that the mystery of God cannot be exhausted by belief in God incarnate. The former, I argue, makes a space for a wide variety of valid images of Jesus (see chapter 7); the latter allows for the possibility – though Christian theology cannot explicitly discuss it – of salvation via other religions. I want to argue that for contemporary theology the latter is a necessary position to maintain.[4]

As chapter 6 will demonstrate, therefore, having 'mystery' in one's theological equation before explicitly Christological reflection necessarily relativizes what one has to say about the Christ event, which itself is an implication of God's grace being mediated through an incarnation rather than any other manifestation. Similarly, having a 'rhetorical' stage *after* one's Christological reflection argues against simply imposing a certain understanding of Jesus Christ upon every social context; it argues for a necessary, secondary mediation between the Word/word articulated theologically, and the situation in which its audition occurs. That mediation takes the form of Church as sacramental narrative, understood as flexibly as possible. And that rhetorical address is the effective channel via which contemporary theology is tested and applied to the world in which it lives.

It follows that I am using 'rhetoric' in a classical sense, as the art and/or technique of *persuasive* discourse; and, as I will argue in chapter 8, when it is understood in this way a number of interesting things arise which impinge upon contemporary theology's fascination with this term. It is essential that my definition of rhetoric in this book is clear: it is simply the second 'bell', necessary to complete the work of mystery as first 'bell' and of event as neck of the theological hourglass. Without such rhetorical address, theologians are left in the unenviable position of making simply oratorical statements to the already converted, a situation which reinforces the worst prejudices of both churches and societies about the certainty with which theology too often functions.[5]

[4] Here, evidently, I am influenced by John Hick's work, amongst others (see Hick 1989). Whereas Hick uses the expression 'the Really Real', however, I prefer 'mystery' as simpler, more flexible, and true to my own Christian heritage; it is indicative of the Anglican tradition, confirmed here as my own specific context.

[5] As Lewis Ayres has pointed out to me, this emphasis makes my theology 'liberal' rather than 'catholic', because I am arguing for the primacy of society at large as the arena of theological debate, rather than a church. I accept this point, but want to maintain that for contemporary theology – as previously throughout *modern* theology – it is that social context in which critical theology must operate and be tested – something which might help us to redefine the qualifier "catholic". See Milbank 1990 for a radically different argument.

Mystery, event and rhetoric: these three terms structure the way in which I think critical theology functions, and make a necessary distinction between the stages of reflection which occupy both modern and systematic theology. If one looks for a parallel in recent thought one might identify Nicholas Lash's symbolic, linguistic and institutional,[6] or perhaps von Balthasar's conceptuality of aesthetic, dramatic and logical. But my rationale for this distinction is to facilitate Tim Kerr's demand, that critical theology 'take revelation seriously'.[7] As the raw material which my mystery–event–rhetoric taxonomy seeks to understand and communicate, I now turn to this point.

'Taking revelation seriously'

The first thing to be said here is that 'taking revelation seriously' necessarily involves the Christian theologian in making truth claims about something he or she believes is *real*; on this I want to agree with Barth against theologians like Don Cupitt who attack theological realism. It seems to me that this is the only way of recognizing the eschatological quality of God's action in Jesus Christ, in which one confesses and witnesses as a believer that God's action in the world makes a definitive statement about that world. As Dalferth's marvellous essay (1989) makes clear, therefore, if Barth is an eschatological realist, it is because this necessarily acknowledges the particular character of God's revelation in Jesus Christ as the presence of eternity in time. This is why my theology is critical (*Krisis*) theology.

Naturally, such eschatological realism functions quite happily as the basis of much Christian faith and piety. Within a theological context, however – again, as Dalferth shows – it must be subjected to ontological, epistemological and semantic critique. When this occurs, what one finds is that 'taking revelation seriously' entails acknowledging

[6] Fergus Kerr (1979, p. 237) made the following illuminating comment on Nicholas Lash's inaugural address as Norris Hulse Professor in Cambridge: '[Lash] ... defines the work that he wants to do not as the philosophy of religion (MacKinnon's emphasis) but as what he calls *critical theology*. It is perhaps not unduly summary to say that this means systematic theology (a rarely practised enquiry in the ancient English universities) which is critical of its own grounds and disturbing to the faithful (a rare phenomenon in confessional institutions). The task of the critical theologian in this sense is – or would be – to reflect, theoretically and critically, upon the first-order levels of more or less spontaneous religious (in this case, Christian) existence as they are found in symbolic, linguistic, and institutional forms'.

[7] In his essay 'Time for a Critical Theology' (in Mulder 1979, p. 60) Hugh T. Kerr writes: 'a critical theology, taking seriously the revelatory dimension of the gospel, could be our best safeguard against selling out completely to a "religionless Christianity" which is no more distinguishable from secular humanism'.

the specific limitations which a confessional theory of truth place upon theological understanding and communication. It entails, consequently, an acknowledgement that confession cannot be reduced either to correspondence – because *eschatological* realism simply cannot be verified or falsified – or to consensus – because eschatological *realism* is not universally accepted as the most apposite way to speak of God's being and presence.[8]

If this is the case, then it follows that 'taking revelation seriously' involves the critical theologian in accepting certain methodological contraints upon her work, which shape her rhetoric, her Christology, and ultimately the way in which she speaks of God as the mystery of the world. Taking revelation seriously, on this understanding, makes theology an inexact science, one whereby its statements and claims are limited because of the limitations of God's confessed mode of self-revelation, namely incarnation. This consequently returns theology to the question of God's concealment, now with an eye to its methodological implications.[9]

All theology therefore originates in revelation; this much is axiomatic. Simultaneously, however, this means that all theology originates in concealment, and that thereby all theology originates in a tension between what is known and unknown. For this reason one cannot speak of theology as 'faith seeking knowledge', but rather 'faith seeking understanding' – Anselm's expression, implicit within which is his awareness of the mysterious origins of faith. Moreover, this acceptance of the unknown origins of faith and thereby theology makes it impossible for the theologian to regard her 'results' with any degree of certainty; for on the contrary, theology as an inexact science is founded upon the principle of uncertainty. Classically, this principle goes by the name of analogy. In everything that follows, therefore, I will be pursuing an analogical method to speak of God's mysterious revelation in Jesus Christ, and that analogy – elaborated in chapter 6, as a

[8] On this question of defining Christian truth, see Pannenberg 1991, pp. 8–17. I am not convinced that Pannenberg's answer satisfactorily recognizes the confessional theory of truth which is central to Christian theology, but he certainly discusses the issue more thoroughly than any other living systematic theologian.

[9] As will become clear as this book unfolds, and particularly in chapters 6 and 7, I want to deploy something very similar to Wittgenstein's theory of language games to explain how different theologies can be equally true, though they say very different things in very different contexts. I think I can do this partly because such a theory reflects what I take to be the linguistic situation of humanity as it struggles to communicate in a pluralistic world, and partly because of the understanding of revelation, truth and incarnation which I have elaborated in this Introduction. At bottom, therefore, it is a hermeneutic question (see Geffré 1987, pp. 59–64). I am indebted to discussions with John Hick and Michael Goulder on this issue.

direct result of the investigations of Part I – will direct and motivate the particular rhetoric I employ in chapter 8.

Why will my argument proceed in this way? First, because it is consistent with certain of the basic premises of the Christian tradition, and also of the Biblical witness: 'The wind blows where it wills, and you hear the sound of it, but you do not know whence it comes or whither it goes; so it is with every one who is born of the Spirit' (John 3:8).[10] Second, and as importantly, because I live and work in a social, political, economic and cultural context in which two things – Christian pluralism and interfaith dialogue – have paramount importance for the systematic theologian, a situation and challenge which I am happy to embrace, but which carries with it many responsibilities. It is not appropriate to elaborate my own position as an Anglican theologian in this context, where I am concerned with theoretical questions of truth and method; but it is important to acknowledge that I argue as I do *not* because I seek to relativize the Christian faith, or my own place within its theological tradition, but because I can identify no *a priori* viewpoint from which I can legitimately relativize any other religious tradition.[11] Such are the constraints of taking revelation seriously – that one takes seriously the profound limitations the Word of God places upon one's abilities to reflect its meaning and significance. Finally, all I have attempted in this book, systematically, is to work out the methodological implications of this fundamental and axiomatic truth.

[10] In an earlier draft I included some further material here on Jesus' encounter with Nicodemus, an interpretation which will now be included in the first volume of the *Christian Origins* series, edited by Lewis Ayres and myself (Routledge, in progress). In passing, however, I should acknowledge here the influence of two texts on my reflection: Goulder 1991 and Ashton 1991, particularly pp. 374–7.

[11] That I could identify *a posteriori* criticisms, particularly ethical ones relating to certain religious conduct, is of course a given. Hence, I can attack the behaviour of David Koresh and the Branch Davidian sect from the viewpoint of my own Christian faith, because I can argue that their conduct was unethical and resulted in tragic consequences; but I cannot say *a priori* that God did not communicate with David Koresh, and I cannot judge *a priori* the quality of Koresh's understanding of any such communication.

Part I

The Roots of Critical Theology in the Twentieth Century

1

Harnack and Barth, On First Principles: The Roots of Critical Theology in the Twentieth Century

1

Harnack and Barth: On First Principles

In the beginning was the Word, and the Word was with God, and the Word was God (John 1:1)

My general aim in Part I is to say something about the roots of critical theology in modern theology, thereby acknowledging the origins of my own way of speaking of God in the intellectual context in which I have grown up, and which I have studied. More specifically, I have chosen to begin Part I with a consideration of certain aspects of Karl Barth's work for two reasons: first, and notwithstanding the interesting question of Roman Catholic Modernism, for many people the story of twentieth-century theology originates with Karl Barth; and second, because Barth did indeed return modern theology this century to its proper debate about first principles, and thereby to the mysterious origins of God's Word of revelation, Jesus Christ. For both historical and theological reasons, consequently, any consideration of the roots of critical theology in the twentieth century must consider Barth's work.

Simultaneously, however, and because I want to write about critical theology's intellectual context, one must recognize Barth's own such world; and, in terms of the web of ideas and relationships from which he arose, the most important factor here is German liberal Protestantism, both because of the way in which it helped shape Barth's early work, and his strong reaction against it. In this sense it is an important truism that Barth's *Romans* project would have had far less impact, and far less meaning, without its tense relationship with liberal Protestant theology.

Given this, I have chosen to focus upon the encounter between Barth and Harnack in 1923, rather than an elaboration of the *Romans* books, for three reasons: first, the 1923 debate is far more precise a statement of Barth's position, and liberal theology's opposition, than one finds elsewhere; second, it is a good deal more interesting to examine Barth attacking another set of ideas, rather than producing a huge text; third, this encounter centres upon the key issue of first principles, of the origins of Christian theology, which establishes my concern for mystery. For these reasons, therefore, I want to consider the 1923 debate between Barth and Harnack as it speaks of certain questions of truth and method, prior to both Christological and ecclesial reflection. In this way I want to establish a set of guidelines which will direct my interpretation of the subsequent theologians in modern theology, discussed in the following chapters of Part I.

The Christian life

1923 in outline

The first explicit reference to the confrontation between Barth and Harnack was Barth's letter of 23 January 1923 to Thurneysen,[1] in which he wrote: 'Have you read Harnack's "Fifteen Questions" in *Die Christliche Welt*? As soon as it came to my attention I asked his excellency whether he had me in mind, in which case I would be ready to answer him blow by blow' (Busch 1976, pp. 127–8). Barth then quoted Harnack's reply to this question:

> My dear Colleague! I wrote down those questions six weeks ago on a sudden resolve and at *one* stroke, without literary preparation, on the basis of a whole complex of impressions which I have received during the last year, partly from books and essays, partly from conversations, and which have filled me with anxiety about the future of our scientific theology.... I have read only *one* article of yours (Busch 1976, p. 128).

On this correspondence, Barth commented to Thurneysen: 'So I used the *dies academicus* on 18th January to puzzle out the "Answers to Prof. von Harnack" and to get them on paper. They are, as Rade wrote me, already "on the press" and so will meet you shortly in *Die Christliche Welt*' (Busch 1976, p. 128).

This is the basis of the initial skirmish between Barth and Harnack in 1923. Additionally, however, there was a further communication from Harnack to Barth, which the latter repeated in a letter to Thurneysen of 18 May 1923. Harnack, as reported by Barth, wrote:

[1] Barth and Harnack had clashed previously, in 1920, at the Aarau Students Conference. Barth delivered a paper entitled 'Biblical Questions, Insights and Vistas', which received scant treatment from Harnack (see Busch 1976, p. 115).

> I have read the sermon that you were so kind as to send me, and I thank you very much for it. When I remark concerning it that I see in it an especially powerful and clear witness to a Christian experience that is not at all strange to me, yet that I can grant this experience no exclusive validity and must assert that it represents a stage of development that can and must be transcended ..., I realise that such a standpoint cannot be acceptable to you .... One must hold to the reality of history (Busch 1976, p. 144).

Harnack is clear: Barth's work is not theology. Rather, it is itself a phenomenon of the Christian religion, a witness to personal faith in the mystery of God, but one which in Harnack's opinion must be transcended, both historically and theologically. Theology for Harnack is a question of the scientific study of history itself, and the particular history of Christianity. From that study, and their education in and by it, people learn what they need to know about living in the world, in the service of God.

This debate's character, therefore, becomes quite apparent. It is not so much about the nature of the Christian God, or Christianity's perception and understanding of revelation, as about the way in which one can speak of that revelation's truth, of how one witnesses to God's mystery revealed in Jesus Christ. Barth's position in the *Romans* books was straightforward: revelation is real and transforms all human existence. Harnack's response, however, indicated above but elaborated in greater detail in the debate itself, is to marginalize Barth's statements and then argue that theology occupies a special level of discourse. If Barth is right, then Christian theology is solely about truth. If Harnack is right, then Christian theology is solely about method. But if they are both right, then Christian theology must speak of truth and method *together*. The debate turns upon how one responds to this issue.

Harnack's Fifteen Questions

Harnack's initial foray was entitled *Fifteen Questions to the Despisers of Scientific Theology*. Here, in summary, is Harnack's position (see also Rumscheidt 1989, pp. 85–7):

(1) Is there really only 'one' revelation, 'one' Bible? Is this true with respect to the great diversity of Christianity? If not, then do not Christians require historical criticism to clarify and understand their experience?

(2) Moreover, for an understanding of the Bible, do we not need both an inner openness, *and* historical knowledge and critical reflection?

(3) Is the experience of God different from the awakening of faith? If it is not, do we not need preaching guided by critical reflection to assist such faith and experience?

(4) If one makes a distinction between God and the world, even on the level of experience, how can one avoid a radical, quietist withdrawal from the latter?

(5) Additionally, how can one speak of God and the world as opposites, when the unison of the two is the core of the gospel? And how is this equivalence possible without the highest valuation of morality?

(6) If God and the world are opposites, how do you educate people to become better Christians?

(7) How do we protect society and culture from atheism, if God has nothing to do with society and culture?

(8) If one rejects the ideas of Kant, Goethe, and others, how do we save their culture from barbarism?

(9) But if the converse is true, and all culture is in the process of being overcome dialectically, how can one recognize this without historical-critical reflection?

(10) If the knowledge that God is love is the goal of religion, how can one deprive people of this goal by keeping them between door and hinge, by limiting them to what is a point of transition?

(11) If the Christian message is one of liberation, how can one erect barriers between God and what is good, true and beautiful? Should we not relate each to the other by means of critical reflection?

(12) And how can one preach a paradox? Surely one must preach against sin so as to overcome it?

(13) How can one wish to rebuke and destroy reason? Does this not lead to gnosticism?

(14) Linked to this, is critical reflection not necessary to identify a correct Christology, and to protect against the construction of an imagined Christ?

(15) Finally, is it not true that the only genuine theology is a scientific one? What persuasiveness and value belong to a theology which is not, fundamentally, scientific?

These are Harnack's original questions to the despisers of scientific theology. As he claimed in his letter, Harnack did not explicitly direct his questions against Barth; but it is certainly true that his remarks and arguments betray specific references to Barth's work, notably *Romans* II. The position of the individual between door and hinge, for example, is a clear reference to Barth's text, as are the remarks in questions 13 and 14 concerning the despisers' rejection of rationality and its consequences for Christology. Most significantly, however, the tone of Harnack's questioning is established by his initial remark concerning the unity of Bible and revelation, a clear reference to the foundation of Barth's entire position. In this respect, Barth's excited and aggressive response, as reflected in his letter to Thurneysen, is understandable.

But what is Harnack saying? Harnack is identifying, positively, a specific model of theology, and, negatively, criticizing a religious phenomenon for masquerading as theology. Positively, Harnack constructs a model of theology in which one identifies the basis of religion in the message of the gospel, then teaching this to people by relating it to the highest achievements of culture and society. Implicit in this model is the conviction, first, that education is the task of the theologian, and second, that society and culture have reached such a stage of development that one can speak of their goodness, truth and beauty in the same way that one speaks of the Christian religion. For Harnack it is axiomatic that historical research and critical reflection reveal that such a relationship between religion and culture is not only possible, but also what God actually wants, as expressed in Jesus' life and message. Harnack is not speaking of mystery at all, therefore, but rather *knowledge*, given by Jesus the teacher, which dispels all obscurity and mystery. This knowledge, and the God who reveals it in Jesus' is Harnack's first theological principle.

Negatively, Harnack rejects a position which regards Christianity, the Bible and revelation as solely one thing, namely the Word of God. This posits too much for Harnack, too reductively; Christianity is simply not like that, he argues. On the contrary, it is a *known* mystery, and the way it is known is in terms of its essence, identified by science and reason. This, moreover, is a right which has been won for humanity by its development since the Enlightenment. To ignore it is not simply obscurantist; it is also recognizably gnostic. Ultimately, argues Harnack, the theology which wants to speak of one, and only one, revelation, is the theology which regards itself as something akin to the keeper of a sacred flame. This is not a genuine theology; it is a false religion, one which turns true knowledge into ignorance and which, as such, must be resisted.

Barth's Fifteen Answers

Barth's response to this challenge was immediate, and by May 1923 the debate was fully engaged. In his answers to Harnack's original questions, Barth gives one of the most succinct statements of the first principles of his theology. Here, in summary, is its content (see also Rumscheidt 1989, pp. 87–91):

(1) Simply because one rejects the contemporary scientific theology does not mean that one despises scientific theology *per se*. If the one revelation is the subject of theology, then its 'scientific' character can only be the recollection that its object was once subject and must become so ever again.
(2) Moreover, inner openness and critical reflection may be equally help or hindrance; but it is the *Spirit* which moves faith, not a faculty of humanity, whichever it might be.
(3) The experience of God is completely different from faith, therefore. Nor does faith arise through preaching. On the contrary, preaching arises through faith; and the task of preaching is at one with the task of theology. Critical reflection is simply preparatory to this task.
(4) The cross is the utter contrast between God and the world and cannot be avoided, and so a radical protest against the world by the Christian cannot be avoided. This is the meaning of a correct understanding of the doctrine of creation.
(5) Similarly, the coordination of the love of God and the love of humanity reveals the utter distinction between the old creation and the new. God takes life before God gives it; that is what love means.
(6) And that is why theology has nothing to do with education: one can only come to God via the cross and resurrection, not via a taught understanding.
(7) Again, statements about culture and society, in relation to the experiences of God, may have a certain relevance; but this is not the meaning of the gospel. What they achieve is always a contingent question, interesting perhaps, but not directly relevant to faith.
(8) Rather, real statements about God are ones which proclaim revelation and judgement, instead of culture and religion. The question of barbarism with respect to Kant and Goethe, raised by Schleiermacher, is therefore simply irrelevant.
(9) It follows that one may be able to identify a dialectical development within the sphere of culture and society; but in God's truth there is only an Either/Or. The way from the old to the new creation is not a stairway; it is a being born anew.
(10) If knowledge of God is knowledge of the highest, how can one

claim to be in possession of it? Faith is always also unfaith; we are saved in hope, not knowledge.

(11) Similarly, the relationship between God and what we *call* good, true and beautiful, is one of *Krisis*, not continuity. Only in the light of the cross can one see and understand the truth about such things.

(12) This is unfortunately simply the case: the fact that God wills to save a fallen world unworthy of salvation is a paradox. A genuine theology, and not a spectator one, must walk in curious ways.

(13) When such a spectator theology walks in what is familiar, rather than what is terrifying and unclear, it results simply in a psychology of feeling and a secularized philosophy of religion. This can be seen in contemporary theology.

(14) For this reason, the basis of Christology can only be faith. Critical reflection and historical research do indeed provide certain foundations; but they are not God's, and so they are not part of Christology proper. The task that historical-critical research can undertake for theology is to frighten people into understanding the otherness of the gospel.

(15) Finally, this can only mean that science must be the servant of theology; it cannot be a relationship between equals. Or should the present fortuitous *opinio communis* of others really be the instance through which we have to let our work be judged as to its 'persuasiveness and value'?

The sole focus of Barth's statement is the revelation of God's will in Christ; anything else, which might pass for religion on the basis of reason and knowledge, is not revelation. The task of theology, therefore, is the task of preaching; to show people, in faith, that there is only one genuine question, and only one genuine answer: Jesus Christ, crucified and risen, in whom people live anew in the power of the Spirit. This is the mystery of nature and grace. Any other question, no matter how interesting and how illuminating for our understanding of the world, is irrelevant to God. Barth thus rejects any notion that theology is education, which though rightly regarded as one aspect of the daily life of the Church, has nothing to do with the primary proclamation of the gospel.

The difference between Harnack and Barth is therefore clear. The former regards the gospel as a pedagogic message, of teaching the individual to be a better person, restoring them to the image of God as they are justified by Jesus's death and resurrection. In this sense the task of theology is to understand the message that is to be taught, to analyse its historical foundations, and to facilitate its communication. One might say for Harnack that theology is concerned with articulating a message which can be understood and rationalized by and for people as they live their lives culturally and socially. It is building upon God's achievement in Christ, and in so far as that work is ultimately mysterious, so faith is concerned with knowledge of mystery; but it is *knowledge*.

For Barth this is simply nonsense. Or rather: it is sin. Jesus Christ is not a teacher of religion, dispensing practical advice and assistance to those in need of development. Jesus Christ is the eschatological prophet, messiah, the Son of God, the Word. Barth's Christology is reductive, which for Barth must be understood positively: the 'Christ event' is one of salvation which is the decisive turning-point not of history (that was the mistake of *Romans* I), but of the world and everyone in it. This event *is* mystery, *in toto*, and so everything that is immanent in God, argues Barth, is always economic; i.e. revealed in the incarnation of the Word.[2] By contrast with Harnack, who regards Jesus of Nazareth as another human being, albeit supremely religious (*pace* Schleiermacher), about whom one can discover many things so as to understand his message and significance, Barth understands 'the Christ' by analogy with his soteriological model. The dependence here upon Reformation theology, in particular Melanchthon's famous dictum that 'to know Christ is to know his benefits', is striking.[3]

The debate between Barth and Harnack continued in *Die Christliche Welt* during the summer of 1923: Harnack wrote an open letter on Barth's initial answers, which is a model of clarity; Barth responded with his own open letter to Harnack, which is less elegant. Finally, Harnack broke off the exchange quite abruptly: 'To my disappointment I cannot continue the discussion now and in this journal, since the number and weight of the problems are too great to be dealt with briefly and in this place' (Rumscheidt 1972, p. 52). Nevertheless, the debate raised five important questions, which I now want to consider in the following order. What is: the message of the gospel?; the scope of Christology?; the meaning and place of religion?; the task of theology?; the role of education in that task?

I will consider these questions in turn, developing a clear impression of how mystery appears in the light of the Harnack–Barth debate.

[2] On the identity of the immanent and economic in Barth, see Roberts 1991, pp. 35–7 (although Roberts does not employ this terminology, the point is made); see also Sykes 1979, pp. 17–54; Winzeler 1982, pp. 187–90; Bochmuehl 1988a.

[3] The same is also true of Harnack, of course, though to a lesser degree. On the relationship between the origins of Lutheranism and modern theology, see Beyer 1992.

In so doing, it is not my intention to arrive at a final judgement concerning who 'won'. Rather, I want to identify certain specific parameters relevant to the rest of this book, which will help to shape my understanding of the way in which mystery can function as the first principle of theology, and how these ideas are established early in the twentieth century. The process is cumulative, and no one answer to any of these questions can be taken to be normative; but together they go some way towards preparing the ground not only for the subsequent chapters in Part I, but also for chapter 6, on mystery itself.

Mystery as first principle

One other way of viewing the Harnack–Barth debate, of course, is to see it as a disagreement about authority; for first principles are authoritative, otherwise they have no claim to priority. Harnack understands reason and scientific analysis as the ultimate authority of modern theology because these things dispel mystery (in the sense of confusion) and reveal God's will regarding human conduct, as first expressed in the life and teaching of Jesus of Nazareth. Barth, by contrast, understands mystery itself as the ultimate authority of any theology of the Word, because *this* mystery is eschatological, and therefore something other than this-worldly. For Harnack, first principles in theology are methodological, because they govern one's procedure; for Barth they are true, because they are pre-existent with the Word. As will be demonstrated, this divide informs the entire development of modern theology since 1923, and remains instrumental for any understanding of the present state of the discipline.[4]

The message of the gospel

Significantly, the Scriptural authority that Harnack and Barth appeal to is, respectively, Synoptic and Pauline. In itself this difference demonstrates the fundamental distinction between Harnack and Barth: the former regards the gospel as something *taught* by Jesus; the latter understands it as an *event* revealed in Christ, proclaimed ever anew as Christ crucified and risen. In terms of the message of the gospel, one can say that for Harnack it is a call to a new way of life; for Barth, by

[4] Importantly, the Christological distinction here is that between 'above' and 'below'; i.e. the viewpoint from which one approaches the task of speaking of God's presence in Jesus Christ. On this question, see Lash 1980.

contrast, it is a new life, a new creation in Christ (II Cor. 5:17). Both men agree that the gospel is of ontological importance for humanity; but they disagree radically about how that importance is to be understood, communicated, and appropriated by both individual and society.

The importance of this disagreement is emphasized in Harnack's response to Barth's own initial reply, his *Open Letter*:

> Your sentence '... the gospel has as much and as little to do with barbarism as with culture ...' can be understood only as a radical denial of every valuable understanding of God within the history of man's thought and ethics .... Does this not exclude the belief that one's being a Christian happened ... on a stairway on which eternal values had already been given? Remember Augustine's account of his becoming a Christian! (Rumscheidt 1972, pp. 37–8).

For Harnack the gospel is itself a message to humanity which makes sense of humanity's ethical beliefs, because the gospel is the expression of God's will for humanity, in such terms that humanity can understand and realize it. Harnack's interpretation of the gospel regards it as being continuous with human reflection upon such ethical concerns, so that a progressive evolution in the individual's – and by extension, society's – conduct occurs, rather than a decisive, once-and-for-all shift achieved by external force.

Barth rejects this continuity because it leads to idolatry. He argues that it is impossible to elevate anything human, be it salvation history, as in *Romans* I, or reason and morality, as in Harnack's *What is Christianity?* (1957), to such pre-eminence. It is God alone – the Unknown God – who wills to save the world. This is the message of the gospel; it is one of discontinuity, of *paradox*. This is what Barth means by mystery:

> The Scriptures themselves witness to revelation. One does not have to believe it, nor *can* one do it. But one should not deny that it witnesses to revelation, *genuine* revelation that is, and not to a more or less concealed religious possibility of man but rather to the possibility of God, namely that he has acted under the form of human possibility – and this is *reality* (Rumscheidt 1972, p. 44).

Barth argues that there can be no sense in which the individual is capable of moving independently *from* this world *to* God. Nor can any one do this with the assistance of a *taught* gospel, as Harnack claims. Rather, the gospel is an Either/Or: one falls, with the old creation, or rises, as the new. This is the mystery of faith as grace, as pure gift: revealed and concealed in Christ, attested to in Scripture, it comes directly from the darkness of God's being and is for Barth, thereby, the sole mediation of something entirely Other than this world. Unlike Harnack, therefore, who regards mystery in human terms, as something irrational which hinders humanity's exercise of reason, and which scientific theology dispels, Barth understands mystery as the first principle of theology. It is its genuine source, and as such exercises a determining authority over all its subsequent expressions. Mystery as grace becomes the structuring power of Barth's entire theology, because the presence of God is mediated solely through Jesus Christ.

If, by contrast, one follows Harnack at this point, one regards the gospel as the new covenant, replacing the old. It is a new ethical code revealing and facilitating a new life for humanity, replacing the old Law which had been given to Moses. Harnack's position is intelligible as ethical monotheism; Jesus is not so much the new Adam as the new Moses. His theology, therefore, if it is to be consistent, must centre upon the communication of this covenant, and the teaching of he who brought it. This Harnack achieves, most famously, in *What is Christianity?*[5]

There is obvious Biblical support for Harnack's position. Matthew's Gospel, for example, presents such an understanding of the gospel, and Matthew 5–7 is perhaps the best evidence for regarding the gospel as a new covenant, replacing the old Law (see Gerhardsson 1982, pp. 32–60). This interpretation of the gospel, moreover, is advantageous to theologians like Harnack because it leads directly to concerns about its religiosity, practicality and efficacy. Simply, a gospel which is primarily an ethical code presents the individual with a very clear path, with definite guidelines leading to definite results. As Harnack might have observed, a paradox, such as Barth's, does not help one to live well and religiously.

The problem with such an interpretation, as Barth recognized, is that it domesticates the presence of eternity in the world; it reduces the question of eschatology, of God's will and action to save humanity, to a matter of right conduct. Barth argued that this was simply wrong, because it meant abandoning belief in the Otherness of God so as to affirm the relevance of religious experience and behaviour on behalf

[5] The problem of course, is that Harnack's way of understanding Jesus effectively makes Christianity the new 'chosen people' and, more importantly, a German interpretation of their status becomes normative through liberal Protestantism. Though he dies before the rise to power of Hitler, therefore, there is at least a sense in which his work is implicated in the prejudicial ideology of German Christianity which lead to the evils of national socialism (see Ericksen 1985).

of humanity's perceived qualities. Mystery cannot be reduced to something accessible in the world, argues Barth, even if it is something good and attractive which people agree sounds like the life which God might desire for humanity.

Harnack's retort to this is that Barth's Otherness cuts God adrift from the world, leaving humanity isolated:

> By answering my questions like this, in terms of what Christianity still lacks and of what we all know, you shatter what we already possess, for you make the Christian's confidence ... in which he is allowed to live, an illusion, and his joy, which is to fill his life, you turn into frivolity (Rumscheidt 1972, p. 38).

'Definitely', replies Barth; for this is what the gospel achieves, the destruction of all worldly certainty. But, writes Barth: 'I do not sever; I do repudiate every continuity between hither and yonder. I speak of a dialectical *relation* which points to an *identity* which cannot be established nor, therefore, presumed by us' (Rumscheidt 1972, p. 49). Again, it is this identity in difference that constitutes for Barth the authentic mystery of faith. Mystery and the Christ event are brought into complete union in Barth's early theology, a structure which can be identified in far more fluent and developed form throughout Barth's three efforts at dogmatic theology, where the identity of the economic and immanent, of what is *revealed* and *concealed*, is pivotal to his position's exposition.[6]

The distinction between Harnack and Barth on the question of the message of the gospel, therefore, concerns the relationship between time and eternity, this world and God; it is on this question – of eschatology – that the debate turns. It is a matter of which interpretation – Harnack's ethical code or Barth's dialectic of revelation – preserves the eschatological nature of the gospel. Here, there can be no doubt: Harnack's testimony is inconsistent with the thoroughgoing eschatology of the New Testament, and of the gospel itself. Eschatology is, as Barth attested, concerned with the real presence of something Other and if this is ignored, or argued away, then the first principles of Christian faith (and so theology) disappear.

This does not mean that Barth's own interpretation is entirely correct, even though he does recognize the priority of eschatology in the gospel (see Introduction above). The disquieting thing is why Barth regards the eschatological gospel as the sole subject of theology *per se*,

[6] This can be seen at different stages in each of Barth's three dogmatic projects: see Barth 1991, pp. 131–67; 1982a, pp. 64–8; 1957, pp. 179–204.

when it is clearly the motor of religious belief and practice, to which theology cannot be reduced. The gospel is an eschatological message of hope and salvation; but it is only so understood in, by and through faith, which is religious and therefore part of the relationship and experience of and between individual, community and God. There is a confusion, consequently: having identified correctly the message of the gospel, Barth expresses it solely as an absolute statement, when in truth it must be more fluid and subtle, able to generate and support differing theological arguments. In so doing he undermines his theology's ability to speak of the mystery of faith in anything other than Biblocentric terms, which is unsatisfactory because it is not the way people actually live. All of the pressures in Barth's theology are ultimately to conform to one single understanding of what God wants for humanity, pressures which crush and distort the *per accidens* distinctions which one finds in social and practical contexts. In this respect, mystery for Barth does not pervade human existence; it dominates it utterly.

The scope of Christology

The place where one would expect to witness these pressures to conform, at least in terms of Christian doctrine, is Christology, because the production of solely one image of Jesus Christ, as the medium by which God and humanity are joined, is generated by a particular understanding of the way in which people should relate to God. The real question with respect to Christology, then, is its scope: how much latitude is it allowed to communicate divine mystery, and how much scope may its recipients be allowed to interpret that image for themselves?

The disagreement between Harnack and Barth on this question can be succinctly expressed. In his open letter to Barth, Harnack writes:

> my suspicions are heightened because of the context in which you use the Pauline 'we know Christ no longer according to the flesh'. So, we do not know the historical Jesus Christ of the gospels any more? How am I to understand that? By the theory of the exclusive inner word? Or by which of the many other subjectivistic theories? (Rumscheidt 1972, p. 37).

Harnack's argument is straightforward: what becomes of Jesus of Nazareth in Barth's Christology of a Christ 'event'? It is because Harnack holds true so positively to Jesus, that he devotes so much attention to the question of the exegesis and interpretation of history. For Harnack, it is Jesus himself who teaches us about mystery, who removes mystery (and confusion) by the perfection of his message.

Barth's retort to Harnack is precise: 'The definite article before "Christ" is of no consequence to me at all' (Rumscheidt 1972, p. 42). Despite this reply, however, the suspicion remains that Barth has reduced the question of Christology to a moment of incarnation, meaning crucifixion and resurrection, but that there is no sign then of the historical life of Jesus of Nazareth. In this one detects the Hegelian undertones within Barth's theology generally, and the two editions of *Romans* in particular, where 'event' seems to be reduced to 'concept', *Begriff* (see Findlay's preface to Hegel 1977b, pp. vii–xii). With that, the question of whether Barth's 'mystery' and 'event' are in any way Christian, or simply philosophical, becomes urgent; for the real question here is how, practically, the individual and community appropriates this tense identity of the economic and immanent within its own existence. How can one answer Jesus' question: 'Who do you say that I am?' (Mark 8:29), if the sole permissible vocabulary seems to be reductively conceptual?[7]

Given Barth's own religious presuppositions his emphasis here is intelligible, echoing the tenor of *Romans* II: God the Wholly Other, revealed in Christ, for judgement. This is not an understanding of the gospel which requires a detailed discussion of the life of Jesus, even though Barth would want to assert that the historicity of Jesus' earthly life is always presumed. As stated, *the* Christ is Christ crucified and risen, proclaimed and then encountered as God's Word of judgement:

> According to this testimony, the Word became flesh, God himself became a human-historical *reality* which took place in the *person of Jesus of Nazareth*. But from this it by no means follows for me that this event can also be an object of human-historical *cognition*; this is excluded because and in so far as *this* reality is involved. The existence of a Jesus of Nazareth, for example, which can of course be discovered historically, is not *this* reality (Rumscheidt 1972, pp. 44–5).

Harnack, conversely, cannot believe or accept that faith arises without a personal encounter with the historical individual, Jesus of Nazareth. One may wish to clarify the level upon which this encounter

[7] I will develop this argument more fully in chapter 7, there explicitly in relation to the problems of Christology. Here I am really addressing a perceived lack in Barth's early work, though it serves to illustrate the most obvious criticism of language about 'mystery' and 'event', i.e. that it is essentialist.

occurs, argues Harnack, and how one interprets it; but the Christian *religion* begins and ends with the declaration of Peter at Caesarea Philippi, which would be meaningless without the figure of Jesus himself before Peter. Harnack's ethics, his understanding of society and the conduct of the individual within it, his understanding of *politics*: this is governed by a personal relationship between two people, one of whom is the Son of God. It is unsurprising, then, that his theology, as a form of social theory, should so resemble liberal anthropology and its origins in Kant's philosophy.

It is here that the Harnack–Barth debate focuses upon one of the key issues of critical theology, namely its spirituality, the degree to which mystery *per se* is felt and experienced, individually and socially, independently of its revelation in Christ. Granted that Barth rejects religion completely, in favour of an either/or, yet one recognizes in his work (particularly *Romans* II) an implicit understanding of the Christian religion: it is one of audition and witness, encounter, decision and judgement, which Barth identifies with the eschatological framework of the gospel. Barth thereby attends to the fact that the gospel comes first to the individual, of whom is demanded decisive action and commitment as, almost simultaneously, such action and commitment are demanded of society as a whole. Both Harnack and Barth, for all of their difference, agree on one thing: God in Christ as gospel and judgement, and subsequently as kerygma and teaching, confronts the individual with life and death.[8]

It would seem to be Harnack rather than Barth, however, who has understood the next, necessary stage of the Christian religion, the move from the individual to the collective, in which more is revealed sacramentally than solely in the Christ event and its immediate ramifications. Barth's argument on this question seems astonishingly crude: his bald assertion is that the gospel comes first to the individual, but that it is the world *in toto* which is judged. This may be correct; but it leaves no room for the role and position of the individual in her own community to be developed socially and culturally, as is demanded in modern society. The individual is simply judged: participation or otherwise in a specific collective does not arise as a separate problem for Barth.[9] The pressures to conformity in Barth's

[8] I think the important point here is whether one thinks this shift occurs 'simultaneously' or 'almost simultaneously'. If the former, then the gospel is really a social message. If the latter, then the possibility of a Protestant distinction between faith and works is preserved. I think at heart both Barth and Harnack want to maintain the latter understanding, contrary to the thesis of those who regard Barth's work as inherently political.

theology, and specifically his Christology, too quickly reduce the gulf between the individual and the communal to insignificance.

Harnack, by contrast, confronts the individual with a gospel which leads her directly to her community, on the basis of certain specific ethical directives. For Harnack the primary concern is to understand the nature of Christian spirituality – of the way in which one responds to mystery socially and individually, both with and without the Christ event – as one in which the individual is called and judged, certainly, but in which this judgement leads inexorably to participation in a particular situation. One may wish to question certain of Harnack's theological statements; but his understanding of the spiritual nature of the Christian religion in terms of this relationship between individual and community is secure.

Ultimately, it is Barth's failure to reflect upon the nature of Christianity as an eschatological spirituality, rather than simply an eschatological event, which makes it difficult for his theology in the 1920s to say much that is practical or even effective.[10] In terms of my understanding of critical theology, consequently, it is Harnack rather than Barth who reveals a fundamental principle: that the Christian religion requires Jesus *of Nazareth*, not solely a Christ *event*, but that, paradoxically, it is instrumental to Jesus' own mission and message that he points beyond himself, towards a reality to which even the *incarnate* Son is not entirely equal (which is why theology requires the doctrine of the Trinity). The economic is not, therefore, precisely the same as the immanent; there must be room, socially and individually, for faith to respond to Jesus by moving away from Jesus. This is fundamental to the entire process of creating and interpreting images of Jesus; and, whilst it does not endorse Harnack's own Christology, it does reveal the scope of Christology to be much wider than in either of Barth's two *Romans*. Spirituality must be the passage which connects mystery and event. In so far as Barth overlooked this, his theology remained strangely uncritical both of the Christian message, and the contingencies of the world it addresses.[11]

[9] McFadyen (1990, pp. 57–8, 279–80) has reacted against this (implicitly) with considerable clarity and imagination, recognizing in the later Barth a fuller understanding of the status of the personal.

[10] This is paradoxical, given the heavy emphasis Barth laid upon his preaching 'in the Spirit' in his early ministry and publishing career – the point being, however, that simply claiming the Holy Spirit is not the same thing as spirituality (see Freyer 1982 and Rosato 1981).

[11] The interesting parallel here is between Barth and Rahner on the identity/difference of immanent and economic (see Marshall 1987; see also chapter 6 below).

The meaning and place of religion

These arguments about spirituality, about what it is to be religious and therefore to have faith, are pivotal to the 1923 debate, and also to the immediate background to Barth's writings of this period, since *Romans* II is dominated by his condemnation of religion. In terms of the history of ideas, one can limit this to a rejection of the tradition of romanticism in Christian philosophies which had its origin in the work of Friedrich Schleiermacher, specifically his *On Religion: Speeches to its Cultured Despisers* of 1799 (see Schleiermacher 1988), which in turn was heavily influenced by Kant's post-Enlightenment moral philosophy (see Velkley 1989). This history of ideas approach has the support of Barth himself, who on numerous occasions condemned a dependence upon religious feeling or experience and an intuition of the Absolute. One recognizes Barth's rejection of this understanding of religion in his debate with Harnack as being something entirely intelligible within that historical milieu.

There are other abstractions of religion which Barth, similarly, would wish to reject. For Barth the crucial point is that it is not given to humanity to proclaim abstractions, but to address the concrete reality of the Word and the world's judgement. Simultaneously, however, Barth implicitly affirms *one* religious model; i.e. the sermon and its audition within an ecclesial context. Granted that for Barth the task of theology is the same as the task of preaching, yet his emphasis upon the audition of stories about God's revelation in Christ for the judgement of the world, occurring within a church and at the hand of a minister, is a religious model.[12] What happens is that Barth's model squeezes the life out of religion, catching it between an absolute understanding of the gospel (which is correct), and an authoritarian model of theology (which is not). What results is an attenuated understanding of religion in which the relationship between the individual and the collective – which is *the* ecclesiological question, and therefore fundamental to theology – is reduced to the existential moment of decision, in which the individual lives or dies, rejecting religion entirely as the false offering of the devil.

Despite Barth's strictures, however, there are other models of religion which theology must consider when addressing the question of mystery. Given that Barth is correct to emphasize a gospel of revela-

[12] The conflation of theology and religion which occurs here in Barth's thought should not be allowed to obscure this basic fact. Barthian theology has for too long propagated the untruth that its position is entirely a–religious, as if this were possible within the Christian faith.

tion and judgement, correct to condemn a purely subjective understanding of religion, but wrong to reduce the question of religion to a model of sermon, audition and decision, what are the possibilities? Here, Harnack provides a way forward. At the very end of his exchanges with Barth, Harnack writes:

> There is no future... in the attempt to grasp a 'Word' of this kind as something so purely 'objective' that human speaking, hearing, grasping, and understanding can be limited from its operation.... But since for centuries it has again and again been presented, the only thing to change is its background, it may be justified individually and must, therefore, be treated with respect. *But can it create a community and are the blows justified with which it beats down everything which presents itself as a Christian experience*? (Rumscheidt 1972, p. 53; my italics).

Can Barth's theology move from the individual to the collective?; can it address, persuade and construct?; can it be *rhetorical*, in my sense? Harnack's answer is 'No', because Barth fails to appreciate the breadth, range and sheer catholicity of the Christian religion. There is no genuine rhetoric in Barth's theology, argues Harnack, solely oratory, because Barth has no spiritual basis upon which to speak of the way in which the individual and society are moved, separately and together, to *be* Christian.[13] Barth has solely a reductive, destructive Word, which when uttered demolishes the very world in which humanity has to live. As Harnack observes, this is so unhistorical as to be an unhelpful way of considering the place of Christianity within a world where mystery itself is emphatically *not* regarded solely in Christological terms.

This would seem to be the crucial point on this question. Without accepting Harnack's own, constricted understanding of religion, one can still acknowledge that Barth's position removes from Christianity many of its traditional bases and foundations. Where are the sacraments in Barth's early theology?; worship and liturgy?; experience and emotion?; ethical conduct and good works?; spirituality? They are noticeable only by their absence. By moving directly from gospel to sermon, Barth demands an unworkable hermeneutic: the direct, unmediated proclamation of the Word. This cannot be the necessarily mediated foundation of Christian theology which, rather, must be identified in a spiritual understanding of mystery, *before* moving on to Christology. Without this theology itself is reduced to the construction of a system of knowledge as, arguably, one finds in Barth's *Church*

[13] One of the most interesting passages written on this aspect of Barth's theology is Ralph C. Wood's chapter 'Barth's Evangelical Theology of Culture' (1988, pp. 57–79).

Dogmatics. This is the gnostic danger which Harnack identified in Barth's theology as early as 1920 and which Barth rejected, even as he unwittingly embraced it.

As Harnack recognized, therefore, the authentic proclamation of the gospel is initially a religious matter; it must be, not only because it is concerned with concrete situations within Church, but also because it addresses the fundamentally spiritual nature of humanity:

> The task of preaching is the pure presentation of the Christian's task as a witness to Christ. You [Barth] transform the theological professorship into the pulpit ministry....On the basis of the whole course of church history I predict that this undertaking will not lead to edification but dissolution (Rumscheidt 1972, p. 36).

Harnack's statement, though couched in the analysis of a church historian, is acute: Barth is not a theologian, in Harnack's sense, because he does not give sufficient attention to the diversity and profundity of Christianity, operating instead with an attenuated understanding of the relationship between individual and Church. Indeed, Barth himself is a religious phenomenon. Harnack writes 'Would it not be better for him to admit that he is playing *his* instrument only and that God has still other instruments, instead of erecting a rigid Either/Or?' (Rumscheidt 1972, p. 53).

Developing Harnack's argument, however, one can say that to name Barth a religious phenomenon is *not* a reductive statement. On the contrary, it recognizes Barth's stature as the most significant Christian religious prophet since Martin Luther in the sixteenth century. But simultaneously it must place some limitation upon the scope of Barth's work. *Romans*, in either of its guises, is not a work of critical theology; on this one must be clear. It is, rather, a text produced by faith and for faith. One might certainly recognize in it the power and work of the Holy Spirit, even to the extent of the *testimonium Spiritus Sancti internum*; but this does not make it critically theological. If Harnack is correct, Barth's reductive drift actually endangers theology by making it impossible for the theologian to escape from the straitjacket of an authoritarian understanding of Christianity. Granted the magnificent clarity of Barth's statement of the gospel's essence, people are still people; they are, and alway will be, spiritual *before* they hear sermons and encounter the Christ event. It is the task of theology not only to recognize this fact, but also to build upon it rhetorically.[14]

[14] This is the point at which Rahner's theology is superior to Barth's, because of its explicit recognition and understanding of the slides between mystery, event and rhetoric (though always regarded from the viewpoint of grace); see chapter 3 below.

The task of theology

What, then, is the task of theology? If it is to be *critical* theology, its task is to reflect upon the mystery and event of Christianity, guided by faith, hope and love, and working thereby to understand and educate rhetorically believers as to the implications of their faith, hope and love. Or, in more Biblical terms: to wait, in faith and hope, for the coming of the Lord, at all times watching for the signs of the times (see Mark 13:4). Critical theology is an eschatological occupation, on the borderlands of faith and society, as Barth realized; but eschatology is no longer a simple business, and Barth's error was to think it was.[15]

It should be acknowledged that neither Barth nor (even) Harnack would agree with this definition of the task of theology. At one point in his open letter to Barth, Harnack writes: 'You say that "the task of theology is at one with the task of preaching"; I say that the task of theology is at one with the task of science in general' (Rumscheidt 1972, p. 36). As far as theological method is concerned, Harnack depends upon science, with all of the empirical and objective criteria which it employs. Barth rejects this, because theology must be more than merely a rehearsal of established facts if it is to *mean* anything.

Granted, however, that critical theology must build upon a spiritual understanding of mystery and how people are aware of this in their lives, after Harnack, and that these foundations are named for Christianity as the gospel of event and judgement, after Barth, what then can be the methodology and structure of a critical theology? Or, better: how does critical theology undertake its task? Both Harnack and Barth supply their own answers to this question. For Harnack theology functions as an historical science; it establishes facts, judges them, and then presents them to the waiting public:

> You see in contemporary scientific theology an unstable and transitory product which has been in the making since Pietism and the Enlightenment and that it has the value of an *opinio communis* only. I see in it the only possible way of grasping the object epistemologically (Rumscheidt 1972, p. 36).

Barth, in contrast, regards the 'scientific' character of theology solely in terms of its ability to express the Word of God anew to believers.

[15] In this respect, I am almost inclined to agree with postmodern commentators who argue that the twentieth century constitutes a decisive loss of innocence for humanity, and that consequently one can now speak of the eschatological nature of existence from a secular viewpoint. This is a complexity which critical theology must address rhetorically; see chapter 8 below.

Barth writes, therefore, in his answers to Harnack's original questions, that: 'The "scientific character" of theology... [is] its adherence to the recollection that its object *was once subject* and must become that again and again, which has nothing to do whatever with one's "heuristic knowledge" and "experience" in themselves' (Rumscheidt 1972, p. 32).

There is no similarity at all between these views. What this means for the present chapter is that a way beyond Barth and Harnack must be discovered if a deeper understanding of critical theology is to be identified in the structure and dynamic of the 1923 debate, as a way forward for this entire book.

What is the task of critical theology? It is to *communicate* the message of the gospel in terms of mystery, event and rhetoric, the last-mentioned of which is itself understood as a form of sacramental narrative, something which mediates the relationship between faith and society as they engage with each other in the lives of individuals and communities. Critical theology, therefore, is concerned with questions of understanding and interpretation and is hermeneutic in character, being centred upon the quest for meaning. This does not imply, however, that it is concerned solely with questions of *Biblical* interpretation, as many hermeneutic theologies have been rather narrowly defined. On the contrary, critical theology is hermeneutic in so far as it interprets not only the Bible, but also tradition, Church, faith and particularly society. The hermeneutic 'circle' thus relates the theologian not only to the Bible, as one source of authority, but also to Church in its broadest possible sense, and the world in which it lives (see Caputo 1987).[16]

The reason this understanding of theology is different from Harnack's is that it does not operate under the rubric of science, in the sense of objectivism and empiricism. A hermeneutic theology, on the contrary, seeks to go beyond the subject/object dichotomy and is not, therefore, concerned with the discovery of facts. Rather, it is concerned with being meaningful. One of the necessary implications of this position is *pluralism*, the acceptance of a variety of equally meaningful different theological viewpoints, each of which can be genuinely critical. Whereas

[16] I will make a point throughout of referring to 'Church' without the definite article, for two main reasons. First, I want to emphasize ecclesial pluralism; I want to reject the reification which lies behind the use of the expression 'the Church'. Second, I want to emphasize the active nature of this name Church, understanding it more as a verb than as a noun rather in the way Nicholas Lash (1988, p. 296) employs 'Easter' after Gerald Manley Hopkins. I hope that these two reasons protect my understanding from being mere affectation, and that as the book progresses they will be able to stand as a valid way of undertaking ecclesiology. My influence here is Schillebeeckx 1990.

Harnack recognizes only one way of doing theology, the scientific establishment of facts, critical theology as *hermeneutic* theology explicitly recognizes the possibility of many different ways of speaking of God and God's relationship with the world. This is the most important quality of the *open* rhetoric of critical theology in terms of its methodological *character*: its effectiveness and applicability is determined by the establishment of its first principles in the process of naming mystery by reference to a specific event.[17]

This is why it is so important to locate the question of what is absolute in Christianity firmly on the side of faith, and *not* theology itself. Barth is correct to argue that the gospel is a message of revelation and judgement; but he is wrong to make revelation the sole subject matter of theology *per se*. Theology cannot say anything about revelation; it can only reflect upon what revelation means in the world, because the ultimate meaning of revelation is concealed to the world. The reason why Barth makes this mistake would appear to be clear, though surprising: he establishes the gospel itself in his own Reformed, dogmatic foundations. Barth regards the message of the gospel, and in particular Paul's mediation of that gospel, through the lens of a distinction: the infinite qualitative distinction of Kierkegaard, which, however, is correctly traced back to Luther and Calvin. This only serves to distort what Barth is attempting to state. Harnack is correct, therefore: Barth's is a position which can be justified from within the history of the Christian Church, and as a religio-ecclesial phenomenon; but it is not the only way of speaking about God, and nor is it the only way of understanding the Christian religion.

One way to circumvent this problem is to accept in all seriousness Anselm's axiom, that critical theology is faith seeking understanding; thereby faith itself is established in the spiritual first principle and origin, mystery, which is fundamental to being human in this world. The mysterious nature of this conviction, and its function as the origin of any speech about God (the naming and appropriating process), is subverted in the context of the 1923 debate when Barth's understanding of the relationship between God and the world is accepted – a surprisingly Enlightenment understanding, given his opposition to Harnack's scientism. Barth's model is, in reality, one of knowledge seeking faith seeking knowledge, not faith seeking understanding. This results in dissolution, as Harnack realized in 1923.

[17] On this question of theology's character, see Cunningham 1991, pp. 98ff. Though I do not agree with Cunningham's remarks in their entirety, I recognize the importance of the question he raises at this point.

The role of education

Of course, Barth too wanted to maintain what is absolute in Christianity against the vagaries of human knowledge and interpretation; but in identifying theology as preaching with the gospel itself, Barth jeopardizes the latter's autonomy. If all religion and theology are to be established finally in faith alone, as a pure gift of God, then there can be no identity of religion or theology with such faith. On the contrary, instead of an identity there is a difference: if faith is to come into the world and into the life of both individual and society as mystery, then it must be a singular event which yet requires interpretation from a variety of different viewpoints if it is to be meaningful in the contemporary world. Everything else must be established in that conviction if Christianity is to have any independence whatsoever.

Yet again, therefore, what is critical theology? Negatively, a critical theology is not the message of the gospel; it is not religion, either personal or communal; it is not a statement of experience; it is not apologetics, dogmatics, ethics or Biblical studies; nor is it sociology, politics or economics. (All of these, to a greater or lesser extent, are to be found within Christianity and its reflection.) Rather, a critical theology is the way in which faith, in the shape of a specific community, explicitly, rhetorically, turns itself towards the society in which it lives, addressing the perceived – on the basis of faith – relationship between God and that society.

There are two important implications which stem from this definition. First, it means that critical theology is a very limited subject, with its parameters set quite clearly by the explicit limits, in various forms, of Christianity, and specifically the Christian community which it might serve. Critical theology has a wide-ranging brief, charged with addressing every aspect of reality as humanity perceives it, because it is given a clearly defined role as the community in question's means or avenue of communication with the larger society in which it finds itself. In terms of the model which Barth develops in *Romans* II, a critical theology finds itself as the hinge between the Christian religion, as expressed in a particular community, and the society at large.

Second, it follows that the task of the critical theologian is directed not simply towards the individual, but towards the community as a whole. This appears straightforward; but the history of twentieth-century theology, at the very least, is replete with examples, such as Rudolf Bultmann and Paul Tillich, of theologians who concentrated solely upon the individual to the detriment of their understanding of the community.[18] The role of theology as rhetoric, therefore, is not to teach the individual, but to teach the *community*.

Both Barth and Harnack failed sufficiently to appreciate this point in 1923, Barth by rejecting education altogether, Harnack by misdirecting its application to the values of a specific culture. On my understanding of critical theology, however, the message of the gospel is communicated to the individual solely via faith, and it is axiomatic for the Christian understanding of faith that it involves directing the individual towards the collective, be it church, community or society, in which the individual finds herself. This can all be expressed very simply: the task of a critical theology is to take over in *time* at the point where the Christian religion, as the *eternal* message of the gospel and its historic witnesses, comes to an end. A critical theology addresses only its own culture and society, on the fringes of its own community. It is a contextual theology.

There is a consistency supporting this understanding, therefore. Theology must be religious, because all of its foundations and materials – its first principles – are reflected in Christianity in the form not only of the eternal gospel, but also of the community and its rituals and practices. It must also be practical, however, because it is directed towards the engagement between the community and culture and society. Indeed, it must ultimately be nothing but practical, because its sole task is to address the relationship between Church and worldly issues, in the light of faith's understanding of the relationship between God and the world; i.e. the gospel of revelation and judgement, in Christ. This is fundamental to everything I cover in Part II.

Preliminary conclusions

There can be no sense in which this analysis of the Harnack–Barth debate provides any definitive information regarding contemporary theology's operation; analysis is not the same thing as repristination, and the guidance of the past cannot suffice for the present. Instead, one must simply draw some preliminary conclusions concerning the general shape and structure of critical theology, which will guide the discussion in the rest of this book, as well as being in themselves tested in the individual chapters which follow. What one can at least decide

[18] A position argued against Tillich by Gunther Wenz (1979); on Bultmann, see Jones 1991, pp. 68–77.

at the moment, therefore, is how favourably critical theology seems as a working model.

There are seven major points to arise from this chapter. I will consider each in turn, though acknowledging that they are interdependent, since the structure of critical theology only functions when all are regarded as integral to one model.

First, Anselm's axiom that theology is faith seeking understanding must apply to all theology. This not only preserves the independence and integrity of theology as a discipline positioned on the borderlands of faith and society, but also safeguards the mysterious and primary nature of faith as a pure gift of God's love and salvation. There may be various different presentations of faith, and even different interpretations; but there can be no valid attempt to go behind it. A gift is the only origin of the new life in Christ, and ultimately the only first principle of critical theology. At the beginning of belief, therefore, as Barth realized, there is only mystery.[19]

Second, the message of the gospel must be an event of judgement and revelation, in the power of the Holy Spirit and the gift of faith and, therefore, in the long shadow of Pentecost. The establishment of authority in Christianity must be derived from the outpouring of the Holy Spirit; without this event, there would be no historical religion called Christianity. The meaning of the cross and resurrection, from the viewpoint of faith and thus in terms of the gospel, is always the subject of address to both the individual and community. The power of that address, however, as it is named by faith, is the power of the Holy Spirit and of Pentecost.

Third, the scope of Christology must attend to the question of the historical Jesus. Failure to do this leads directly to the emblematic Christology which one recognizes, for example, in liberal English theology (past and present), where the cipher of divine love is sketched in terms of idealized qualities with little reference to the life of Jesus of Nazareth (but see Newlands 1980, pp. 65–79). This naturally and significantly raises the question of the role of Biblical exegesis and interpretation in the establishment of a credible image of Jesus, then to serve within a Christology. I will address this matter in detail in subsequent chapters.

Fourth, any understanding of the Christian religion, if it is itself to be authentically critical and thereby reflective of the real lives of Christians, must be catholic; it must reflect as deeply as possible upon the

[19] Whether or not this mystery is recognized as a religious mystery, however, and what it might be if it were not religious, is not so certain; see chapter 5 below.

greatest length and breadth of human religiosity, rather than reifying one particular set of presuppositions and naming them 'religion'. This means that theology today must forge links with its close relative religious studies, a move advocated by John Hick (1993), and practised by David Tracy (see chapter 5 below).

Fifth, the chain of authority, from rhetorical expression back to mystery, must be securely established if theology is to function successfully. This means that when theologians speak publicly about their work's impact, of its relevance for social and ecclesial issues, they must be able to demonstrate both how their statements relate to the particular images of Jesus Christ they articulate, and the understanding of human existence and religiosity which deems Jesus Christ a necessary Word to articulate. It is a question, consequently, not of relating Christology and rhetoric to Biblical and episcopal authority, but rather to a wider and deeper frame of reference, within which humanity as such finds some treatment (see chapter 3 below).

Sixth, the role of rhetoric in theology, which is the communication of the implications of authority and therefore of the gospel and of mystery, is to address the community *in toto*. This reverses the traditional Christian understanding of pedagogics whilst maintaining the teleological thrust of Christianity as an eschatological religion and/or movement. Critical theology, therefore, in so far as it is public discourse, cannot focus solely upon the individual, but rather must address itself to the relationships Christianity faces in a pluralistic world. This is the specific agenda of modernity (see chapter 2 below).

Seventh, theology, on the basis of its religious foundation and its rhetorical motor, must engage with society and culture, the interpretation of which necessitates an engagement with the social sciences. Theology, consequently, is itself an *applied* science; it is meaningless without this reference beyond itself and beyond Christianity to the world at large, because Christianity is a religion of application – evangelization – to the world in general. Failure to recognize this fact reduces Christian faith to the level of a codified historical message which, devoid of its eschatology, simply takes its place as one liberal ideology amongst many others.[20]

These seven points exhaust what I want to say about critical theology on the basis of the Harnack–Barth debate of 1923. Overwhelmingly they focus upon the vital question of first principles, and how

[20] On the question of theology's applicability to a world of constant change, I am broadly in sympathy with John Milbank (1990, pp. 326–79) when he writes of 'the differential flux' in which Christianity and theology find themselves, if for no other reason than the expression indicates something of the imprecision inherent to the processes of application.

this finds expression in both Harnack and Barth in their treatment of the related ideas of mystery, knowledge, revelation and understanding. In the course of this exposition, however, the other themes of critical theology – event and rhetoric – have also been discussed, albeit less comprehensively than mystery. I now want to turn towards the treatment of these problems in the subsequent history of modern theology, and more precisely the slide from mystery to event which occurs as Christology and the economic becomes the sole medium for reflection upon the nature of mystery itself, the immanent being of God. This means turning now to the theology of Dietrich Bonhoeffer.

2

Bonhoeffer: Naming the Crisis of the World

Now is the judgement of this world, now shall the ruler of this world be cast out (John 12:31)

The point of the present chapter is to see how one theologian, Dietrich Bonhoeffer takes the Harnack–Barth debate a stage further, moving beyond the establishment of first principles about mystery *per se* towards a clearer understanding of what revelation reveals *per accidens*. I am concerned, therefore, to understand how Bonhoeffer names mystery, and to appreciate why he names mystery 'Jesus Christ'. Here I want to introduce the notion of a 'slide' between mystery and event; i.e. the movement from theological metaphysics towards theological epistemology and the naming of mystery as a specific, known individual. This is the next stage of my argument in modern theology.

Towards the end of his life Bonhoeffer wrote: 'Let me just summarise briefly what I'm concerned about – the claim of a world that has come of age by Jesus Christ' (Bonhoeffer 3/1967, p. 343). With these words, written in 1944 to Eberhard Bethge, Bonhoeffer announces two of the principal themes of his late thought: the need to recognize the claims of modernity upon theology; and the uniqueness of Christ as the medium of God's revelation. Christ and the world, therefore, intimately and positively related; this is the specific concern of Bonhoeffer's late writings from prison. They are, moreover, themes which Bonhoeffer (1966) addressed in *Christology*, a text based on lectures given in 1933. These are the two sources I want to discuss.

In concentrating upon this much studied area of Bonhoeffer's work, however, I do not want to construct a systematic theology out of the fragmentary ideas of his final letters and papers (or the equally fragmentary notes which make up his *Christology* text). Rather, my intention is to discuss the potential of some of Bonhoeffer's ideas in terms of the slide between mystery and event. The structure of this chapter, therefore, is straightforward. An initial section considers the historical and intellectual relationship between the general aims of Bonhoeffer's work and the Harnack – Barth debate of 1923. In the light of this foundation I want to examine Bonhoeffer's preliminary discussion of the Christ event, his *Christology*. Then, as the central part of this chapter, I will consider Bonhoeffer's famous letter from prison of 16 July 1944 before finally, and as a link with chapter 3, questioning the potential and relevance of Bonhoeffer's most speculative reflections.

From 1923 to 1944

Fides qua creditur and *fides quae creditur*

Despite the clearly fragmentary nature of so much of Bonhoeffer's thought, certain key themes keep recurring. One of these is his distinction between *actus directus* and *actus reflectus*, which is found in his earliest work and which continues to be of central importance until his death in 1945 (see Feil 1985, p. 28).[1] The definition of these expressions is simple: *actus directus* and *actus reflectus* correspond in Bonhoeffer's theology to faith and reflection. Generally, Bonhoeffer accepts the customary definition of the *actus reflectus* as reason or the intellect, the principal object of discussion in the western philosophical tradition since Kant. But Bonhoeffer's understanding of the *actus directus* is much more specific. This is faith directed towards Christ, the *fides directa in mysterium*, so that 'faith directed towards mystery' is always named as faith directed towards Christ. This is important, as Bonhoeffer writes: '"God revealed in the flesh", the God-Man Jesus Christ, is the holy mystery which theology is appointed to guard' (1973, p. 28). Bonhoeffer thus gives Christological content to the *actus directus*, recognizing and affirming the requirement to speak of Jesus as the mysterious goal of humanity's faith, given by God as grace. For Bonhoeffer mystery always has an economic being – it is real in Christ.

Bonhoeffer's early distinction between the *actus directus* and the *actus reflectus* is mirrored in his final writings by one between the *fides directa* and the *fides reflecta* (3/1967, p. 373), where the thrust of his distinction between these two is to clarify what he understands as the person and work of Christ and their universal relevance. In

[1] On the place of this distinction in Bonhoeffer's early thought, see his *Act and Being* (1962), pp. 180–4, and on this text see Marsh 1992a and 1992b.

these two pairs of expressions, one recognizes not so much a static dualism in Bonhoeffer's theology as a dynamic attempt to interpret the themes of classical Christology in terms of how people are given the grace to encounter Jesus Christ as their salvation. Faith reflects, and in so doing seeks understanding; but the understanding that faith seeks – the understanding it is directed towards by grace – is itself located in the eternal person and work of Jesus Christ.

Structurally, therefore, one can identify a simple distinction in Bonhoeffer's theology, one which clears the way for an emphasis upon the Christological nature of faith whilst simultaneously maintaining an important, though comparatively unarticulated, role for human reason. A contrast between nature and grace thus seems important for Bonhoeffer; and yet it is one expressed via the philosophical language of historical existence and reflection upon it. This is the sense of the 'directedness' of faith. Directed towards God in Christ, certainly; God in Christ not as an external reality, however, but as the decisive turning-point of life. In this way, for Bonhoeffer the divine mystery comes to the very heart of the human mystery (a point central for Rahner, of course; see chapter 3 below).

Bonhoeffer makes the intellectual significance of this *fides directa in mysterium* clear when he writes:

> Mystery is something uncanny because we are not at home in it, because it tells of a manner of being at home different from ours. To live without mystery means that one knows nothing of the mystery of one's life, or other peoples' lives, of the world (quoted in Feil 1985, p. 5).

Faith is directed towards Jesus Christ; but the Christ event itself – the person and and work of Christ – is directed, as revelation, towards something greater still: the mystery of the Godhead, which in creation, through the Word, is the mystery of life itself. At the very heart of Bonhoeffer's theology, consequently, is an identity of faith, Christ and mystery, economically revealed through incarnation, cross and resurrection. One cannot bypass this event, either cognitively or pedagogically, because of the identity Bonhoeffer stipulates between life and faith, nature and grace, in Christ.

The bare bones of this argument echo many of the issues raised in the debate between Harnack and Barth. Indeed, the contrast between *actus directus* and *actus reflectus*, as well as *fides directa* and *fides reflecta*, signals the relative positions of Barth and Harnack respectively, since there is a certain symmetry between Barth and Harnack. When the former glorifies Christ as Son and Saviour, the latter reduces him to the status of teacher; when Barth indicates a divine mystery comprehensible solely as eternal Yes, Harnack rejects mystery in favour of scholarship.

I want to argue, however, that Bonhoeffer's position is an advance upon Barth's rigid theology, and certainly upon Harnack's reductionist tendencies. For Bonhoeffer, faith and reflection are two parts of the one human response to God's will – a will uniquely expressed in Christ, but simultaneously requiring an acknowledgement by the individual and community. Here one can invoke another important distinction in the Christian tradition, that between the *fides quae creditur* – 'the faith which one believes' – and the *fides qua creditur* – 'the faith by which one believes'. The former echoes the *fides directa*; the latter the *fides reflecta*. Together, however, they express the necessary relationship between God and humanity which describes the existence of both as mystery. On this question, one might argue, the neglect shown by both Barth and Harnack to one side of this equation reflects negatively upon the other, which they are trying to vindicate. Harnack never had the opportunity to rectify this situation; but Barth's entire effort in the *Church Dogmatics* might be interpreted as an attempt to identify an analogical method by which to speak positively of the mystery of life in the world, as well as of an eschatologically real event.[2]

What one finds in Bonhoeffer's theology, consequently, is not a combat or dialectic between two antithetical ideas or images of divine action and its interpretation, but rather a conciliatory attempt to bring God and the world together. It might be too much to speak of Bonhoeffer's *natural* theology; but his very positive view of creation evokes an altogether different response to that of Barth's negative theology. Bonhoeffer's Christ is definitely the mystery *of* the world, a very important qualification.

This does not mean that Bonhoeffer places too great an emphasis upon the world's participation in revelation and salvation; he remains a Protestant theologian, one therefore concerned to maximize the relevance of the person and work of Christ for the salvation of humanity. Rather, it means that Bonhoeffer seeks to establish the idea or necessity of a Christ *event* – of the incarnation as dynamic process, presently meaningful as revelation – within a more general understanding of God's role as the mystery of the world (see Jüngel 1983, pp. 57–63), to regard the world as the necessary *locus* of revelation, because concealment is revelation's true home. In Barth's theology this *locus* is

[2] On this question in Barth, see Pugh 1990. A similar phenomenon can be identified in Rahner's theology, particularly the ideas which coalesce around the notion of 'conversion to the phantasm'; see Rahner 1968. On this question in Rahner, and its relationship to eschatology, see Phan 1988 and Sheehan 1987.

provided by the doctrines of the Fall and original sin, which are regarded as themselves eschatological events; in Harnack's, by the evolution of reason (which, following Kant, might also be spoken of eschatologically; see Kant 1963). For Bonhoeffer, however – particularly in 1944 – this *locus* is understood as the world come of age. It is in this idea that Bonhoeffer moves theologically to balance the relationship between God and the world, and to interpret that balance – again in 1944 – Christologically. Mystery, therefore, is the necessary precursor for any understanding of the Christ event; but the crucial question for Bonhoeffer is what real status one gives to that mystery, the concealment from which revelation emerges.[3]

The spirituality of mystery

How does Bonhoeffer take his first steps towards answering this question? In an early work he wrote:

> In the act of belief, which Christ himself creates within me, in as much as he gives me the Holy Spirit who hears and believes within me, he also proves himself the free Lord of my existence. Christ 'is' only 'in' faith, yet he is master of my faith (1962, p. 141).

This discussion of a personal relationship with Jesus, constituted in the gift of the Holy Spirit, is found throughout Bonhoeffer's work. Its emphasis upon the *cor curvem in se* – the 'heart turned in on itself' – is a clear echo of Bonhoeffer's understanding of the necessary status of mystery as constituting both divine and human existence. It is, therefore, an anthropological emphasis; and in theology, if an anthropological emphasis is not simply to collapse into philosophy, it must be combined with an explicitly spiritual understanding of human existence, such as one finds in Bonhoeffer's theology.

This assertion is significant. Bonhoeffer, like Barth before him, appears to condemn religion for what he calls its intellectual state as a human construct (see Feil 1985, p. 175), for being an expression of sinful pride rather than humble obedience to God's will. Whereas Barth's rejection of religion is absolute, however, Bonhoeffer always insists upon a clear distinction between religion and spirituality,

[3] That revelation necessarily involves a moment of concealment, which is as integral to God as the incarnation, is fundamental to the methodological claims which critical theology wants to make about the way in which one can speak about God (see Introduction above). Bonhoeffer gives this question an important twist, which is why the relationship between revelation and concealment is highlighted here.

rejecting the former, but asserting the latter. For Bonhoeffer religion is a phenomenon of intellectual history, something to be interpreted by analogy with Dilthey's understanding of the *Geistesgeschichte*. Spirituality, by contrast, is the *cor curvem in se*, which can only mean the individual recognizing its fundamentally mysterious being as God's creature. Spirituality for Bonhoeffer is thus about human completeness, its true being before God.

The contrast with Harnack's theology is informative at this point. One might argue that Bonhoeffer's emphasis upon the world is due to his lingering liberalism; but there is nothing in Harnack's position which serves to prepare modern theology for Bonhoeffer's development. For Harnack the personal relationship with God in Christ may have psychological or emotional status, leading theology towards a practical emphasis. This is very different, however, from Bonhoeffer's developed argument, where it is inappropriate to speak of such a relationship psychologically or emotionally. When Bonhoeffer uses terms like mystery and spirituality, rather, he is making ontological assertions about human existence and so employs the terminology of being, of completeness. It is such speculative reflection which Harnack rejects in favour of the historical-critical method, and which Barth subordinates to the oratory of the Word. Bonhoeffer, by contrast, returns speculation to its rightful place at the heart of Christian discourse about mystery, about what it is and what it means for mystery to be revealed and concealed in Christ.

In developing these themes in his work Bonhoeffer turns explicitly to Church's tradition, attempting to understand the Christ event not solely as an articulation of Christian faith, but as the pinnacle of the entire Christian tradition and all of the doctrines it entails. One can recognize this in his treatment of mystery. For Bonhoeffer the idea of mystery only makes sense in so far as it involves not solely the Holy Spirit (present in Church and believer), but the entire Trinity. Similarly, Bonhoeffer's treatment of the world does not make sense without his emphasis upon the doctrine of Church. Finally, and most problematically, Bonhoeffer's understanding of the autonomy of the world is intelligible only because of the sacramental, mediating nature of that autonomy itself: in the world's autonomy – and Christ's witness to it on the cross – God's mysterious being, and thereby the *world's* mysterious being, is revealed.

Very little of this is ever worked out completely by Bonhoeffer; but that is not the point, which is rather that Christ is no longer to be thought of as an extrinsic Saviour, coming to the world but not of the world. Instead, Christ is of the world: the world is the *locus* of the presence of God – grace – realized in incarnation, cross and resurrection, and subsequently in the spiritual life of the believer. This, argues Bonhoeffer, is the only sense that one can make today of the Chalcedonian Definition: that it ensures not so much the divinity of Christ, but Christ's humanity (see Bonhoeffer 1966, pp. 87–9).

One might be tempted to regard this as a vestige of liberal Protestantism, since it seems to be dependent upon an historical understanding of the life and fate of Jesus of Nazareth; but Bonhoeffer is not concerned to spend time discovering evidence about the historical Jesus. Rather, he wants to bring God into the world, historically and therefore meaningfully. How he makes this attempt within the basic distinction between the *actus directus* and the *actus reflectus* is not evident conceptually. It is, however, clearly established in his interpretation of the person and work of Christ in the *Christology*, where the apposite level of such discourse is identified as the approachability of the Christ event.

The *Christology* of 1933

The scope of Christology

At the very beginning of his *Christology*, Bonhoeffer states: 'We must study Christology in the humble silence of the worshipping community' (1966, p. 27), thereby juxtaposing an attitude with a context: the attitude of the believer towards the person of Christ, and the context (community) in which belief finds expression. Axiomatically, therefore, Bonhoeffer establishes the first principles of speaking of Jesus Christ as *fides quaerens intellectum*: Christology must be contextualized within a community orientated towards faith itself. This social and spiritual attitude is significant, because the introduction of such an understanding of faith so early in the lectures is characteristic of Bonhoeffer's entire theology (echoing his distinction between the *fide directa* and the *fides reflecta*). In fact Bonhoeffer deploys this distinction now to assert that Christology is not concerned at all with the idea of a Christ event – in an attenuated sense – but with a person whose work is to win salvation for all believers. It is in encountering this figure that God's grace is revealed; hence it is vital to approach that encounter with the correct question.

Repeating Barth's criticisms of Harnack's scientific theological method, Bonhoeffer rejects such interrogatives as 'How?' and 'Why?', regarding them as questions intent upon establishing facts and data rather than approaching the meaning of what occurred eschatologically in Jesus. Instead Bonhoeffer makes the 'Who?' question *the* question of Christology, because only this question mediates the necessary relationship between the believer and Christ. He writes:

> The question 'Who?' is the question of transcendence. The question 'How?' is the question of immanence. Because the one who is questioned here is the Son, the immanent question cannot grasp him. Not 'How are you possible?' – that is the godless question, the serpent's question – but 'Who are you?' The question 'Who?' expresses the strangeness and otherness of the encounter and at the same time reveals itself as the question of the very existence of the enquirer himself (1966, pp. 30–1).

For Bonhoeffer this approach to Christology is intended to establish the fundamentally mysterious grounds of speaking of Jesus. Despite his sympathy for Barth's position, therefore, Bonhoeffer can write: 'The question "Who?" is the religious question' (1966, p. 31). Transcendence – as Bonhoeffer categorizes the "What?" question – *is* mystery; transcendence is the necessary boundary of human existence beyond which it cannot proceed, but towards which it is always turned. He writes: 'The mystery of the "Who?" remains hidden. The ultimate question of critical thought is involved in the dilemma of having to ask "Who?" and yet not being able to' (1966, p. 32). The *fides reflecta* thus addresses the mystery of grace itself, as the hidden reality which cannot be known, simply glorified in Christ by the *fides directa*. The mystery of the "Who?" is the basic parameter or limit of creation.[4]

In the space of a few pages, therefore, Bonhoeffer has elaborated the principal themes and scope of his Christology, namely to relate the questions of human existence and its eternal tasks to the mysterious being of God. Doctrinally, if one were to speak of the work of Christ soteriologically, then for Bonhoeffer in 1933 salvation is the victory Jesus wins over humanity itself and, most particularly, its desire to live without mystery. He writes: 'In the end, there are only two possibilities of encountering Jesus: either man must die or he kills Jesus' (1966, p. 36). Again one returns to the idea of a dialectic between the humility of faith and the arrogance of human reason directed to and for its own ends, an issue centring upon the spirituality or otherwise of the individual or community in question.

Much of this is reminiscent of the dialectical theology of Barth's two *Romans* books: the Christ event as person and work constitutes

[4] Bonhoeffer features only twice in Tracy's *Blessed Rage for Order* (1975), but there is an important sense in which they agree on this aspect of the limitedness of human existence; see chapter 5 below.

the pivot around which human existence turns; Christ himself is the eternal question-mark which hangs over the lives of every believer and every community, because the spiritual crisis which Christ brings as gospel is a crisis of creation and therefore of the world (so that one can speak of an identity of Spirit and world through grace). Bonhoeffer's Christology, however, has advanced further than that of the early Barth. He writes: 'Jesus is present as the Crucified and Risen One' (1966, p. 43). The "Who?" question, which elicits an immediate response both from God and the believer, is answered not conceptually but figuratively, in the broken yet miraculously healed body of Jesus of Nazareth. This is the genuine nature of an Easter faith, so that speaking of Christ as event and therefore as something which transforms creation is always pictured in the Sacrament of One who mediates grace and mystery. Now deliberately echoing the Chalcedonian Definition, Bonhoeffer continues:

> Even as the Risen One, Jesus Christ remains the man Jesus in space and time. Only because Jesus Christ is man is he present in time and space. Only because Jesus Christ is God is he eternally present everywhere .... I do not know who this man Jesus Christ is unless I say at the same time 'Jesus Christ is God', and I do not know who the God Jesus Christ is unless I say at the same time 'Jesus Christ is man' (1966, pp. 45–6).

Jesus, therefore, must be *faced*, in the deliberately ambiguous sense of that expression.[5]

In this way Bonhoeffer deepens his understanding of the scope of Christology, which is to embrace the mystery of human existence within a clear understanding of divine mystery as the *sine qua non* of all theology. This anthropological thrust in Bonhoeffer means that speech about God is simultaneously speech about humanity and vice versa (a point also made by Bultmann and Rahner). At this stage, however, it is unclear how one ought to speak of humanity. Granted that Bonhoeffer wishes to speak of the mysterious, graceful revelation which occurs as the Christ event, and that this revelation is of decisive significance for the salvation of the believer, yet questions remain: is that believer to be regarded individually or collectively?; does one employ the terminology of the subject or collective to describe the activity of faith in the believer?

A decision between these two antitheses, of course, is by no means necessary; one could quite reasonably insist upon a 'both/and' rather

[5] Thus one enters the world of Emmanuel Levinas (1969, pp. 194–7), who writes on this problem philosophically, but in a way open to religious appropriation. On this aspect of Levinas's work, see Hand 1989, pp. 82–4, and Valevicius 1988, pp. 41–57.

than an 'either/or'. Indeed, Bonhoeffer writes: 'He who alone is the Christ is the one who is present in the community *pro me*' (1966, p. 48). The question, however, is not simply terminological; it also has distinct implications for any understanding of the authentic nature of both mystery and event, in so far as they are revealed in Jesus Christ.[6] If it is correct to say that to speak about God is to speak about humanity and vice versa, then one must identify the character of the two subjects of that speech. 'Mystery' and 'event', consequently, are certainly theological categories; but they require contexts in order to be intelligible within a systematic and critical theology. Bonhoeffer, so far, has related the two in a traditional manner; but he has not yet made any explicit claim for their contextual status, other than the broadly anthropological.

Contextualizing mystery and event

The *pro me* structure of Christ's person and work, which at first sight indicates an emphasis by Bonhoeffer upon the relationship between Jesus and the individual, is in fact more complex. For Bonhoeffer it implies three things: that Christ is pioneer, head and firstborn of the brethren who follow him; that Christ is for the brethren by substituting himself for them; and that because Christ acts as the new humanity, it is within him and he within it (Bonhoeffer 1966, pp. 48–9). Far from concentrating upon the individual, therefore, the *pro me* structure of Christ indicates the collective body of all believers. This is important because the *pro me* is indicative of the intentionality of the Christ event towards believers, which in turn is theologically necessary: the Christ event is an event of salvation because of this intentionality.

Is the collective, however, to be understood abstractly or concretely? Bonhoeffer seems to give an unequivocal answer: 'Christ is the community by virtue of his being *pro me*' (1966, p. 59). The intentionality of the Christ event is thus directed explicitly towards not an abstract collective, but the particular community or Church. The ecclesial nature of Bonhoeffer's 'community' is justified by the liturgical terminology he employs to elaborate upon the true meaning of the Christ event.[7]

[6] I do not want to suggest that Bonhoeffer seeks – or that critical theology should attempt – to speak of the Ding-an-sich of divine mystery, even if the immanent is really the economic. Rather, such speech is always governed by the image one presents of the person and work of Jesus (see chapter 7 below).

[7] On these questions in Bonhoeffer's theology, see Gerhard Muller's two excellent monographs (1979, pp. 88–94, and 1980, pp. 217–29).

Developing this understanding of the relationship between Christ and Church, Bonhoeffer writes: 'Truth happens only in the community' (1966, p. 51), which is an important statement because of the theological claims it makes. For Bonhoeffer 'truth' is not simply a correct understanding of the intentionality of the Christ event. It is also a quality predicated of God. Fundamentally, therefore, Bonhoeffer appears to be claiming – implicitly here, certainly – that in so far as truth is both an event, Christ, and a quality predicated of God's being, this mystery is pre-set in Church. Or better: the partial relation of mystery, as the truth of God's being and therefore as the Christ event, is something which occurs communally. Liturgically this implies, as Bonhoeffer goes on to recognize, that the presence of Christ must be celebrated within Church sacramentally; but it also has important doctrinal implications. Doctrinally it implies a coherence between the life of the community and the life of the Godhead, articulated by the idea of the Trinity, and established in the Christ event as genuine revelation. Truth is thus something which occurs both in Church and in eternity: Jesus Christ.[8]

This is an important and exciting idea. Correctly understood, it seems to offer a coherent alternative to the *analogia fidei* developed by Barth in his Anselm book, in which he offered a renewed interpretation of the *analogia entis* (see Pugh 1990). Bonhoeffer understands the being of God as Trinity in terms of the being of believers as Church: each finds its true expression in Christ. Employing a metaphor deployed by Hans Urs von Balthasar (1972) to represent Barth's theology, one can say that for Bonhoeffer the Christ event is the narrow neck of the hourglass, through which any revelation and therefore discussion of either human mystery or divine mystery (its two bells) must pass. Today mystery is revealed (and concealed) in Church, argues Bonhoeffer (an idea with profound implications for questions of inter- and intrafaith dialogue; see chapter 6 below).

As was seen in chapter 1, the temptation when speaking of mystery and event is to discuss them in the singular. Both Barth and Harnack thus succumb, addressing Jesus Christ as a singular event and the divine mystery as a singular quality, synonymous with grace and being. Similarly, the appeal of God in Christ to the believer was expressed in individualistic terms: call, repentance and redemption lend themselves to such a description, as indeed does spirituality, the quality of Chris-

[8] This is the basis of the idea of the perfection of mystery as the Trinity (see chapter 6). On the relationship between the doctrines of the incarnation and Trinity, see MacKinnon 1987, pp. 145–67.

tian devotion which most characterizes Bonhoeffer's understanding of the religious disposition.

Certainly, on whatever level one wishes to locate such discourse – existential, psychological, emotional, historical, essential, sacramental, spiritual – there is a strong sense in which the nature of mystery and event can be addressed in terms of an appeal to the subject. Indeed, one can go further: the Christ event is a *singulare tantum*, discrete in time and eternity. Mystery itself, consequently, must also be a *singulare tantum*, as it is revealed economically. These claims are axiomatic for the Christian faith; without them such faith degenerates into simple liberal humanism as, arguably, one recognizes in Harnack's theology.

An axiom of faith, however – by definition, a religious belief – is very different from a theological understanding. Granted that such axioms are normative for ensuing theological inquiry, yet there remain grounds for flexibility in their application to the search for understanding. This is what one sees in Bonhoeffer's *Christology*. Concisely, Bonhoeffer applies a collective or communal understanding to the axiomatic uniqueness of both the divine mystery and the Christ event: 'Truth happens only in the community' (1966, p. 50). This means that the questions of fundamental meaning in theology – concerning mystery and event – are not challenged solely as to their application to the community as a whole, by means of anthropological terminology. It also means that anthropology itself is to be understood socially. For Bonhoeffer human existence is social existence as it responds to God's Word, because God's grace and mercy are themselves expressions of the will and being of the Trinity. Theology establishes this understanding by means of analogy; God establishes it by the economic procession of the three Persons of the Trinity in revelation and concealment, in Jesus Christ. Theologically, this implies that if a community is to live in Christ, then it must also live in the Trinity. For Bonhoeffer this means that being in Christ involves the community in a constant process of becoming, of moving forwards in incompleteness towards eternity, which is the only possible eschatological being open to humanity. Socially, humanity lives *towards* the Trinity, as it is known in Christ (see Boff 1988).

When Bonhoeffer writes, therefore, 'Here Christ stands, in the centre, between me and myself, between the old existence and the new. So Christ is at the same time my own boundary and my rediscovered centre, the centre lying both between "I" and "I" and "I" and God' (1966, pp. 61–2), it is clear that he is not reducing faith or theology to a reflection upon the individual's relationship with God. On the contrary, the paradox of Christ being both centre and boundary extends beyond humanity itself, into eternity: Christ is centre as question-mark, but also boundary as the necessary development or procession of Church from the old to the new (see II Cor. 5:17). Bonhoeffer, therefore, characterizes Christ's office as centre in the following three ways: as the boundary of humanity; as the boundary of history; and as the boundary of nature. Christ's presence – grace – as Word, Spirit and Sacrament is thus a transforming power not only for human existence, individually or socially, but for the entire creation.

Such is the basic position of the *Christology* text. Bonhoeffer is gradually pushing back the limits of theology's discussion of the Christ event in order to say more and more about the mysterious nature of the God who acts in that event. What Bonhoeffer has achieved, at least in preliminary form, is the relation of both mystery and event to a number of different areas – existence, history, nature – in order to narrate the meaning of mystery and event ontologically; i.e. as the *complete* identity of Spirit and the world. The implication of Bonhoeffer's conclusions is that henceforth any rhetoric in theology – any sacramental narrative – must find its application in the context of the world at large. Bonhoeffer has established the largest possible stage for theology.

What Bonhoeffer had not achieved in 1933, however, was any degree of sophistication in his understanding of the specific personality of Christ; he did not elaborate completely the figure of sacrifice who achieves salvation and thereby makes mystery the genuine basis of a new beginning for humanity. What one finds, rather, is a programme or blueprint for expansion: the development of the meaning of the Christ event until it fills both boundary and centre of the social existence, history and nature of humanity and the world. This is the promise of Bonhoeffer's *Christology*, but one which went undeveloped in 1933.

How does Bonhoeffer solve this problem? By reflecting upon the real meaning of the Christ event as a personal event. In so doing he offers a clear picture of the nature of God's mystery as the true nature of humanity, with particular reference to modernity. Bonhoeffer calls this 'the world come of age', and his most famous ideas on the subject are found in his posthumously collected *Letters and Papers from Prison*, in particular the letter to Bethge of 16 July 1944 (Bonhoeffer 3/1967, pp. 357–61).

A letter from prison

It is important to keep this text in perspective, for it is not a universal panacea to be advocated for all theological ills.[9] On the contrary, Bonhoeffer's letter of 16 July 1944 is almost too problematic for consideration. As a reflection upon mystery and event, however, it may be considered in the present context, precisely because of its fragmentary and experimental status.[10] Because I am still only working around the problems of mystery and event and how they are related, and not offering a comprehensive system of theology, Bonhoeffer's ideas provide a useful lead. They cannot be prescriptive, but here at least Bonhoeffer returns to the themes which influenced his *Christology*, eleven years earlier.

The letter begins slowly, concentrating upon personal news; it is only halfway through that it turns, quite suddenly, to more philosophical themes. Philosophical, indeed, rather than theological: at this stage it is with the background to theology proper that Bonhoeffer is concerned. Signalling his change of subject quite explicitly, Bonhoeffer writes:

> On the historical side: there is one great development that leads to the world's autonomy. In theology one sees it first in Lord Herbert of Cherbury, who maintains that reason is sufficient for religious knowledge. In ethics it appears in Montaigne and Bodin with their substitution of rules of life for the commandments. In politics Machiavelli detaches politics from morality in general and founds the doctrine of 'reasons of state'. Later, and very differently from Machiavelli, but tending like him towards the autonomy of human society, comes Grotius, setting up his natural law as international law, which is valid *etsi deus non daretur*, 'even if there were no God'. The philosophers provided the finishing touches: on the one hand we have the deism of Descartes, who holds that the world is a mechanism, running by itself with no interference from God; and on the other hand the pantheism of Spinoza, who says that God is nature. In the last resort, Kant is a deist, and Fichte and Hegel are pantheists. Everywhere the thinking is directed towards the autonomy of man and the world (3/1967, p. 359).

The key ideas here are readily apparent and have often been noted by commentators. Pre-eminent is the notion of intellectual or moral validity, 'even if there were no God', which with Grotius Bonhoeffer

[9] A good example of this dubious manipulation of Bonhoeffer's work is the short essay by William Hamilton (see Hamilton and Altizer 1968, pp. 118–23).

[10] I believe that Bonhoeffer, unlike many contemporary theologians, resists the temptation of being too synthetic (see also Introduction above) because he has a genuine understanding of the mystery and concealment of God, and a real spirituality.

sees entering reflection at the expense of the genuinely mysterious, spiritual basis of human existence. In terms of Bonhoeffer's preferred distinction, the *actus reflectus* replaces the *actus directus*, beginning with Grotius and continuing into modernity. Leaving aside the question whether or not Bonhoeffer's reading of specific philosophers is correct, one thing is clear: he is establishing a distinction between the burgeoning power and integrity of human reason, and the apparent waning of genuine religious belief.

There is, however, a greater subtlety to this text. Midway through this passage Bonhoeffer writes: 'Later, and very differently from Machiavelli, *but tending like him towards the autonomy of human society*...' (my italics); i.e. Bonhoeffer specifies a particular aspect of human life, rather than simple existence *per se*. He does so, moreover, at the point where he begins to speak of Grotius, leading to the famous expression, *etsi deus non daretur*. The implication here is that it is not simply the rise of human reason which indicates the intrusion of atheism into modernity, but rather the development of the autonomy of society itself which threatens traditional theological definitions. It is an autonomous society, therefore, functioning in modernity according to laws 'even if there were no God', which is the true origin of these reflections for Bonhoeffer (see Bethge 1970, pp. 973–7).

If the preceding interpretation is correct Bonhoeffer's focus here, generally overlooked, is in fact of paramount importance, because it is the social which in theology defines not simply the authentic nature of human existence *coram deo* (in Church), but also by analogy the being in Trinity of the divine mystery itself as it is revealed in the world. Any movement by humanity away from an understanding of society which regards it as being dependent upon God, consequently, is not solely a move towards autonomy; it is also a development which denies God's being. For Bonhoeffer it is not simply the movement away from the *actus directus* and towards the *actus reflectus* which requires a new understanding of God's revelation in Christ; it is the entire debate about the nature of society itself. If society has genuinely redefined itself in modernity, argues Bonhoeffer, then God can either no longer be understood by analogy with the social nature of humanity, or the very autonomy of society must reveal something hitherto overlooked about God's revelation in Christ as the articulation of God's being in Trinity. Since for faith the former is unthinkable, Bonhoeffer is left with only one resort: he must reflect upon the theological implications of the autonomy of society. Leaving behind, therefore, the simple understanding of community one finds in his *Christology*, and absorbing the impact of modernity, Bonhoeffer returns with renewed vigour to the interpretation of the Christ event, now to elaborate the mystery it reveals economically in terms of the paradoxical coming-of-age of modernity. Bonhoeffer thus begins to reflect upon how society alters the way theology can speak of God, because the autonomy of society says something about God's being.

Bonhoeffer's acknowledgement of this situation is made clear when he writes:

> God as a working hypothesis in morals, politics, or science, has been surmounted and abolished; and the same thing has happened in philosophy and religion (Feuerbach!). For the sake of intellectual honesty, that working hypothesis should be dropped, or as far as possible eliminated (3/1967, p. 360).

Theology must accept the historical context in which it has to operate, for such is intellectual honesty. For Bonhoeffer this is not problematic. Indeed, it is not even open to discussion. It simply is, as the natural predicament of the modern theologian.

Bonhoeffer's acknowledgement of this situation, however, is not solely intellectually honest. It is also the product of his conviction that God's will is revealed even where it appears most concealed. The acknowledgement of this fact is not simply intellectual assent. It is repentance, the reorientation of life itself in the face of the reality of grace. Bonhoeffer writes:

> Anxious souls will ask what room there is left for God now; and as they know of no answer to the question, they condemn the whole development that has brought them to such straits.... There is no such way – at any rate not if it means deliberately abandoning our mental integrity; the only way is that of Matthew 18:3; i.e., through repentance, through *ultimate* honesty (3/1967, p. 360).

Ultimate honesty: for Bonhoeffer's theological rubric this can mean nothing more nor less than *eternal* honesty, which makes of repentance an eschatological concept. And not only an eschatological concept, it is also a mysterious one: it opens to reflection the authenticity of both human existence and the divine will, because genuine repentance is the true and necessary response to the Christ event, revealed by God.

Clearly, for Bonhoeffer the acceptance of the autonomy of society is an acceptance of God's mysterious will. Or better, and in the words of Bonhoeffer's *Christology*: the genuine answer to the 'Who?' question can be made only in terms of the autonomy of society, with all this means for human understanding of the divine mystery. Whoever God is, Bonhoeffer argues, God comes in Christ as the expression of a being who wills society's autonomy and therefore radical independence from God. Bonhoeffer thus continues, famously and densely: 'And we cannot be honest unless we recognise that we have to live in the world *etsi deus non daretur.* And this is just what we do recognise – before God!' (3/1967, p. 360).[11]

That this is God's will is confirmed by Bonhoeffer's next statement: 'God himself compels us to recognise it' (3/1967, p. 360). Theology must always be *fides quaerens intellectum*; the significant question is not that this is the case, but rather how understanding is to be reconciled with the situation accepted in modernity as social reality. This Bonhoeffer affirms by relating the autonomy of society to the ontological status of humanity itself: 'So our coming of age leads to a true recognition of our situation before God' (3/1967, p. 360).

Bonhoeffer's, therefore, is nothing more than a preliminary conclusion, for any ontological statement about human existence – because of its genuinely mysterious nature – is also always a statement about God's true being, as willed and revealed in Jesus Christ. Bonhoeffer writes:

> God would have us know that we must live as men who manage our lives without him. The God who is with us is the God who forsakes us (Mark 15:34). The God who lets us live in the world without the working hypothesis of God is the God before whom we stand continually. Before God and with God we live without God (3/1967, p. 360).

How do we know this? asks Bonhoeffer. Because it has been revealed in the cross of Christ:

> God lets himself be pushed out of the world on to the cross. He is weak and powerless in the world, and that is precisely the way, the only way, in which he is with us and helps us. Matthew 8:17 makes it quite clear that Christ helps us, not by virtue of his omnipotence, but by virtue of his weakness and suffering (3/1967, p. 360).

The normal theological label for such a theory is *kenosis*, the self-emptying of God in Christ, culminating in the Godforsakenness of the cross, when the Son obeys the will of the Father even unto death (see chapter 7 below). Bonhoeffer wants to radicalize this understanding, however. He wants to interpret the Christ event as revealing more of God's will than simply its desire to become its opposite, death or non-being. That interpretation makes of God's free act a necessity, in the

[11] On this question, I am greatly influenced by Rowan Williams (1988).

sense that a being or event or concept requires its opposite to achieve definition.[12] Rather, Bonhoeffer seeks to express Christianity's faith – that God in Christ, in the cross and resurrection, reveals God's genuine will to save – in broader terms. Bonhoeffer, consequently, describes God's willed action in terms of human existence. This is the philosophical foundation of his turn towards the general question of atheism and the autonomy of the modern world, *etsi deus non daretur*.

Bonhoeffer's is a risky strategy, because an acceptance of the intellectual necessity of atheism immediately raises the question of the very existence of God altogether, as seen in the work of those 'death of God' theologians who have appealed to Bonhoeffer on precisely this question. Bonhoeffer seeks to avoid this difficulty. Or rather, he never raises it: he remains within the general parameters of a faith seeking understanding. For Bonhoeffer the question of atheism is thus always a question of God's will. It is straightforwardly a sign of the genuine wholeness of God's love that it even broaches the question of divine non-existence, on the cross, in order to save humanity. What one finds in Bonhoeffer's letter is not a theory of human independence in terms of the projection of religious goals and ideals onto an external, divine being, but rather a general, speculative metaphysics of God's being, expressed via an event: Jesus Christ's life, death and resurrection, conceptualized and encountered through the autonomy of society. This is theology moving towards an acknowledgement that in modernity society effectively governs Church's rhetorical address to the world.

It is in this sense that Bonhoeffer writes:

> Here is the decisive difference between Christianity and all religions. Man's religiosity makes him look in distress to the power of God in the world: God is the *deus ex machina*. The Bible directs man to God's powerlessness and suffering; only the suffering God can help (3/1967, p. 361).

Leaving aside Bonhoeffer's simplistic representation of other religions, one yet recognizes the power of the theological insight that 'only the suffering God can help' – that it is only in the cross that *Christians* find God's will truly, eschatologically, revealed. For Bonhoeffer, finally, the entire relationship between the unknown God and the known humanity (in the autonomy of society) is mediated through the narrow pathway of the incarnation, an argument which gives to the person Jesus Christ absolute power and authority, precisely in his powerlessness.

[12] Jüngel (1983, pp. 55–104) brings out the similarities – and differences – between Bonhoeffer and Hegel (1977a) on this question, by relating them together in one section entitled 'Talk about the Death of God as the Theological Answer to the Question: Where is God?'.

The reductive drift of Bonhoeffer's Christology

Given the metaphysical tenor of Bonhoeffer's comments in 1944 one can speak of a broadly reductive drift in his Christology, since the narrowness of his emphasis upon the cross precludes a developed theological interpretation of the personhood of Christ (in terms of genuine humanity). Instead, the personhood is effectively collapsed into the work of Christ. Already in his *Christology* Bonhoeffer had identified at this point his dependence upon Melanchthon's dictum, that to know Christ is to know his benefits, as the founding principle of Christology (1966, p. 37).

Granted, however, that Bonhoeffer is clear about the origins of his own particular Christology, yet it is justified to enquire whether or not it is successful in addressing the needs of both the historical situation, and the interpretation of the Christological doctrines. It is evident that what is required here is an examination of Bonhoeffer's two axioms: that religion is something deleterious; and that atheism is the correct description of the autonomy of the world.

Philosophically, it seems obvious that an emphasis solely upon the Christ event as the unique mediation between God and the world, as the only way in which the unknown God is revealed, makes of that event something necessary. Revelation thereby becomes not a voluntary act of God but a first-order act of definition on God's part, and the expression of God's definition of the world. It is, therefore, an inflexible theological model, and unnecessarily so; for what it seeks to preserve and articulate can be preserved and articulated by other means. The social nature of the world, its emphasis upon communication of meaning and intent, and the generation of relational understandings between groups and individuals, works against an exclusive interpretation of God's relationship with the world. The very nature of the world argues for spontaneous articulation and dialogue as the best model for interpretation, in place of the unidirectionality of Bonhoeffer's Christology, because the religious and social pluralism of the world – which itself reflects something of the revelation and concealment of mystery – must be acknowledged to contextualize any interpretation of the Christ event.

This argument requires development, something I want to undertake in detail in chapter 6; but the basic themes can be elaborated here. The attractions of Bonhoeffer's late, fragmentary ideas is that they return the question of Christology to the more general arena of the question of modernity. In so doing, however, Bonhoeffer fails to grasp the real opportunity, which is to understand that event naturally; i.e. in terms of the creative fate of the world. Instead, deploying Grotius' *etsi deus non daretur*, and employing the historically questionable notion of the world's increasing atheism, Bonhoeffer once again narrows the focus of his enquiry; once again, he produces a reductive Christology. Not only does this not address the considerable difficulties involved in advocating such a Christology 'from above' without historical reflection, but it does not address the diversity and flexibility of humanity's concern for the divine. Its reductive drift is thereby aimed not only at Christology, but also at religion, which is unsatisfactory if one accepts the premise that the spiritual nature of mystery is reflected – if not explicitly revealed – in a wide variety of different religious traditions.

What one finds, therefore, is that Bonhoeffer's ideas inhibit theological development at the very point where he seeks to open dialogue, namely the fate of the world. This is not his intention; but in overlooking the complexity of society and humanity, in terms of the plurality of cultures and contexts in which people seek to speak of God, Bonhoeffer's thought is reductive. In this sense, one might argue, the real autonomy of the world in modernity is best expressed not in terms of atheism but pluralism. Again, if one seeks to articulate the being of God by means of the interpretation of the Christ event, then it is the legitimate possibility of many such interpretations that reveals something of the divine tolerance, therefore will, therefore being. It is the thrust and drive towards religiosity, towards a relationship with the divine, which seeks its (to Christians) sole answer and genuine revelation in Christ, which constitutes the mystery of the world in terms of the entire creation; but Christ cannot, *theologically*, appropriate mystery *in toto*.[13]

In terms of Barth's polemical stance in modern theology – something which is evidenced in Bonhoeffer's work – the implication here is that the *analogic fidei*, the analogy of faith which is comprehended in Christ alone, in some way requires the *analogia entis*, the analogy of being – which in turn it perfects – in order to address the entire world. One must therefore discuss naturally the world in order to understand God's address to the world in Christ. For Bonhoeffer this

[13] On this question I am influenced by the work of John Hick (1989, pp. 5–9) and Paul Badham (1990, pp. 1–14).

would mean devoting considerably more attention to what he refers to as the *actus reflectus* or reason.[14]

For my distinction between mystery and event, one can see – from both Barth and now Bonhoeffer – that too quick a leap towards Christology serves only to devalue it, whatever the good intentions of the author, because any interpretation of the doctrines of Christ requires an *a priori* understanding of humanity and its spiritual quest which reflects upon its fundamental nature. Mystery, therefore, *is* natural. If this is accepted for a doctrine of God and the incarnation, then there can be no reason why this is not the case for a doctrine of humanity.

Without accepting Harnack's own particular model of religion, consequently, once again one can reiterate his misgivings about dialectical theology – but this time, additionally, elaborating those misgivings in terms of the necessity of a philosophy of the world to complement Christology. In the next chapter I will develop this argument in dialogue with two theologians, both very significant in the era from 1960 to the mid-1990s, but who come from very different traditions: Karl Rahner, theological father of the Second Vatican Council (1962–5), and Professor Jürgen Moltmann, a Reformed theologian from Tübingen. In this way I intend to develop further the general scope of this book, concentrating now upon the specific problems associated with the interpretation and communication of the Christ event in and of itself.

[14] One sees the same intention, though in differing ways, in the theologies of Karl Rahner and Hans Urs von Balthasar. Rahner turns to such a rational analysis of human transcendence – on the basis of a Kantian/Maréchalian analysis of knowledge and will – in order to form the background against which to understand faith (see Sheehan 1987, Part I). Von Balthasar, more traditionally but less philosophically, turns to such an understanding of human nature as mediated through the thought of Erich Pryzwara and Henri de Lubac (see Kehl and Loser 1982, pp. 17–22, 31–42).

3

Moltmann and Rahner: The Presence of Eternity

And this is eternal life, that they know thee the only true God, and Jesus Christ whom thou hast sent (John 17:3)

One preliminary conclusion to be drawn from chapter 2 is that the movement towards a social understanding of such categories as mystery, event and rhetoric has been a very gradual one in twentieth-century theology. Harnack's liberalism, attacked and condemned by Barth because of its failure to appreciate the immediate confrontation of the individual by the Word, gives way in Bonhoeffer to a communal interpretation. Even here, however, such themes as community and society are strictly defined by Bonhoeffer's Protestant ecclesiology, reinforcing the already strongly dialectical nature of his narration of the Christ event and its meaning, and thereby dominating his 'philosophy of theology';[1] i.e. the framework within which Bonhoeffer considers questions about God. Bonhoeffer's rhetoric, consequently, remains within certain carefully defined parameters. It never develops into a full anthropology within which he might suggest, implicitly or explicitly, a general theory of the relationship between faith and society.

The question I want to consider in this chapter is how one might develop a full anthropology in this way, within the context of explicitly Christological reflection; it is, therefore, a question of how one moves theologically to a level of general redescription, upon which one can discuss matters like the relationship between God and the world in the light of revelation, and from which one can address society at large. In late twentieth-century theology one can identify this question in a wide range of theologians – Metz (1980) or Pannenberg (1991), for example. In focusing upon the unlikely coupling of Moltmann and Rahner, however, and thereby explicitly concerning

[1] The expression is MacKinnon's (see Kerr 1986, p. 171).

myself with the centrality of the Christ event, I want to achieve two things: first, an understanding of the differing levels of discourse upon which such reflection occurs, something cast into relief by the obvious differences between these two thinkers; and second, a movement of the Christological question away from its own explicit parameters, towards an engagement with a specific social context. This will lead into chapter 4.

Jürgen Moltmann

Moltmann's philosophy of theology: The Crucified God

More than any other theologian since Bonhoeffer, Moltmann has made his experiences in prison camps pivotal to his understanding of the doctrines of Christ (see Moltmann 1980, pp. 6–7), clearly defining this position in his most famous work, *The Crucified God* (1974), in which such theological categories as mystery, grace and, most significantly, the saving event of the cross, are related to the issues of suffering and oppression in society: 'Christian theology cannot be a pure theory of God, but must become a *critical theory of God*' (1974, p. 69). For Moltmann such a critical theory of God, one which mediates between faith and society, must begin and end in a certain understanding of Golgotha. In terms of my general rubric, the *mystery* which concerns theology is God's expressive love, in which God absorbs suffering into the Godhead via the Trinitarian event of the cross. The hard edge of Moltmann's theology is that mystery can be interpreted only on the basis of a critical theory of society; i.e. how society functions and how faith relates to it. Moltmann has developed the implications of this insight throughout his subsequent writings.

The philosophical support which Moltmann claims for this understanding of the relationship between faith and society comes from the work of T. W. Adorno and Max Horkheimer, particularly the former's *Negative Dialectics* (1991). Using this text (published in German in 1966) as a springboard in the same way that his *Theology of Hope* (1967) used Ernst Bloch's *Principle of Hope* (1986; 1949), Moltmann develops a philosophical theology distinct from the German Protestant parameters of the Kantian – Hegelian tradition. He writes:

> The criticism of the Church and theology which we have been fortunate enough to experience, and which is justified on sociological, psychological

and ideological grounds, can only be accepted and made radical by a critical theology of the cross (Moltmann 1974, p. 2).

In this way Moltmann brings together Christ and society in one symbiotic relationship, a clear development of Bonhoeffer's late position.

The point of this development is to move theology away from the arid debates about epistemology and ontology which dominated it up to and including dialectical theology. Such reflection, argues Moltmann, leads theology to ignore the true nature of the world in which people live. In order to appreciate the practical realities of Christian social life, Moltmann reverses the traditional order of philosophy and theology: instead of starting with a theoretical framework which is then applied to the surrounding world, Moltmann begins with practical problems, only then seeking to identify the theoretical implications of his data. He writes: ' It follows from these reflections upon the concrete political problems of Christian life, that the question of identity comes to a head only in the context of non-identity, self-emptying for the sake of others and solidarity with others' (1974, p. 17).

The philosophical justification which Moltmann claims at this point gives an interesting twist to the traditional definition of theology as faith seeking understanding. If, with Moltmann, one agrees that theology can begin with the concrete political problems of Christian life, then what one has is a theological methodology which starts from understanding, and then moves on to establish that in a particular interpretation of Christian faith. Understanding seeking faith, consequently, becomes the guiding principle of Moltmann's theology; that would seem to be the logical implication of his allegiance to *negative* dialectics (after Adorno).

What one finds in The *Crucified God*, then – and the same is true of Moltmann's later books – is a concentration upon the development between society and faith, practice and theory, to establish a *relevant* understanding of God's message to humanity, something which reiterates Bonhoeffer's remarks in 1944. Such a dynamic interpretation of this relationship, which according to Moltmann overthrows the static conceptions of faith and society found in earlier theologies, mirrors the political nature of humanity. He writes: 'Theologies which are drawn up in order to achieve a connection with the surrounding world, to which they wish to make Christian life relevant, must give serious attention to the necessity to be relational' (1974, p. 11). It is this notion of relationship which Moltmann wishes to develop as the prior, contemporary requirement to speak of God in Christ, on the cross.[2]

Despite his protestations to the contrary (1974, p. 11), therefore, Moltmann is effectively allowing society to establish the agenda for faith.[3] He writes: 'If the title "Christ" refers to the redeemer and liberator, then practical "Christian" action can only be directed towards the liberation of man from his inhumanity' (1974, p. 23). Moltmann's 'if... only' construction here betrays his basic presupposition, that in the quest for relevance authority now resides not in tradition, or doctrine, or any other form of orthodoxy, but rather in a relational understanding of action within society, which elsewhere is described as orthopraxy (see Schillebeeckx 1987, p. 30). It may well be true, as Moltmann suggests, that this development in modern theology is necessary; but it is very important to recognize how far Moltmann's critical theory carries him at his point.

If one wishes to speak of a philosophical structure to Moltmann's theology, consequently, one must articulate his understanding of the contemporary world in which he lives. This is the first implication, as Moltmann sees it, of beginning theology in the work of Adorno and Horkheimer (and Bloch), rather than Kant and Hegel. There is no attempt at all in Moltmann's work to identify any metaphysical basis for theology; that would mean the imposition of a theoretical model which he is keen to avoid. Instead, structure and framework – if one can speak of them at all – are for Moltmann consequences of approaching the social nature of human existence and reality from its own perpective, namely historically.[4]

As acknowledged, Moltmann is heavily influenced by critical philosophy, particularly Adorno. Simultaneously, however, he wants to claim an exclusively Christian foundation for his methodology, in keeping with the axiomatic approach typical of modern Protestant theology:

> Christian theology must be theology of the cross, if it is to be identified as Christian theology through Christ. But the theology of the cross is a critical

[2] The radicalization of this understanding of relationship in European Protestant theology since Barth and Bultmann has in many respects been a reaction against these theological teachers, something most strongly emphasized in the work of Dorothee Sölle. For her recent reflections upon this situation, see Sölle 1990, p. 16.

[3] This would seem to be entirely contrary to Milbank (1990), in which astonishingly Moltmann's theology is not mentioned.

[4] Moltmann uses 'history' quite loosely, without the reflection upon *Historie* and *Geschichte* which one finds in a theologian like Bultmann. It is clear, however, that 'historical existence/experience' for Moltmann is something people enjoy socially, and therefore with the concomitant questions of political and material significance about which Moltmann wants to write.

> and liberating theory of God and man. Christian life is a form of practice which consists in following the crucified Christ, and it changes both the man himself and the circumstances in which he lives. To this extent, a theology of the cross is a practical theory (Moltmann 1974, p. 25).

Because Christianity is a religion which began in an historical event, and which even in that very event was profoundly social and political, so it can and must be critical of the historical context in which Christians live. To this extent Moltmann has a crude, implicit anthropology, unarticulated but heavily dependent upon broadly socialist principles, which defines the parameters of his theology quite rigidly.

Moltmann therefore arrives swiftly at the functional basis of *The Crucified God*: a robust, if curtailed, synthesis of critical theory and historical-critical exegesis of the New Testament. The justification for this approach is to be found, as already indicated, in Moltmann's own experiences of God during and immediately after the Second World War, and by extension in the witness to Christ of all those who are oppressed and suffer. Similar to Barth's rejection of Harnack, then, Moltmann opposes any theology which has nothing to say about the predicament of those who are awaiting, in hope, the *eschaton*:

> As the people of the crucified Christ, the Church originated in the particular earthly events of the oppression and liberation of Jesus, and exists in the midst of a divided and mutually hostile world of inhuman people on one side and dehumanised people on the other (1974, pp. 52–3).

Without his emphasis and methodology, Moltmann argues, not only can theology not do justice to its own foundation events of the death ('oppression') and resurrection ('liberation') of Jesus of Nazareth; it can have nothing to say to the world in its present circumstances. Today, all theology is genuinely critical, and thereby practical, only in so far as it addresses this predicament. Such is Moltmann's basic position.

The Crucified God gives a clear definition to the notion of critical theology which is central to the present study, in that it seeks to articulate a fundamental relationship between faith and society. Does it do justice, however, to the eschatological nature of such Christian faith? In its attempts to be materially historical, does Moltmann's theology do justice to the Christian belief in the immanence of the future (eternity) in the past and present (Pannenberg's criticism)? Or does it simply elaborate a social and practical way of behaving, which is advocated in the name of the cross because the cross seems – aesthetically and existentially – to signal the apotheosis of certain ethical qualities? These questions are important because Moltmann's theology of the cross does attempt to be comprehensive, to seek to define the Christ event universally as the first principle of Christian thought.

Comparison with earlier theologians at this point is illuminating, because it is at this juncture of time and eternity, of history and eschatology, that theology in the twentieth century has most often encountered difficulties. The clearest example here is Karl Barth, whose movement from *Romans* I to II is such a shift from materialism to an eschatologically – realist understanding of the Word of God. Moreover, Barth clearly makes this move because he thinks that no philosophy can provide a satisfactory structure for what theology has to say about the cross and resurrection; hence Barth's oft-mentioned failure to develop any philosophy of theology, because he thinks there can be no adequate such philosophy. From the viewpoint of Barth's mature theology, Moltmann's assimilation of Adorno (and Bloch) is the mistake which the older man made in *Romans* I. The general point is clearly that mystery demands a more sophisticated interpretation than Moltmann's materialism provides, even if it is established in an understanding of the Christ event.[5]

By contrast Dietrich Bonhoeffer, in his last letters and papers from prison, attempts to construct a speculative, metaphysical framework in which to understand both the cross of Christ and, by extension, the relationship between God and the world, today come of age in terms of society's autonomy. Moltmann, certainly, shares Bonhoeffer's commitment to a belief in the cross as the *singulare tantum* around which humanity turns; but he clearly does not want to leave these reflections on the level of general speculation, as Bonhoeffer seems to do. Rather, Moltmann turns away from writing explicitly about the universality of Christ, until he has identified the particularity of Jesus and his fate. In this respect one can almost write of Moltmann, Barth and Bonhoeffer as Russian dolls: each fits neatly inside the next, as each apparently moves on to a 'higher' level of speculation and metaphysical framework. One can argue this point not simply theoretically, in that the style of each of these theologians is geared to a different level of analy-

[5] The real point here is that a theological understanding of mystery must say as much about concealment as it does about revelation, because faith is not knowledge, and grace is not naturally something which gives complete awareness of God's will and being. The danger with Moltmann's emphasis upon what is revealed in the cross and resurrection is that it fails to give sufficient weight to the fact that so much of God is concealed in the cross and resurrection, and that even a personal encounter with the Revealer – in Bultmann's sense – still does not secure any position from which one can then speak with certainty of the meaning of these events and this person. The methodological point here – that theology's hermeneutic task is necessarily limited by the truth of revelation – is important for how I want to move from general theological statements about mystery towards Christology proper (see chapter 7).

sis and discussion, from the deliberately contextual work of Moltmann to the speculative metaphysics of Bonhoeffer. One can also argue it historically, in that their relevant experiences as theologians in Germany helped to move their work away from the tendency towards totalitarianism. This is clearly the case in Moltmann's laudable emphasis upon the validity of different types of theological model; but one can also argue that such an awareness lies at the heart of Barth's *Church Dogmatics* IV.[6]

Granted the validity of this argument, however, Moltmann's theology is subtler than such a preliminary inspection reveals; for the particularity of Jesus' death is itself the pathway into a different universalizing analysis of Christ's significance. Moltmann's strategy – to speak of God not in universal terms which can be made practical, but in practical terms which are then claimed, in faith, to be of universal significance – is dependent upon what he has to say about Jesus' fate. It is the *cross*, therefore, which constitutes both a scandalizing opposition to oppression and injustice in society – in Jesus' own life – and a statement, in faith, about God's elective love of the world.

The particularity of the cross

One of the most important implications of Moltmann's philosophy of theology is that he must be concerned with questions of historical-critical research, for only then can he adduce any authoritative basis for the practical arguments he wants to advance: 'the first task of Christology is the critical verification of the Christian faith in its origin in Jesus and his history' (Moltmann 1974, p. 84). In all of his work, therefore, most clearly in *The Way of Jesus Christ* (1990), Moltmann has followed the path of Rudolf Bultmann in constructing systematic theology upon the foundations of Biblical – specifically New Testament – criticism, an approach which still leaves a considerable degree of flexibility at the theologian's disposal because, as Moltmann's later work indicates, there are many different ways in which one can appeal to the historical Jesus in support of a theological argument (see Moltmann 1990, pp. 38–9). In *The Crucified God*, however, Moltmann is much more specific: 'the understanding of the crucified Jesus must be the origin of all Christology, for otherwise his death on the cross would mean the end of all Christology' (1974, p. 124). Christology

[6] I would argue that in his later work Barth had moved much further, methodologically, from his early position than is generally realized, even to the point that his late theology is inherently pluralist. On this question, see Ford 1981, pp. 33–46: I would not claim that Ford agrees with my argument, but I think he has recognized the implication.

cannot simply construct an image of Jesus, emphasizing his mission and message and his activity as a teacher (as Harnack attempted), which does not take as its pinnacle Jesus' obedient death on the cross.[7] In this sense Moltmann, like Rahner, argues that Jesus' voluntary death is the final act of his earthly life, the final confession and witness of Jesus to his being the Son and thereby to his relationship with the Father: 'The problem intrinsic to every Christology is not merely its reference to the person called by the name Jesus, but also the reference to his history, and within his history, to his death on the cross' (1974, p. 86). Methodologically, therefore, Moltmann establishes his Christology in an attempt to understand the mission and message of the historical Jesus.

This emphasis upon the role of historical-critical research in understanding Jesus' life and death necessarily involves Moltmann in a discussion of the kingdom of God, because it is the kingdom which gives Jesus' activities eschatological significance, which makes of Jesus the presence of eternity for all humanity. What one finds in *The Crucified God* is Moltmann's attempt to regard the eschatological significance of Jesus' life in terms of his historical activities, and his historical activities in the light of his eternal meaning as Son. Clearly, therefore, Moltmann is attempting to write for Christian faith; but he is also seeking understanding via the terminology of the kingdom, within a previously established framework of critical theory. This, as Moltmann (1977 and 1981) acknowledges, has considerable implications for his understanding of eschatology's practical dimension in the present.

Moltmann's reliance upon the historical-critical method, however, hinders his development of an imaginative and therefore genuinely theological Christology. History, in Moltmann's sense, would seem to establish clear parameters, beyond which lies territory unmapped by either research or hermeneutics. This is a small point at this stage, and it does not cause Moltmann any particular problems in his Christology; but it does highlight something which is going to be increasingly important as this book progresses. Concisely, the adoption of the historical-critical method in the construction of any image of Jesus, and thereby the appropriation of objective criteria for establishing histori-

[7] The question of whether Jesus' death was really a willing one is still obscure to me; 'yet not what I will, but what thou wilt' (Mark 14:36) would seem to indicate that the Son's will is constrained by the Father's, in the power of the Holy Spirit, something which makes sense only in terms of the doctrines of the incarnation and Trinity. (The point here is that although the Son chooses to obey the Father, it is still the Father's will which prevails over that of the incarnate Son.) Nevertheless, for the sake of understanding one can acknowledge Moltmann's argument here.

cal truth ('accuracy'), militates against any interest in methodological pluralism. Moltmann's definition of history is therefore exclusivist because it establishes boundaries, albeit implicitly, beyond which lies material which Moltmann considers theologically irrelevant.

In fact Moltmann argues that the historical-critical method is peculiarly liberating:

> If it is true that Jesus' proclamation of the kingdom is associated essentially with his person, and not merely by chance, then no continuities in the field of history, the philosophy of history, the philosophy of language or the history of existential life can bridge the discontinuity which lies in his death (1974, p. 122).

The kingdom of God – Jesus' eschatological meaning and purpose – is not something simply added to his historical life at a particular moment in time. It is, rather, inherent to his person, and when that person suffers death on the cross, albeit a death which is the consummation of a chosen life, the kingdom is thrown into crisis; one, moreover, not only of the world, but also of the Godhead. This is the implication of speaking of Jesus Christ in personal terms, which Moltmann wants his reader to understand: eschatology too becomes personalized, entirely, in Jesus Christ. This is how Christ reveals God on the cross, economically and therefore immanently as the image and story of a particular individual.

Moltmann does not present the reader with a system of theology, therefore, in which the classical doctrines of the Christian faith are adduced rationally and sequentially. On the contrary, he is concerned with the *person* of Christ, but not the 'person' of Christ as it is understood in the Chalcedonian Definition. Rather, Moltmann is operating with a modern philosophy of personhood, one which may articulate the meaning inherent in the two natures doctrine, but certainly not one which is limited to it (see McFadyen 1990). He writes:

> The theology of the cross is not "pure theology" in a modern, non-political sense, or in the sense of private religion. Faith in the crucified God is in the political sense a public testimony to the freedom of Christ and the law of grace in the face of the political religions of nations, empires, races, and classes. Between faith in Christ and the deified rulers of the world, the personal cults and the social and political fetishes of society, Jesus himself stands (1974, p. 145).

Moltmann's emphasis upon personalized eschatology thereby reveals another crucial aspect of the particularity of Jesus' cross: Jesus stands alone. On the borderlands of faith and society, Moltmann argues, Jesus Christ, in the desolation of the cross, is the sole mediation between the eschatological life in which believers share, and the world in which they live. Jesus functions as mediator, moreover, because he is encountered as a person, because it is only on the basis of a personal relationship with another that any one can mediate. In this sense the profoundest implication of the event of the cross for Moltmann is its revelation of the Trinity, which must inform all subsequent understanding of what it is to be a Christian within Church.[8]

The particularity of the cross highlights the uniqueness of Jesus Christ's death, both historically and eschatologically. Historically, because it is the consummation of his life; eschatologically, because it is the consummation of humanity's. The cross, however, also focuses attention upon the particularity of Jesus, both historically and eschatologically. Historically, because as the Gospels testify, Jesus was abandoned to his fate in Gethsemane (see Mark 14:50) by his friends and disciples; eschatologically, because as the Son, the second Person of the Trinity, Jesus is abandoned by the Father, albeit in love. Christ goes to his death in the Father's profoundest rejection, argues Moltmann, which is how the willed being of the Trinity is revealed to humanity as its eternal fate: 'Not until we understand his abandonment by the God and Father whose imminence and closeness he had proclaimed in a unique, gracious and festive way, can we understand what was distinctive about his death' (1974, p. 149). This is the other side of Jesus' immediate personhood – the loneliness of the Son – in which Christians share: 'eschatological faith in the cross of Jesus Christ must acknowledge the theological trial between God and God' (1974, p. 152). Perhaps most profoundly in this text, Moltmann thus relates his understanding of personalized eschatology directly to the being of the Trinity: it is there, in the Godhead, that the mysterious basis of theology's understanding of eschatology becomes clear for Moltmann. In so doing, entirely traditionally, Moltmann places the humanity of Jesus directly in the midst of the eternal mystery of God, thereby preserving the beauty of his own image of Christ.

None of this means, of course, that Moltmann escapes from the obvious criticisms of any theology which seeks to establish Christology in questions of personhood and, by implication, personality; but this is not the immediately significant point, which, rather, is that

[8] Moltmann clearly sees this point, which is why he begins his five-volume systematics with a book about the Trinity and the kingdom of God. In contemporary theology a similar point has been made by McFadyen (1990), with a developed understanding of personhood. For my own reflections upon the relationship between human and divine personhood see Jones 1992; see also chapter 6 below for the implications of this point for how one understands mystery by analogy with time.

Moltmann's is an isolationist Christology: the Son is alone, because the Father has abandoned him (albeit into the power of the Spirit). The particularity of the cross therefore has direct implications for an understanding of personhood, because if isolation is the desolation which the Son must endure for the sake of humanity, then isolation – in all of its as-yet undisclosed meaning – must be something which all humanity experiences negatively. As one would expect, therefore, the overcoming of isolation, in a variety of ways, is for Moltmann the practical sense of Christian faith and, consequently, of eschatology; for it is only in the power of the Holy Spirit, the power of the open future of God, that anything can be achieved *now*. Eschatological power is for Moltmann therapeutic of society, absolutely and hence universally. Such is the practical implication of faith, established in the Triune and personal love of God, and the task of theology is to address itself therapeutically to the needs of people in society. This is why the Christ event is for Moltmann the defining quality of faith's relationship with society.

The cross as focus of faith and society

Moltmann is clearly seeking a classical understanding of the cross in terms of the interrelationships of the three Persons of the Trinity: 'There is a Trinitarian solution to the paradox that God is "dead" on the cross and yet is not dead, once one abandons the simple concept of God' (1974, p. 203). The confession of three Persons in one Being, central to the orthodox doctrine of the Trinity, allows Moltmann to make a distinction between the suffering of the Son on the cross which, though shared in love by the Father and Holy Spirit, is not their immediate experience, and that unifying love, which as the basis of the Father's participation in the cross, is also the foundation of the presence of the Holy Spirit at the crucifixion and subsequently in Church and thereby the world. Moltmann can, therefore, quote Steffen in conclusion:

> The Scriptural basis for Christian belief in the triune God is not the scanty trinitarian formulas of the New Testament, but the thoroughgoing, unitary testimony of the cross; and the shortest expression of the Trinity is the divine act of the cross, in which the Father allows the Son to sacrifice himself through the Spirit (1974, p. 241).

In this manner, and as the necessary implication of his movement away from traditional forms of epistemology and ontology towards the critical theory of Adorno, Moltmann is able to circumvent the traditional shibboleth of divine impassability; for the level upon which he now locates discussion of God's Personhood is not that of being, but rather love understood as expression of will. Moltmann writes: 'The justifiable denial that God is capable of suffering because of a deficiency in his being may not lead to a denial that he is incapable of suffering out of the fullness of his being; i.e., his love' (1974, p. 230). This, certainly, still presents important epistemological problems of its own. How, for example, does one distinguish between love and being? And, indeed, what is being? Or, if they are identical, does this not raise once again, like Samuel's wraith, the problem of fundamental ontology? Nevertheless – and if one accepts Moltmann's own philosophical presuppositions – then his conclusion seems inevitable: 'Because this death took place in history between the Father and Son on the cross on Golgotha, there proceeds from it the Spirit of life, love and election to salvation' (1974, p. 246). The task of theology is for Moltmann that of reconciling the therapeutic needs of people in society with his own definition of grace. Moltmann has undertaken this task ever since.[9]

The problem with Moltmann's formulation is that it still seems to subordinate the Holy Spirit to a mode of being or 'implication' of the binitarian love which occurs between the Father and Son, in which respect the Hegelian background to Moltmann's work, simply because he is a German theologian, is readily apparent (see McGrath 1986, p. 191). Moltmann seems to be aware of this problem: 'Christ is more than necessary; he is free and sets us free' (1974, p. 266). But, although the rejection of necessity as a Christological theme goes some way towards countering the basic tenet of Hegel's position in *Faith and Knowledge* (1977a), the implicit juxtaposition of liberty and bondage plays directly into the conceptuality of the *Phenomenology of Spirit* (1977b). In this respect Moltmann's attempt to identify a basic anthropology – which is the hidden agenda of his use of critical theory – runs into trouble, simply because the classical problems of faith (life and death, time and eternity) and society (liberty and bondage) have been dominant in philosophy and theology for over 150 years. This raises the question: what, if anything, is new in Moltmann's combination of the doctrine of the Trinity and critical theory, *pace* Adorno's negative dialectics?

The immediate background to Moltmann's career gives an initial answer. His texts of the 1960s and 1970s, as Moltmann explicitly acknowledges, articulate the social and political concerns of the

[9] In many respects Moltmann's systematics is a therapeutic theology, addressed primarily to the perceived ills of society (see Moltmann 1992, p. 4).

period. Dominated by discussion of the death of God and the possibility/necessity of a 'theology after Auschwitz', *The Crucified God* is straightforwardly an attempt to tackle the questions that society and history place in the way of Christian faith. Moltmann writes: 'God in Auschwitz and Auschwitz in the crucified God – that is the basis for a real hope which both embraces and overcomes the world, and the ground for a love which is stronger than death and can sustain death' (1974, p. 278). Moltmann's is an apologetic theology, consequently, and as such it exists on the boundaries of society and faith, seeking to reconcile them on the basis of the perceived needs of the former, and the Christomorphic revelation of the latter.[10]

Moltmann therefore confronts faith with society; his is not an attempt to understand faith and society as in any way two sides of one problem, or to understand contemporary society and its issues as in some sense being 'absorbed' into faith. On the contrary, Moltmann's is a theology of conflict: society makes certain vital demands upon the way Christians live, which in turn shape our reflection upon God into socially responsible categories. This, for Moltmann, is what makes faith eschatological: not the justification of faith in sight of society, but rather the necessity of changing the world so that it conforms to Christ's proclamation of the kingdom of God. In this sense a theology of the cross is genuinely political because it expresses the power of change in Jesus' proclamation, which is its socio-political force. Moltmann thus writes: 'The political theology of the cross must liberate the state from the political service of idols and must liberate men from political alienation and loss of rights. It must seek to demythologise state and society' (1974, p. 327). Theology and society are symbiotically related, therefore, from the viewpoint of faith. This is the only way, Moltmann argues, in which theology today can function relevantly within the relationship between those who believe, and the society in which they live (again, ideas which Moltmann works out in his subsequent writings; see particularly Moltmann 1977).

Moltmann's position is not new in modern theology, but if one compares Moltmann's argument with the theologians considered in chapters 1 and 2, certain important points become apparent. First, Moltmann, unlike Harnack and the Barth of *Romans* I, is definitely not interested in writing a critique of theology and culture. Instead, like Barth in *Romans* II, he is elaborating a doctrine of God, from the perspective of eschatology and therefore in terms of the presence of

[10] Moltmann's interpretation of the Jewish holocaust has been heavily criticized; see Metz 1984, Haynes 1991, pp. 103–60, and Eckardt and Eckardt 1988, pp. 102–17: my thanks to my colleague Isabel Wollaston for her advice on this question.

eternity in the world. In this respect that which is socially relevant in Moltmann's theology, as in Barth's, is not so much a goal of his method, as rather a function of the being he believes God to be. This works because Moltmann employs negative dialectics and the doctrine of the cross to reveal both the force of change in society, and God's triune being, which wills society to change because ultimately the kingdom of God is the ideal goal of society.

When compared with Bonhoeffer, however, Moltmann's theology pales somewhat, because whereas Bonhoeffer recognizes the autonomy of society as the necessary status of modernity, the full extent of God's love and thereby being, Moltmann's appreciation of modernity, via society, is functional: he nowhere acknowledges fully the 'coming of age' of modernity in the way that Bonhoeffer does. Moltmann has no place for Grotius' *etsi deus non daretur* because theism is his philosophical conviction, unshaken by anything he writes, either concerning contemporary human existence or the horrors and evils of the Jewish holocaust. This marriage of critical theory and theism only makes sense, argues Moltmann, in a theology of the cross, which is the point of *The Crucified God*.

Moltmann's arguments are deliberately subversive of what one might call 'traditional' theological method; i.e. one which moves from philosophical frameworks towards explicitly theological questions. But as I have demonstrated, this does not stop Moltmann from addressing very traditional Christological issues and formulating normative Christological statements in time-honoured fashion. Consequently, I shall now turn to the work of Karl Rahner, and a far more overtly philosophical theology, to relate Moltmann's ideas to those of his Roman Catholic near-contemporary. The point of this turn, as I stated at the beginning of this chapter, is to understand the methods these two theologians employ to approach Christological reflection, the levels upon which such reflection ensues, and the felicity with which they permit theology to address a particular image of Jesus Christ to a specific social context.

Karl Rahner

The cross as creative event

In The Crucified God Moltmann writes, quoting Rahner: 'In Catholic theology, since 1960 Karl Rahner has understood the death of Jesus as the death of God in the sense that through this death "our death [becomes] the death of the immortal God himself" '(1974, p. 201). Rahner himself writes, in a later text, that: 'it is only by the cross of Jesus as such that the unsurpassability of Christian revelation can be and is established; the theology of the cross is an internal constituent of the doctrine of the unsurpassability of the Christian revelation as a whole' (1983, p. 136). Moreover, Rahner adds: 'the *death* of Jesus is an internal constitutive element of God's eschatological self-promise to the world' (1983, p. 139); and, finally:

> If the cross as Jesus's death achieved to the point of resurrection must be described as the end of the history of revelation, this is not to deny, but implicitly to assert, that in this cross as the victory of God's offer of himself to the world, the Church, too, of course is established as the historical and (as public) institutional palpability of faith in the crucified and risen Christ, a faith without which God's self-promise to the world in Jesus would not be victorious at all (1983, p. 141).

The memorable notion of 'institutional palpability' reveals the fullest, ecclesial and therefore social implications of Rahner's apparent doctrine of the cross, because Christ's death is itself a social event, and not something which occurs solely to one person (even as one Person of the Trinity). For Rahner this means that any understanding of the relationship between faith and society must be in terms of the doctrines of Christ, because for Rahner the economic revelation of the Trinity is always simultaneously the revelation of the immanent Trinity.[11]

In this respect Rahner's theology of the cross greatly resembles Moltmann's, something which is reinforced by Rahner's own explicit emphasis upon the humanity of Jesus: 'It would certainly be a heresy, and one which could not be tolerated within the Catholic Church, if anyone sought to maintain that faith in Jesus as the Christ is absolutely independent of the historical experience and self-interpretation of the pre-Easter Jesus' (1974, p. 192). Rahner moves as far as Moltmann in appealing to the historical Jesus for the authority of his Christology; for both theologians, it is in the particularity of the historical Jesus' fate that the definitive nature of grace is revealed. Rahner, therefore, in the essay already quoted by Moltmann, concludes:

[11] Rahner's basic point here, as noted in chapter 1, has clear similarities with Karl Barth's work, so that the doctrine of the Trinity as a mystery of salvation for us may be formulated as follows: 'the Trinity of the economy of salvation is the immanent Trinity and vice-versa' (Rahner 1966c, p. 87). Whether or not this can be the only possible understanding of immanent mystery – as opposed to the only Christian named response – is open to debate (see chapter 6 below).

> If one looks to Jesus, to his cross and death, and really believes that there the living God has said his last word, decisive, irrevocable and hence comprehensive; if he really believes that there God redeems him from the imprisonment and tyranny of the existentials of his blocked, guilty and doomed existence; he believes something that can only be true and real, if Jesus is what the faith of Christianity confesses. Whether he knows it consciously or not, he believes in the incarnation of the Word of God (Rahner 1966a, p. 118).

Rahner therefore agrees with Moltmann that the Christ event is central to the relationship between theology and society; but the question remains open as to the level upon which one can discuss that relationship.

Rahner's connection to Protestant theology (of a certain kind), moreover, is confirmed – particularly in terms of my argument – by Rahner's intellectual proximity to Bonhoeffer. On the humanity of Jesus, Rahner writes:

> there we who have gone out from the world to God, return with him in his entrance into the world, and are nearest to him there where he is furthest away from himself in his true love of the world; there and in this we are nearest to him because, if God is love, one comes closest to it where, having given itself as love to the world, it is furthest away from itself (1967, p. 43).

Rahner interprets this understanding of the doctrines of Christ, in Trinitarian terms, as the profoundest radicalization of the *kenosis* of the Godhead, the clearest and deepest expression of God's self-emptying on the cross, for the sake of humanity. Thus far, and in agreement with Moltmann, therefore, Rahner – like Bonhoeffer before him – seems concerned mainly to emphasize the authentic nature of the Trinity's movement towards the world, and even then only in very general (though traditional) economic categories. Rahner's doctrinal framework is not new; that is the point.

Unlike Moltmann, however, Rahner is unwilling to answer explicitly social or political questions at any length; he does not go on to develop, as Moltmann does in *The Crucified God*, the material and liberating implications of this understanding of the Christ event. On the contrary, Rahner determinedly shies away from such statements, preferring to locate his resources and significance in the area of fundamental, speculative theology (but see Rahner 1986). What one does not find in Rahner's theology of the cross, consequently – and here Moltmann cannot appeal to Rahner for authority – is any sense in which he looks forwards (in a crudely indexical sense) towards the material elaboration of Jesus' eschatological mission in certain specific socio-political achievements (Moltmann's 'liberations'), although Rahner does assert that faith must hope for an objectively real Last Judgement.[12] Such 'achievements' are not, for Rahner, the best way to identify the social meaning of the Christ event, and so one cannot, in Rahner's theology, speak of a materialist understanding of the relationship between faith and society, as one can in Moltmann.[13]

Granted this very real distinction from Moltmann, despite their apparent proximity and agreement concerning the necessity of the theology of the cross, is it still possible to speak of Rahner's desire to develop the ontological meaning of the Christ event for humanity – the death of a real human being – rather than simply a Trinitarian event? The answer to this question must be 'Yes', because the meaning of the Christ event is to articulate something of definitive significance for the entire world, and for the social nature of human being, but which nevertheless occurred in one single individual. This is the point of Rahner's understanding of the Trinity and therefore of the Christ event.

Rahner's solution to this apparent dilemma is to move on from the particularity of Jesus' cross in order to make truth claims about its significance for the world, and by implication for society. The way Rahner does this is to speak of the cross as a creative event, not simply, traditionally, because it is the cross of the Word, through whom all things were made, but rather because it is the cross of a creature, thereby establishing in faith an integral relationship between Creator and creation. Rahner writes:

> Jesus, the Man, not merely *was* at one time of decisive importance for our salvation; i.e., for the real finding of the absolute God, by his historical and now past acts of the Cross, etc., but – as the one who became man and has remained a creature – he is *now* and for all eternity the *permanent openness* of our finite being to the living God of infinite, eternal life; he is, therefore, even in his humanity the created reality for us which stands in the act of our religion in such a way that, without this act towards his humanity and through it (implicitly and explicitly), the basic religious act towards God could never reach its goal. One always sees the Father through Jesus (1967, p. 44).

[12] 'The Christian understanding of the faith and its expression must contain an eschatology which really bears on the future, that which is still to come, in a very ordinary, empirical sense of the word time' (Rahner 1966d, p. 326). On Rahner's apparent collapse of eschatology into anthropology, however, despite the appeal to a real future, see Phan 1988.

[13] This distinction also bears upon their different interpretations of the incarnation. Note also that Rahner's followers, for example Jon Sobrino, took up a different position from Rahner on this question (see chapter 4 below).

This means that Jesus Christ is God's creative Word and that, consequently, the Christ event is a creative event in and for humanity and the present world.[14]

This is an important point because it implies that the cross of Christ is not, as Moltmann suggests, to be understood as a particular form of social message to humanity (which would, in fact, simply emphasize the specific effectiveness of the event for people who acknowledge it), but rather is to be understood as the foundation event of all creation and therefore of all society *per se*. Hence, for Rahner theology is not to be interpreted as a social message, as Moltmann seems to regard it, but rather as the foundation of any social interpretation at all. In Rahner's theology one cannot speak of a form of liberation theology, as one might suggest of the ultimate conclusion of Moltmann's *The Crucified God*, but only of a theological liberation: all social categories are absorbed into a more fundamental metaphysics of how people actually live in creation. Rahner thus writes: 'Christology is the end and beginning of anthropology' (1966a, p. 117). Change for Rahner, consequently, is not a remedy to creation's present state. On the contrary, it is the continuation of creation's gradually unfolding existence, through the Word, as nature and grace.[15]

In terms of the Christian tradition, the only orthodox way to speak of the creative event of the historical Jesus' cross is via the doctrine of the Word, through whom all creation occurs, which is what Rahner does. He deploys the doctrine of the two natures of Christ to ensure Christ's creatureliness, and thereby his eternal significance as the first amongst all creatures: 'For, according to the testimony of faith, this created human nature is the indispensable and permanent gateway through which everything created must pass if it is to find the perfection of its eternal validity before God' (1967, p. 43). Hence, Rahner concludes:

> We must conceive of the relation between the Logos-Person and his human nature in just this sense, that here *both* independence *and* radical proximity equally reach a unique and qualitatively incommensurable perfection, which nevertheless remains once and for all the perfection of a relation between Creator and creature (1961, pp. 162–3).

The once-and-for-all perfection of the cross and resurrection, however, is an article of faith. The theological question, by contrast, is

[14] On this interpretation of Rahner's Christology, see Rahner and Thüsing 1980, pp. 3–17, Bokwa 1990, pp. 204–12, and Bonsor 1987, pp. 75–8.

[15] See Rahner 1963, pp. 114–49. On this question in Rahner's theology, see Schwerdtfeger 1982.

how one gains access to this creative event. This Rahner does not elaborate (but see below).

In Rahner's theology, consequently, one is justified in speaking of his replacement of Moltmann's society with creation as a whole, and society solely by implication, because for Rahner the cross of Christ, of the crucified God, is to be understood as the definitive event of God's creative will, and only in that way can it be at all social. The notion that the social event of the cross reveals the true meaning of the Trinity, therefore (as in Moltmann; see also Boff 1988), is for Rahner more or less redundant, because it is obvious that if the cross is the event of creation and re-creation, then it must reveal the true meaning of the Trinity! Rahner has simply gone deeper than Moltmann, into the area of reflection upon the foundations of the entire world, of which 'society' is solely one human way of speaking.[16] One can thus argue that Rahner's understanding of critical theology sees it existing on the borderlands of faith and creation, rather than faith and society, which has significant implications for how one regards the parameters of theology's responsibility.

From Moltmann's viewpoint, one might argue here that Rahner leaves no room for the practical questions of what it is in fact that Jesus Christ does that marks him out as the Word of creation; that, by resorting to fundamental theology, Rahner evacuates the cross and by implication the incarnation of Jesus' specific and therefore real humanity, and consequently his potential for being a *human* event of change; that, finally, Rahner's Christology collapses into docetism. This, however, would be mistaken, because Rahner makes it quite clear that the doctrine of the two natures of Christ establishes and ensures the true humanity of Jesus, and so the Word's power for creative activity and development. Rahner writes: 'Thus by maintaining the genuineness of Christ's humanity, room is left within his life for achievement, and the possibility of a real Mediatorship and thus – if you will – of a real Messiahship is preserved' (1961, p. 158). What Rahner tries to achieve is not a prescriptive analysis of what it is that Christ actually does, as in Moltmann, which is socially liberating for people, but rather to establish the *a priori*, transcendental conditions of possibility of the creative Word to be liberating as a human being. If, therefore, one wants to discover the practical significance of Rahner's understanding of the creative event of the cross, one must look towards his representation of what is *a priori* in creation.

[16] In the process Rahner abandons the theological territory gained by Bonhoeffer in 1944, a radicalization of *kenosis* with distinct methodological implications for both Christology and interfaith dialogue; see Part II below.

Love and death as ontological categories

In an important early essay Rahner writes: 'It is because we need this ultimate interpretation of our lives, one which is not to be had elsewhere, that we must study the theology of Christ's life and death' (1961, p. 192). The expression 'ultimate interpretation of our lives' is a key one: it points towards Rahner's concern for universals, for a fundamental theology of origins and first principles, and therefore his concern with ontology (see Sheehan 1987, pp. 155–72). For Rahner the Christ event – the creative event of relationship between Creator and creature, revealed in Jesus – is ultimately one which, correctly understood, reveals the ontological foundations of human existence. This is the general claim of Rahner's understanding of the Christian faith.

The move towards fundamental theology, towards claims of Christ's ontological significance, has attracted the criticism that Rahner evacuates the Christ event, and in particular the cross, of its concrete reality. That Rahner is aware of this problem, however, and that he seeks to avoid it, is clear in his theology:

> One might say: because we are no longer in danger of becoming polytheists, we are now in danger of no longer being able to honour *created holiness* and hence are also in danger of allowing God to pale into an abstract postulate of the theoretical or practical reason, which is possibly still draped in Christian terms (1967, pp. 39–40; my italics).

Rahner avoids collapsing Christology into general theory, collapsing theological ontology into general anthropology, because of the certain grip that he maintains upon the historical Jesus. That is the meaning of the expression 'created holiness'.

Looking towards the Christ event – which for him means the cross and resurrection – Rahner recognizes there the ontological categories of human existence, namely love and death. Rahner's reflection, therefore, is both theological and philosophical: theological, because he seeks ontological understanding on the basis of a faith received as grace, through Jesus Christ; philosophical, because the categories he identifies as being ontological are genuinely ontological and therefore universal. Rahner thus moves away from Moltmann's critical theory of faith and society because he is seeking a more fundamental level of analysis than social and political action, into which Moltmann's understanding of eschatology ultimately collapses. In this way Rahner is able, as a Roman Catholic theologian, to speak of the relationship between nature and grace.

This movement from Christology towards anthropology is illustrated by the way in which Rahner treats the ideas of love and death. 'Love' is not categorized abstractly, but on the contrary is the way in which people should relate to each other. If this understanding of love is to be predicated of Jesus Christ, argues Rahner, then it must be an experience which in his incarnation the Son was capable of experiencing: Jesus had to be able to give and receive love. Rahner writes:

> If Jesus Christ is not to become an abstract idea, a Christ-principle, and hence a mythological figure unworthy of belief, then this concrete, historical Jesus of Nazareth must be capable of being loved; he must not be merely another word for the incalculable sovereignty of the grace of the transcendent God (Rahner 1972, p. 182).

Love is a real, physical, and therefore spiritual experience for any individual, argues Rahner, and on the basis of Jesus' genuine humanity it is a human experience which is part of the Godhead. In line with classical doctrine, love is thus regarded as the medium of profoundest communication between God and humanity, as Paul observed (I Cor. 13:13). Love *is* mystery, revealed and concealed in Jesus Christ; in this way Rahner identifies mystery and event to a degree Barth implicitly acknowledged, but failed to articulate, in 1923. And the love which is in the Godhead and which is revealed as the humanity of Jesus Christ is the love which God has for all humanity, expressed definitively on the cross. Rahner writes:

> God is not to be thought of as merely "over against" the world and its history of virtue simply because of being its first "cause", untouched by the world itself and transcending it. Rather, in the outward movement of his love he has inserted himself into the world as its innermost *entelecheia*, and he impels the whole of this world and its history towards that point at which God himself will be the innermost and immediately present fulfilment of our existence in the "face-to-face" presence of eternal beatitude (1974, p. 200).

This is Rahner's understanding of eschatology, and it is in this way, as was demonstrated earlier, that for Rahner 'Christology is the end and beginning of anthropology' (Rahner 1966a, p. 117).

This is the most important point in my consideration of Rahner's Christology, and where he differs most significantly from Moltmann. Rahner's concentration upon an anthropological notion such as love, so that he turns it into a category of ontological reflection, is justified solely by Christology. Unlike the stereotypical image of Rahner, therefore, he does not first of all construct a philosophy, only to insert Jesus into it at a later date. Rather, and as he explicitly states, Rahner goes first to what is revealed in Christ to understand what is said there about human nature; for it is in becoming human nature that the Word truly saves. Rahner's Christology is itself established in a spiritual awareness of the hypostatic union in Christ, as the grace of creation. If one wants to speak of a movement or dynamic in Rahner's thought, it is one from faith, to spirituality, to fundamental theology (ontological reflection). Only in this way can what one says be truly Christian, argues Rahner.

This process can be further illustrated if one considers what Rahner says about death. Given the structure of Rahner's thought, one would expect the question of death to be articulated in terms of personal experience of death (faith and spirituality), in Jesus Christ's personal experience of death (Christology), in order to say something importanct about how people in general live towards death and its conquest in the graceful resurrection of our human nature (fundamental theology). Rahner writes:

> A piece of this world, real to the core, but occupied by the pure and sovereign power of the dispassionate freedom of God, is surrendered, in the total self-mastery which can be achieved by fallen man only in the act of death, to the disposition of God, in complete obedience and love. This is Easter, and the redemption of the world (1966b, p. 128).

The coherence of this movement can only be secured, for Rahner, in the hypostatic union of Christ, which in turn means in the humanity of Jesus turned towards the Word: 'We have to recognize that even Jesus, as man and in his special character as the bearer of revelation, likewise utters the revelation of God to the extent that he himself in his human subjectivity hears and accepts what he has to say' (Rahner 1974, p. 193). This is the mysterious and therefore graceful overcoming of death in the triumph of love, and the task of theology according to Rahner is to think this triumph by meditating upon its name – Jesus Christ. It is in this way that Rahner secures the Christological foundation of his anthropology or ontological reflection, because only in Christ is it possible to speak of anthropology from a theological perspective.

If one contrasts Rahner's method here with that of many Protestant theologians, certain important points become apparent. Taking Barth as an example, one sees how his theology moves from Biblical interpretation, to Christology, to ecclesiology (the *Church Dogmatics*). In so doing, Barth is methodologically predisposed not to say anything about either spirituality or ontological reflection. Where Rahner is most profound, therefore, Barth is curiously silent, a difference which surely cannot be explained solely because one was a Roman Catholic, the other a Reformed Protestant.[17]

Similarly, Bonhoeffer's theology from 1944 demonstrates a movement from ontological reflection (the autonomy of society), to Christology, to the doctrine of God – almost the reverse of Rahner's method. The order of discourse here is probably not the important point, which is rather that both Rahner and Bonhoeffer have a fundamental relationship in their thought between ontology, Christology and theology. This is necessary if the theologian's theoretical statements are to have real and thereby practical significance for the way in which people actually live.

Returning to Moltmann, one can see that his theology moves from Biblical interpretation, to Christology, to socio-political programme. Unlike Rahner's, therefore, it contains no reflection upon human spirituality as the basis of any approach to the Christ event, and no ontological reflection, and so no universal application to humanity in general. By contrast with Rahner, Moltmann's theology, as seen first in *The Crucified God* but also in *The Way of Jesus Christ*, does not address in any direct manner questions of the universal nature of humanity, either in terms of spirituality (and therefore openness to mystery), or in terms of categories of human existence, as in ontological reflection. In this respect one can only take Moltmann seriously: he really does remove any thought about ontology (and epistemology), replacing it instead with critical theory.

This, however, only poses further questions. Does Moltmann's critical theory achieve its goal of making theology practically applicable to the way in which people really live in society? Or does it fail where Rahner's ontological reflection succeeds, in giving to fundamental theology a basis for understanding how *everyone lives*, and therefore, by implication, how everyone lives *socially*?

Ultimately this is a question about the task and *locus* of theology and of what it is to be a theologian. Does one, like Barth, regard theology as Church theology, indebted to the tradition and worship of the community, which means that everyone's understanding of society is inevitably coloured by Christian practices? Or does one, like Harnack, understand theology as functionally the same as socio-cultural theory, in which case the relationship between faith and society is collapsed into liberalism? Does one regard theology as having its first principles in the genuine character of modernity, like Bonhoeffer, in which case

[17] The agreement between Barth and von Balthasar, and the antipathy between von Balthasar and Rahner, may be indicative of a fundamental disagreement on the way in which grace is revealed – and concealed – in the world; see Williams 1986a.

the autonomy of society seems to establish theology's agenda? Or does one, like Moltmann, make an openly partial reading of the Biblical witness, in which case socio-critical theory is seen to be the natural formulation of the Christian doctrine of God? Or, finally, like Rahner, does one move from Christology to ontological reflection, in which truth claims necessarily make Christian claims about the way in which faith and society function together (the former ultimately absorbing the latter)?

The answers to these questions – my reason in writing this book – will be fully elaborated in Part II. To conclude this chapter, however, I shall ask whose theology – Moltmann's or Rahner's – makes the most sense, in terms of understanding the task or role of theology as it works to relate together faith and society via an interpretation of the Christ event.

The task of theology: ontological reflection or critical theory?

Moltmann and Rahner are in agreement concerning the central significance of the Christ event to the Christian doctrine of God; but they disagree considerably as to the structure within which one should understand that event. Moltmann's reliance upon critical theory, rather than ontology or epistemology, means that he is concerned with a materialist interpretation of history, one in which the causal relationships between faith and society are elaborated in terms of their practical, social and political implications. Rahner, by contrast, argues that a renewed understanding of transcendental anthropology will provide theology with the necessary framework within which it can then interpret the nature of those people who, in grace and love, are called by Christ to faith. On Rahner's interpretation, questions of anthropology are necessarily *a priori* to questions of historical interpretation; it is almost as if Rahner is saying 'Clarify questions about the fundamental nature of human existence – which is established in grace and therefore spirituality – and one will then have a way of speaking about what it is for the Son to be both God and human in hypostatic union, and therefore to be universal Saviour'. In other words, in theology one must first speak of humanity, because God addresses Godself to humanity as the eternal Word (and subsequently the Holy Spirit). Moltmann, by contrast, is saying that the really important implications of the Christ event, as the revelation of the love of the crucified God for humanity, are necessarily *a posteriori* to the historicity of that event; or at least, that is how theology must understand its task. In Rahner, therefore, theology operates upon the level of logic, which is what it means to speak of transcendental anthropology. Moltmann, however, collapses theory and practice into one reading of the way in which theology must operate in the contemporary world, because of his reliance upon critical theory.

What Rahner is effectively saying is that if theology takes care of its understanding of the *a priori*, then the *a posteriori* will develop naturally. Or: construct an intelligible and systematic framework, and the practical implications of Christian faith become clear. In terms of the themes of this study, Rahner's conviction can be expressed as follows: a genuinely critical theology understands the relationship between faith and society, and its position within that relationship, because of the claims it makes about human existence in general and the grace of God in particular. No one model of society can therefore be imposed upon a critical theology as it seeks to articulate its understanding of nature and grace from the viewpoint of faith. On the contrary, and as Rahner argues, the task of theology is to exist on the borderlands of faith and society, always relating the two, but always acknowledging its principal allegiance to the ontological and epistemological claims of faith.

This point is important because it gives content to the methodological distinction made above between Moltmann and Rahner. Whereas Moltmann's collapse of theory and practice into one thing – praxis – means that theology cannot divorce itself, even conceptually, from the question of realizing grace in nature and therefore the question of teleology, Rahner's strict allegiance to the transcendental method in theology means that nature and grace can be related, without the need, ultimately, to identify them. This would seem to be fundamental to the methodology of any critical theology; for the collapse of theory into practice means inevitably the collapse of theology into the question of context-bound utopias.

If nature and grace are respected as the origins of theological doctrine, two things follow. First, a genuinely critical theology must address itself to the questions of communication and rhetoric (address), of the transmission of meaning, in the name of human existence. Second, theological method itself becomes entirely reflective, rather than proactive. That this is necessary is vouchsafed by the requirement that theology remain always speech about God; that it is Christian by the fact that such rhetoric always addresses Jesus to the world in which it lives.

These ideas take the argument beyond the positions of Moltmann and Rahner, at least as they are considered in the texts examined in this chapter. The questions raised, however, are directly relevant to the world of political and liberation theologians, who have influenced Moltmann greatly, and who in turn have themselves been greatly influenced – the Roman Catholics at least – by Rahner. What I want to do in the next chapter is take my argument one stage further by interpreting the work of one such theologian, Jon Sobrino, in order to understand the way in which questions of Christology that arise from spirituality and anthropology develop towards the rhetorical address of faith in society. This is the second major slide in modern theology, between event theory and rhetoric.

4

Sobrino: Understanding a Liberated Faith

Truly, truly, I say to you, he who believes in me will also do the works that I do; and greater works than these will he do, because I go to the Father (John 14:12)

The previous chapter ended by moving towards the issues raised when one attempts to address Christological reflection towards a specific social context; and, as I argued, one can see that the beauty of Rahner's Christology is that it allows many different theologians, in many different situations, to say what they want to say about Jesus Christ from within the security of Rahner's spiritual and philosophical frameworks. It is logical, therefore, to continue the general development of Part I by considering the work of a theologian who, whilst working in El Salvador, was yet greatly influenced by Karl Rahner: Jon Sobrino.

The present chapter's aim, consequently, is very straightforward: to examine how Sobrino moves from the more general Christological reflection of a Rahnerian kind, towards embracing the specific issues confronted in El Salvador during the 1970s. Chapter 4 will thus proceed by means of an examination of the philosophical presuppositions which Sobrino brings to his Christology, and how these relate to his spirituality, his understanding of the fundamental mystery of the Christian faith. This in turn will lead to the elements of Sobrino's own Christology, as outlined in *Christology at the Crossroads*, by which time it will be possible to evaluate the relative strengths and weaknesses of Sobrino's position.

Sobrino's philosophical presuppositions

In an important passage in *Christology at the Crossroads*, Sobrino writes:

> Whenever Christian faith focuses one-sidedly on the Christ of faith and wittingly or unwittingly forgets the historical Jesus, and to the extent it does that, it loses its specific structure as Christian faith and tends to turn into religion (1978, p. 275).

In writing this Sobrino probably has at the back of his mind – though he does not make it explicit – not only the debate in Protestant theology concerning the split between the historical Jesus and the Christ of faith, as best typified by Martin Kähler (1964), but also Barth's pointed arguments concerning the dangers of religion as a perversion of Christianity, arguments which achieved seminal form in his questions to Harnack. One finds the same commitment in Sobrino as one found in Barth, to understand the Christ event in such a way that it cannot be misappropriated by any dubious, humanistic influence. Whatever Sobrino wants to go on and say about the Christ event, and the place of the historical Jesus in that event, he is at least clear that it cannot be reduced and domesticated to a personal, subjective experience. If has to be critical at a level which transcends the individualistic. Sobrino writes: 'God appears on the cross *sub specie contrarii*' (1978, p. 199).[1]

Granted that this statement functions as a way of entering the Christological debate, particularly in the slide towards rhetoric – the business of formulating a Christology in order to address it to a specific social context – yet it says something very important about Sobrino's basic position. If God appears on the cross *sub specie contrarii*, then this must mean that there is a dialectical tension between God and the world: the contrast between God and the world which is revealed in the incarnation of the Son is to be understood ontologically, and those two beings are related though opposed, as Creator and creature. Whether or not Sobrino wants to go on and develop this argument in favour of a full-blown metaphysics of the incarnation, still his position here makes an absolute claim: there is a real, rather than simply nominal, difference between God and the world, which is of fundamental importance if one wants to interpret the Christ event meaningfully.[2]

As Sobrino himself concedes, the understanding of dialectics which underpins his Christology at this point is his way of going beyond the

[1] Barth's influence here is very important: although Sobrino does not explicitly lean upon Barth's work, their agreement on Christological principles is apparent. On this aspect of Barth's work, and its relationship with Roman Catholic theology, see Küng 1964, pp. 313–36. Sobrino later developed the same point (1985 and 1987).

[2] The engagement of Christology and creation here opens up the question of natural theology, although the latter's agenda is now interpreted socio-politically. The background in Rahner is obvious, but Sobrino has developed the point in keeping with his own historical context.

epistemological problem of how one actually knows or encounters the Christ event (1978, p. 198). For Sobrino dialectics is combined with analogy – reasoning from approximately parallel cases – in order to move beyond the apparent impasse of speaking today about an event that occurred nearly 2000 years ago. Whether or not this approach is adequate, it is at least common; literally dozens of theologians make similar attempts in the name of constructive Christology.[3]

For Sobrino, consequently, there comes a point in his Christology where he wants to make significant philosophical claims for his theological method: it will say meaningful things both about God's being – mystery, the first principle of all theology, named/appropriated in the Christ event – and also about the society and culture in which such a theology is uttered; it will address both thesis and antithesis of the dialectics of the incarnation *sub specie contrarii*. Sobrino does this, however, not because of any grandiose claims for his metaphysics of knowledge – there is a metaphysics of knowledge here somewhere, although relatively unarticulated – but rather because of the specific circumstances in which he writes and which subsequently he always wishes to address – Latin America. Sobrino's methodological position, his shift towards a critical theology in terms of both similarity and dissimilarity in the relationship between God and the world, is determined by the overriding concerns of his office as a liberation theologian writing in El Salvador. In this sense, Christology for Sobrino is always rhetorical.[4]

What one finds, then, is that Sobrino's philosophical shifts are underpinned by a general presupposition about his own circumstances and those in which Jesus lived and died: 'there is a clearly noticeable resemblance between the situation here in Latin America and that in which Jesus lived', he writes (1978, p. 12). Leaving aside the vexed question as to how Sobrino knows this, and whether or not this knowledge can be verified, his statement provides a very clear starting-point for his Christology; and as Sobrino acknowledges at the beginning of *Christology at the Crossroads* (p. 2), the question of a starting-point is

[3] The philosophical 'marriage' which underlies this development – Aquinas and Hegel – lies at the heart of modern theology, most notably in Barth and Rahner and their followers. On this question, see Küng 1987 (although the point is never adequately developed, Küng recognizes its importance).

[4] Sobrino (1990) expressed eloquent and moving reflections upon this situation in his meditations and prayers upon his friends and co-workers murdered by the death squads and military in El Salvador in 1989.

fundamental to whatever hermeneutics one subsequently wishes to pursue.[5]

The underlying presuppositions in Sobrino's Christology are therefore geared towards an immediate, valid and theologically productive comparison between the historical circumstances of Jesus, his culture and society, and Sobrino, his culture and society. Supporting this identification is the epistemological conviction that the apparent similarities between first-century Palestine and twentieth-century Latin America establish a clear relationship between Jesus and the people who believe in him, so that Sobrino can write: 'In Latin America Christology is *in fact* being worked out by comparing the present-day situation with the historical Jesus' (1978, p. 13).[6]

The unspoken implication of such conceptual work in theology is that there must be a material solution to the comparative writing and reflection undertaken by the theologian; i.e. there has to be a direct shift away from theory, towards practice, in terms of a concrete change in the material circumstances of the writer and/or reader. Sobrino acknowledges as much when he writes: 'Christ really *does not exist* and *is not understood* unless he poses an alternative in peoples' lives' (1978, p. 7). Such an alternative, moreover, cannot simply be an existential or psychological possibility, such as one finds in the theology of Rudolf Bultmann, or, for example, in certain modernist literature.[7] On the contrary, Sobrino is speaking of concrete changes to specific circumstances: no exploitation, freedom from oppression, relative economic prosperity, etc. (see Boff and Boff 1987, pp. 2–3). This is the context in which Sobrino makes Christological statements.

With all of this in mind, Sobrino elaborates the five points relevant to his own theological method: theological milieu of the author; attitude towards the Enlightenment; hermeneutics used by the author; posing of the fundamental metaphysical quandary; and density of the author's Christological concentration (1978, pp. 18–22). As Sobrino acknowledges, his theology's procedure will be governed by his attitude towards – and the circumstances of – the society and culture in

[5] This is known as entering the hermeneutic circle 'somewhere', not necessarily 'at the beginning' (if such a thing is ever possible). On this aspect of theological hermeneutics, see Geffré 1987, pp. 61–2.

[6] Importantly – though he never articulates this point as a metaphysical argument – Sobrino clearly also wants to speak of a spiritual identification of the individual and community with the time and life of Jesus, something which is generated by his own Ignatian spirituality. The two approaches are of course entirely compatible, indeed complementary, because they both serve to appropriate the Christ event religiously; see chapter 7 below.

[7] See Scott 1978 and Gunn 1979. On British literature in this period, see Meisel 1987, particularly chapter 2, 'Two Versions of High British Modernism'.

which he operates: 'The theology of liberation serves as the general frame of reference for Latin American Christology.... From the horizon of liberation, good theologizing means service' (1978, pp. 33–4). The notion of 'service', as will be demonstrated, has at its heart a social and cultural critique which is constitutive of the way in which critical theology addresses its specific historical context. Sobrino consequently moves beyond mystery and event, towards specific questions of Christian rhetoric and the way in which faith addresses the world in which it lives.

Interestingly, Sobrino's method at this point brings him into conflict with Karl Barth, because although Sobrino apparently follows Barth in making his epistemology dependent upon a dialectic of conflict – an infinite qualitative distinction, articulated by Barth, but not by Sobrino – which at first glance is always antagonistic towards society and culture (because they are of the world), in fact Sobrino's own specific society and culture are establishing the agenda for his metaphysics of knowledge. Whereas Barth's epistemology therefore – erroneously – attempts to be absolute, Sobrino's is explicitly relative and thus partial. From Sobrino one learns, seemingly, that such exercises as epistemology and method are of necessity dependent upon circumstance; that there is always a practical basis for being theoretical, a rhetorical necessity guiding Christological reflection. This is the foundation of Sobrino's link between Palestine and Latin America, expressed theoretically as the 'indexing' of Christology in a specific historical context.[8]

Developing this argument one step further, one can identify a real tension between Sobrino's apparent acceptance of a Barthian maxim – the infinite qualitative distinction – and his own subsequent qualification of that maxim for social and cultural purposes (a tension which is established in Sobrino's own understanding of the way in which analogy qualifies dialectic). The real question then becomes not whether Barth or Sobrino is correct, but by what authority Sobrino slides away from Barth's position towards that dialectical materialism which one typically finds in liberation theology.[9] Here one comes across an interesting answer. Both Barth and Sobrino claim the Bible as their ultimate authority; but whereas Barth's is an idealist construct, Christ-shaped, Sobrino's is a programme of social and cultural change. There is more here, consequently, than a simple shift from 'Christ' to 'Jesus',

[8] Some of my thoughts here on indexing, and in chapter 7, were initially developed in a paper for the Cambridge systematic theology seminar (1992), entitled 'Beyond Chalcedon: Index and Intentionality in Christology'. I am grateful to Janet Martin Soskice and David Ford for their constructive comments and criticisms on that occasion.

[9] See Vidales 1980 and Gibellini 1987, pp. 1–2.

as might have been implied by Sobrino's initial comments, quoted above. Rather, it is a question of first principles in theology, and of their authoritative revelation. Again, one might argue that Barth's Bible is Pauline, as demonstrated by his *Romans* I and II, whereas Sobrino's is Synoptic, witness his dependence upon such texts as Luke 4:16–21 and 11:20 (see Sobrino 1978, p. 68); but this would similarly be too simplistic. It is not a question so much of the textual support of Barth's or Sobrino's authority as its origin in an understanding of mystery, because whereas the support of such arguments is nearly always contentious, their origins can be given precise status.

In such a simple contrast of Barth and Sobrino, what one finds is that the real difference between their understanding of the Christ event is not so much one between Christ and Jesus, or ideal and material, or any other such pair of antitheses, but rather between two very different understandings of what the Christian doctrine of eschatology is, and the mystery with which it is identified. Granted that Sobrino and Barth both think eschatology is fundamental to any theological interpretation of the Christian faith, yet they differ as to *how* it should be understood. Since this difference is most illuminating for what I want to say about Sobrino's approach to theology in this chapter, I want to establish more precisely what this difference is.

For Barth eschatology is all about salvation, because God acts eschatologically in order to save fallen humanity. That is the meaning of grace, and that is why, as grace, the Christ event in Barth's theology is understood as eschatologically real. The economy of salvation thus dominates Barth's theological vision because he has an understanding of humanity – an anthropology – which transcends his appropriation of Biblical terminology. The same situation and movement is found in Bonhoeffer, Rahner and Moltmann: for Bonhoeffer the status of that transcendence is basically sociological, 'the world come of age'; for Rahner it is *a priori*; and for Moltmann it functions linguistically-socially. For Barth, however, anthropology is established quite simplistically. It is pre-Enlightenment, and as such owes much to early modern Reformed theology.

For Sobrino, by contrast, eschatology is not about salvation, in the way that 'salvation' always seems to imply a metaphysics of human being or anthropology. Rather, eschatology is about liberation, a term which does not allow itself, at least not in contemporary theology, to be used idealistically. On the contrary, liberation is always from a particular social and cultural situation, understood materially, towards a better one. Such a better one, for Sobrino, is inextricably bound up with theology's understanding of the kingdom of God.

What this means is that the traditional and continually evolving terminology of the Christian faith, which during this century has been particularly concerned with ideal definitions of humanity, society, and culture, is converted or recast in Sobrino's theology into a new form, in which idealism is replaced by materialism. Ideas like society and culture, and theology's relationship with them, consequently, become governing factors rather than incidental elements or simply the *loci* of divine revelation. Unlike even a theologian such as Bonhoeffer, therefore, who speaks explicitly about society and culture determining theology (and a willing God), Sobrino wants to allow society and culture to establish the goals of Christian faith and existence because that is how God's will was revealed in Christ. This challenges not only those ideas and norms accepted in the twentieth century, such as the independence of faith from society and culture (if only nominally); it also challenges the provenance of Christian theology itself. Expressed another way: if the Christ event can be reduced – albeit constructively – to a message of social and cultural change, what does this make of Christian discussion of God as the mystery of the world?

Since this question shapes my interpretation of Sobrino's theology, the next section will consider what Sobrino means by the expression, 'the mystery of God'. If room can be found for this idea, then Sobrino's discussion of theology, society and culture will remain within the parameters of Christian discussion. If not, then it will become increasingly difficult to escape the conclusion that the practical in Sobrino's vision has swamped a disarmingly weak theoretical basis.

God as the mystery of the world in Sobrino's theology

Importantly, Sobrino's theological method is always underpinned by a strong sense of spirituality, so much so that one can speak of the link between the believer and the object of belief – God in Christ – as being established in Sobrino's theology by the action of the Holy Spirit. Thus, whilst the cognitive and historical elements of Sobrino's methodology – his metaphysics of knowledge and his understanding of socio-cultural analogy and/or narrative – go a long way towards establishing the level upon which humanity can interpret God's actions, the fact that one *believes* in those same actions is straightforwardly a consequence of the loving presence of the Holy Spirit (Sobrino 1985, p. 4). This achieves two things for Sobrino's theology. First, it establishes his Christological – and theological – reflection in the doctrine of the Trinity, so that one can speak of Sobrino's position as an orthodox, Catholic appropriation of traditional doctrines of the Christian faith. Second, it brings the Holy Spirit as a powerful, purposive, yet supernatural element into the daily lives of Christian believers, thereby supporting Sobrino's contention that the eschatological realities of which Christianity wants to speak – faith, grace, salvation, judgement, liberation – and which a theologian like Karl Barth maintains cannot be reduced idealistically, can in fact find concrete realization in the material world of people's daily lives. In short, the Holy Spirit is understood by Sobrino as the agent of God's eschatological will, acting in the present situation of Christian believers. It is the believing community's primary experience of the mystery of God, something which determines both their real hopes for the world in which they live, and their intuition of communion with Jesus.

Typically, Sobrino defines his understanding of the mystery of God in both Trinitarian and spiritual terms, so that the mystery of God is the eternal presence and absence of divine power, finding expression through the offices of the Holy Spirit. Consequently, the mystery of God has to be something which is – at least potentially – readily tangible in the material world, working as the continuing presence and witness to salvation (one thinks here of Rahner's notion of 'institutional palpability', with respect to Church). This would seem to be in contrast to the mystery which Bonhoeffer is searching for in his letter of 16 July 1944 to Bethge, where – in terms of his understanding of the Christ event – Bonhoeffer wants to address the maturity of society and culture by speaking of the absence of God, albeit an entirely constructive absence. Similarly, Sobrino's understanding of the material openness to experience of the mystery of God – however incomplete that experience may actually be – is in direct contrast to Barth's position, whereby the glory of God's grace is only preserved by locating it beyond the scope of human experience. On this point, Sobrino remains close to the work of his teacher and influence, Karl Rahner, whose own reflection has as one of its principal foundations a profound sense of Spirit's presence in the world (Rahner 1968).

In fact, in one vital respect Sobrino distances himself from the liberal cultural (and thereby materialistic) theology that one finds in Harnack, achieving this by his concentration upon Christology. Whereas for Harnack Jesus Christ is one avenue by which the mystery of God is to be communicated, so that he is quite happy speaking of other such avenues, for Sobrino the question of Christology is really the only question with which a theologian should concern herself. It is not so much that other ways of speaking of the presence of the mystery of God are ruled out as impossible *per se*, but rather that they cannot be regarded as being urgently relevant in the same way that Jesus Christ's life on earth and its continuing power must be. All of this brings Sobrino's theology back to its social and cultural origin, since one speaks of God *at all* because the gospel is *the* message of liberation for the very poor and oppressed who constitute Sobrino's immediate audience. Christology addresses the life of the Christian because that is why people listen, which makes it difficult for critical theology to be concerned with anything else.

Effectively – and leaving aside the question, for the time being, as to whether or not what he says about it is actually true – what one finds is that Sobrino's understanding of the mystery of God, expressed in Trinitarian terms, is deliberately incomplete; it is revealed only partially, not by any cognitive apparatus, as elsewhere in modern theology, but by a specific community's very real experience of oppression, and its consequent need for liberation. The obvious attractiveness of this thesis – the mystery of God is infinitely greater than any one attempt to understand it, and so can be expressed only tangentially – is offset, however, by the narrowness of Sobrino's explicitly Christological base. Whereas Rahner's understanding of mystery and its experience through transcendental knowledge is arguably too broad, Sobrino's is arguably too narrow; it relies upon too particular an image of Jesus to support its contentions. This must be so; for if Sobrino's theology is going to work, then he has to be able to substantiate everything he wants to say about the mystery of God – as grace, Trinity or anything else – on the basis of the historical Jesus, 'the historical Jesus' being the only point in the Christian tradition at which one speaks explicitly of God incarnate and therefore part of the material world.[10]

All of this means, as Sobrino is quick to acknowledge, that: 'Liberation theology has rehabilitated the figure of the historical Jesus in theology' (1978, p. 79), which is a remarkable – though accurate – claim, given the history of twentieth-century theology.[11] The consequences for Sobrino's theology of such a rehabilitation, however, are considerable, because not only is Sobrino now dependent upon the historical Jesus as the sole authority for everything he wants to say about the

[10] One can do this because a little bit of the temporal is now part of the eternal, thereby identifying the spiritual and material in the eternal will of the Trinity's creative and recreative power – everything being understood by analogy with the complete identity of time and eternity in the incarnation (see chapter 6 below).

[11] Käsemann (1964) has a similar view, but it must be doubtful whether his influence has had anything like the same effect as the work of liberation theologians in Latin America – and elsewhere, for example Edward Schillebeeckx in Europe or Albert Nolan in South Africa – in making this issue central to contemporary theology.

mystery of God and the world in which it is experienced; he is also dependent upon the so-called scientific tools and methods of historical-critical research to establish the figure of the historical Jesus. The irony of the situation – a Latin American theologian employing western methods and terminology to portray a figure who denounces implicitly western forms of exploitation – is not lost on Sobrino; but it is nevertheless a problem for his theology which must be addressed.

Sobrino's image of Jesus

Jesus' way to the cross: principal components

The circularity of Sobrino's position becomes readily apparent when one realizes that the philosophical and theological frameworks that he deploys go to shape his image of Jesus, as much as – as he explicitly claims – his image of Jesus shapes his methodology. That is, he is – consciously – in the midst of a hermeneutic circle. Sobrino's way out of that circle, typically, is adventurous: he earths certain key ideas in a basically theistic vision of the status of the world.

Sobrino makes the point early in *Christology at the Crossroads* that God's power should predominate over anything static, so that the primary quality of Jesus Christ's life on earth must be a powerful and dynamic force (1978, p. 43). In the New Testament this can only mean the kingdom of God (Mark 1:12), and Sobrino makes it clear that it is in this light that Jesus' earthly life must be understood:

> Both his [Jesus'] miracles and his forgiveness of sins are primarily signs of the arrival of the kingdom of God. They are signs of liberation, and only in that context can they help to shed light on the person of Jesus (1978, p. 48).

Importantly, therefore, Sobrino makes an explicit link between the *person* of Jesus – which will ultimately be the basis of any Trinitarian Christology, however attenuated – and the kingdom of God as a power for change. It is this power for change, states Sobrino, that makes Jesus' message eschatological and therefore graceful: 'By preaching the approach of God in grace, Jesus opens up to sinners the only future left open to them' (1978, p. 49). Sobrino thus brings the question of the mystery of God – 'the approach of God in grace' – back to its true home – for liberation theology – in the arena of human oppression and thereby, methodologically, social and cultural criticism.[12]

By this route Sobrino arrives quickly at his basic position, namely that three things – the mystery of the grace of God, the power of the kingdom as the present reality of that mystery, and the historical Jesus – are all directed towards an explicitly social and cultural *locus*, one in which change is the primary cause of discussion and action:

> With an essential relationship to the kingdom of God, Jesus cannot help but denounce certain features of social life that are inconsistent not only with the definitive kingdom but also with an anticipatory stage of it (1978, p. 52).

One should certainly take Sobrino's use of the word 'essential' here quite seriously; more than simply 'necessary', Jesus' relationship to the kingdom is essential because both his person and the powerful expression of God's grace are elements of the economic (and immanent) mystery of God. Sobrino thereby remains upon avowedly Trinitarian and Catholic ground as he relates the historical Jesus, by means of his understanding of the kingdom, to his *a priori* theological framework.

Separating Jesus' ministry into two major parts, dividing at Peter's declaration of faith at Caesarea Philippi, Sobrino (1978, p. 41) argues that Jesus realized that the ultimate consequence of his mission in the power of the kingdom would lead to the sacrifice on the cross, and that the story of Christ's agony in Gethsemane – which Sobrino accords extraordinary significance – witnesses to Jesus' own obedience to the dynamic will of the Father:

> The agony of the garden is poles apart from any serene perplexity. It is the total, absolute crisis of the logic of the kingdom with which Jesus commenced his public life (1978, p. 99).

'The logic of the kingdom': this expression reveals the sum total of Sobrino's understanding of Jesus' way to the cross. All of the elements of that journey are subsumed under this logic in such a way that, finally, all that is left is the kingdom: the figure of Jesus drops away from the drama, having revealed the divinely chosen way of access to the mystery of God's grace. Jesus mediates so that the reality of God's

[12] The important point here is not that people can go out and realize the kingdom of God by doing good works, but rather that the kingdom must be a *present* reality if it is to mean anything in the daily lives of people ground down by poverty and oppression. That the kingdom also indicates a real future for Christian faith as well as a present reality is of course axiomatic for Sobrino (as it was too for Rahner).

grace, the mystery of the world and therefore the power of creation in Spirit (God), can become *present* as *liberation.*[13]

That, at least, would be one reading of Sobrino's Christology at this point. It would, however, ignore the important and related question of Jesus' role in the movement or conversion of the individual and community towards faith. How does Sobrino move from his picture of the historical Jesus, in Palestine 2000 years ago, to Latin America in the late twentieth century? Granted that one recognizes the nature of his philosophical and theological frameworks – and the way in which they shape these questions – nevertheless the precise character of this hermeneutic slide is of particular significance, because it is the exposition of that slide from event to rhetoric which is fundamental to Church's address to the world.

The slide from history to the contemporary

Sobrino's initial – only? – answer to this question is disarmingly simple: 'The problem of conversion becomes the whole problem of how we are to participate in the kingdom of God, how we are to cooperate in its fulfilment' (1978, p. 56). As has been demonstrated, for Sobrino this means participating in a message of real, material liberation from the oppressive circumstances in which people find themselves. Thus, he continues: 'Because his [Jesus'] God exists only in so far as he 'reigns', thereby liberating people and creating human fellowship, access to God is only possible in a liberative praxis based on following Jesus' (p. 59). Sobrino can write this, because as he argues: 'Jesus is aware of the fact that in and through his own person the kingdom of God is drawing near' (p. 68); but what it actually means for Sobrino's theology as a whole is even more significant. Sobrino writes: 'Jesus is bold enough to assert that eschatological salvation is determined by the stance a person adopts towards Jesus' own person' (p. 69). 'Following Jesus' is, for Sobrino's understanding of the Christian faith, the one way in which people can help to realize God's kingdom on earth, and thereby work to end oppression and to give liberation to the poor of the world: 'The novel feature in Jesus' teaching is the salvific function of discipleship' (p. 70).

For Sobrino's theology – the extent to which it brings faith and understanding into creative tension with society and culture – the moves

[13] Boff (1980, p. 207) makes this point very well: 'Christ did not leave this world with the resurrection. He penetrated it in a more profound manner and is now present in all reality in the same way that God is present in all things'.

made here are curiously restrictive. There are two logical implications of Sobrino's position, for example, which would seem to obstruct the realization of the kingdom of God which he seeks. First, only those who follow Jesus explicitly can participate in the gradual inauguration of the kingdom, because it is the *graceful* nature of that kingdom which is *not* open to someone who does not confess Jesus Christ as Saviour and convert to a life of discipleship in his service. Second, that which constitutes liberation itself is expressed within the parameters of an explicitly Christian – indeed, Biblical – faith. Such a theology will produce an impressive array of images, a constructive rhetoric with which to convince people of its significance (as witnessed by the popularity of liberation theology in the western world); but will it be consistent with the sheer variety and complexity of contemporary society and culture? However highly developed his philosophical and theological parameters (though not always articulated), how can such a theology as Sobrino's escape the straitjacket of a conservative, Biblical pietism?[14]

These issues will form the basis of the rest of this chapter, but at this point I want to pause briefly to consider the implicit limitations of Sobrino's position, specifically in terms of his Latin American context. Only then will it be possible to continue with the present analysis of his image of Jesus, and the way it slides into rhetoric.

As noted above, Sobrino places the question of conversion right at the centre of his understanding of what it means to follow Jesus. Moreover, he clearly feels that the meaning of such a discipleship is entirely straightforward, if impossible without grace: it is all about realizing the kingdom of God in the present. Granted the parameters of his philosophical framework, one can say that this realization can occur materially; this would be something open to both a cognitive and descriptive analysis. Simultaneously, and given the parameters of his theological framework, one can say that such a participation in the realization of the kingdom of God can only be rewarded by a participation, upon whatever level, in the graceful mystery of God (which need not have any obvious side-effects, because it can occur at the same time as everything else in human experience). With these two qualifications, Sobrino's theology is intelligible to any human individual or community. It is about power and authority, and where they are invested.[15]

[14] Of course, one might argue that liberation theology does not need to escape this restriction– although the attack upon it by evangelical fundamentalism in Latin America argues for the development of a more flexible theological understanding.

[15] This point is made again and again in the case of Leonardo Boff's silencing by the Vatican (see Cox 1989); on Ratzinger, see Messori 1985.

Is it, however, at all acceptable to someone who does not share a social and cultural context in which oppression and liberation are the dominant criteria for judging religious truth? Or better: could someone who does not share such a context, on Sobrino's analysis, participate in the kingdom of God? The answer would seem to be 'no'; or at least, that is what is implied by Sobrino's rubric.

This is one of the most significant difficulties facing liberation theology, namely the extent to which it becomes simply a rite of passage into a different vision of social and cultural utopia. Hence, although the general drift of Sobrino's theological method – mystery and event combined in healthy relationship – must be correct, his rhetoric is not, seemingly, a genuine encounter between faith and society *per se*. It is, rather (and the similarity with Barth is striking), an idealized vision of such an encounter; it speaks in essentialist language about a relationship which is posited as vital for human existence, but which can ultimately only be given the archaic name 'kingdom of God'. The question must be posed, therefore, whether or not this very western version of theological methodology – in which concepts culled from Biblical criticism are deployed in orderly fashion, to convince people to a certain course of action – can any longer be advanced. Is there room in the relationship between faith and society for such concepts as 'grace', 'kingdom' and 'the historical Jesus'? Can Christology be maintained as the major avenue by which people come to an understanding of the mystery of God? Does rhetoric need to be 'about' Christology at all? These are the wider questions which have arisen out of this consideration of Sobrino's *Christology at the Crossroads*, ones which will occupy the remainder of this entire study. First, however, I want to return to Sobrino's own text, to see if therein lie answers to these particular questions.

The place of the kingdom

Sobrino's theology relies upon having an audience which can understand and is willing to accept the terminology of grace, kingdom and Jesus, because rhetorically these are the building blocks by means of which he articulates his understanding of the relationship between mystery and event, and thereby the ultimate importance of his Christology. Sobrino's appeal, therefore, is to an audience well versed in the vocabulary of a Biblical understanding of what it is to be liberated and hence saved. Without such an audience his rhetoric would fail, which demonstrates that Sobrino, like most people, wants to be understood.

Some of the more far-reaching methodological implications of this situation for theology will be considered both in the next chapter, concerned with David Tracy's *Blessed Rage for Order*, and in chapter 8; but there is one particular aspect of this problem which directly impinges upon Sobrino's representation of Jesus, and which can therefore be considered at this point. This is the matter of the *locus* or place of the kingdom of God. Simply, the question is: as part of the rhetorical address of Sobrino's theology, where does he locate the kingdom, and how does this appeal to his specific audience?

Sobrino is entirely familiar with this problem, and tackles it at the beginning of *Christology at the Crossroads*, quoting Leonardo Boff:

> Jesus makes a radical statement about human existence, its principle of hope and its *utopian* dimension. He promises that it will no longer be utopia, the object of anxious expectation (cf. Luke 3:15), but *topia*, the object of happiness for all people (cf. Luke 2:9) (Sobrino 1978, p. 44).

Boff's point, fully endorsed by Sobrino, is important. Whilst maintaining the overtly eschatological terminology of the kingdom (hence the explicit references to Luke) Sobrino, following Boff, converts its utopian and therefore otherworldly language of hope into the *topical* language of material expectation. Doing interesting things to the question of time and its status in Christian faith and understanding, Sobrino collapses the *locus* of the kingdom into the arena of present achievement. What looks like reductionism, therefore, is simply a byproduct of Sobrino's commitment to speaking of the possibility of grace – as kingdom – in this world (a point also found in Rahner).

The rehabilitation of the historical Jesus by liberation theology, which Sobrino is at pains to acknowledge and praise, is consequently a double-edged sword. What one really finds is the rehabilitation of the question of the historical Jesus, in order to arrive at a very discrete image of that individual. The issue of the place or *locus* of the kingdom of God serves simply to confirm this analysis: the kingdom, like Jesus himself, is placed directly in a world defined by the social and cultural concerns of Latin America, a process of theological redefinition which mirrors the Christian life of people in this world.[16]

In and of itself such theologizing is not particularly problematic;

[16] This is part of an ongoing process of redescription, which has recently been directed at the doctrines of the Trinity and God respectively (see Boff 1988 and Gutierrez 1991). It is interesting to note the strategy and tactics of liberation theology as it goes about this matter.

after all, since Kant's essay 'The End of All Things' writers have been willing and eager to draw different pictures of the historical Jesus, and in this respect theologians like Sobrino and Boff, Gutierrez and Segundo, bear a striking resemblance, methodologically, to the liberal Protestant 'Jesuology' which was condemned first in Schweitzer's *The Quest of the Historical Jesus* (1954), and later in dialectical theology as a whole. The fact that the bourgeois liberalism of a writer like Harnack, or even Kant himself, has been replaced in Sobrino or Boff by an explicitly socialist mentality (ironically similar to the very early Barth), does not alter the fact that their methodological roots are fundamentally the same. An appeal to historical-critical research is an appeal to historical-critical research, however it is described by the writer doing the appealing; one *expects* a theologian to attempt to justify the epistemological grounds upon which she builds her system!

The problems with liberation theology's position, however, appear when one considers it in relation to some of the other theologians who have been examined in chapters 1–3 (here I am anticipating the next chapter on Tracy). Karl Barth, for example, attempts to bypass the inherent difficulties attached to the historical-critical method by finding his theological authority in an absolute understanding of revelation, so that for Barth the question of the *locus* of the kingdom of God simply cannot be asked; it is part of the divine mystery itself. (This is one of the main reasons by Barth was so opposed to Harnack's liberalism, something which, one can conjecture, would make him equally opposed to liberation theology.)

The same could be argued for Karl Rahner's theology, in which questions of the *locus* or place of concepts like the kingdom of God, or indeed the historical Jesus, find little real meaning, having been evacuated of material sense in favour of function upon a transcendental level of analysis. Rahner's *a priori* philosophical framework operates upon a level which makes questions of *locus* or place irrelevant; one might equally well ask for the *locus* of the law of gravity as ask for the *locus* of eschatological grace in Rahner's understanding of the relationship between God and humanity.

Though the situation is somewhat different with Bonhoeffer's letter of 16 July 1944 to Bethge, or either of Moltmann's two Christologies (where there is a much clearer recognition of the need to create *images* of the Christ event), the problem here is, of course, the fundamental question for any theology: is what one says actually true? With a theologian like Barth one knows that the concept of truth is being understood in a specific, analogical sense. Similarly, with Rahner one knows that truth is a logical quality which really means 'is it internally coherent? Does it *make sense*?' With Sobrino, however, and liberation theology in general, the question of truth has been handed over to the vicissitudes of contingency. Truth now has the status of a verifiable object, and with that slide comes the implied one, that such concepts as the kingdom, grace and Jesus himself, also have the truth status of verifiable objects. The measurement of that truth status, certainly, wants to be in the hands of the social and cultural context of Latin America; but in reality the genuine responsibility for such evaluation yet resides in the iron grip of objective science. In this respect, for a theologian like Sobrino a certain form of ecclesial rhetoric – which is strongly informed by objective and material analysis – begins to dominate theology.

This can be seen if one looks at the example of the locus of the kingdom of God. This side of eternity, nobody really knows what the kingdom of God is like; the best one can manage is the metaphorical, apocalyptic language one finds in the New Testament (see Rowland 1982). Effectively, however, Sobrino turns loose the question of knowledge – and its metaphysics – upon the kingdom, based upon historical-critical research into certain key, Biblical passages. (This may seem a crude way of describing Sobrino's activity, but it is in effect what liberation theologians do.) The results are the cognitive claims that Sobrino (and Boff) make about the kingdom, namely giving it material, normative status in his interpretation of the relationship between God and the world. The *place* of the kingdom of God, consequently, its *locus*, is in the world, and evidence to the contrary – operating on a judicial model – is disregarded because of the evidentiary rules with which Sobrino operates. This is not necessarily wrong, and all theologians quote selectively from the New Testament. But it is definitely rhetorical; it is designed to persuade.

This means that questions such as place, nature, extent, authority, etc., which ordinarily are not allocated to Christian theology, take on a new and signal meaning in the world of liberation theology. The kingdom becomes a distinct place and therefore has, by extension, a definite entrance (cf. what was said earlier about conversion). Entry to that kingdom becomes an authority established in a certain knowledge and activity. Sobrino, consequently, comes full circle, as he must do: a metaphysics of knowledge becomes the coping-stone of his theology. Or at least: that would seem to be the end point of his methodology, not so much a clear and systematic development towards a definite goal, but rather a spiral progression around the practical desire to find good reasons for adopting a particular attitude towards the situation in Latin America (and thereby constructing a theological metaphysics).

The kingdom in action

How, then, does one follow Christ towards the kingdom of God? As Sobrino himself writes, the answer to this question is fairly straightforward:

> Going to God means making God real in history; it means building up God's kingdom here and now. No abstract concept of the deity can teach us that fact, however; we must learn it from the concrete figure of the historical Jesus (1978, p. 307).

As Sobrino emphasizes throughout his theology, therefore, orthopraxis must take priority over orthodoxy (1978, p. 45). Entrance to the kingdom, the path of conversion, is fundamentally socio-political; and for Sobrino, socio-political action is categorized in the Christian understanding of love:

> When Christians talk about love of God ... they are talking *materially* about real, historical love for human beings ... without the praxis of love people cannot experience the God of Jesus, and hence they cannot pray to the God of Jesus (1978, pp. 172–6).

One might add: and without prayer to the God of Jesus – remembering the role Sobrino ascribes to spirituality – Christians cannot really be part of the true kingdom.

In itself a very simple move, Sobrino's emphasis upon this praxis of love completes his economy of the image of Jesus: 'Christian life as a whole can be described as the following of Jesus' (1978, p. 391). The relationships between mystery, event and rhetoric are established in Sobrino's theology, therefore, upon the twin foundations of his philosophical framework – which gives him an objectivist metaphysics of knowledge – and his theological framework – which gives him a spiritual understanding of the relationship between God and the world. In this light the key concepts which Sobrino wants to deploy – chosen from the New Testament and centring upon eschatology, the kingdom of God and the historical Jesus – are always considered from the viewpoint of what one might call 'doing' theology, orthopraxis. It is very much the case that Sobrino has a practical reason for being theoretical, with considerable positive consequences for the shape, style and structure of his theology.

Sobrino's theology is very consistent, and succeeds in evoking an entirely credible response to the situation in Latin America, for which it was principally written. Simultaneously, however, it raises fundamental questions for both the future shape of theology as a whole, and the present study. In short: is spirituality today's preferred way of seeking the divine mystery? What is the future of Christology in the light of liberation theology's strong dependence upon objectivism? And finally, does Sobrino's theology herald the ultimate priority of rhetoric in the contemporary world? These are the questions to which I now turn.

The implications of Sobrino's theology

Spirituality and mystery

Prima facie, the evidence from all of Sobrino's various texts suggests quite clearly that he regards spirituality as the common denominator between individuals, and by extension communities, which makes them religious; leaving aside until chapter 6 the question as to whether or not such anthropology is still valid in the contemporary world, it is the principal limit which Sobrino places upon his discussion of humanity. From his understanding of spirituality Sobrino can move on towards all of the themes – love, liberation, action and their opposites – which he wants to use to talk about his vision of God's will, as revealed in Jesus Christ, and how people encounter it. Moreover, the emphasis upon spirituality relates Sobrino's anthropology to his understanding of the Trinity, because the Third Person of the Trinity is the ultimate ground of human spirituality in this world. In every respect, therefore, Sobrino's theology establishes spirituality as the way of speaking of God's mysterious being as Trinity. It is the *way* people encounter the presence of eternity – grace – in time, and it is personalized for Christian faith as Jesus Christ (cf. Bonhoeffer's *cor curvem in se*).

This method has certain important advantages when it comes to relating a liberation theology such as Sobrino's to the context of pluralism in which contemporary reflection finds itself, and the necessary dialogue with other faiths which is fast becoming one of the principal duties of the Christian theologian, particularly when as significant a writer as John Hick (1989) has argued that spirituality is the most adequate basis for addressing the *similarities* of the world's differing religious beliefs.[17] A theology such as Sobrino's, though it is not explicitly concerned with interfaith dialogue, can thus find its own avenues towards such discussion. (This point is surely important for the relationship between Christianity and indigenous religion in Latin America.) As significantly, the deployment with objective authority of such key categories as love, praxis, knowledge and liberation, must inevitably involve a theologian like Sobrino in the extensive task of precisely such dialogue; that, after all, is the function of rhetoric (in the understanding of this present study), and presumably one of the main reasons why Sobrino wrote *Christology at the Crossroads*.

Simultaneously, however, the foundation of Sobrino's understanding of spirituality in the Trinity is problematic: such a close association of a general human quality with a central doctrine must inevitably bring Sobrino's anthropology into tension with those who cannot accept its theological basis. This is doubly paradoxical: not only is Sobrino's theology implicitly criticized for its restrictiveness, as opposed to liberality; but it is also one clear example where orthodoxy, in the shape of the doctrine of the Trinity, is governing with authority orthopraxis, in the shape of Sobrino's general anthropology. Sobrino's practical theology is being controlled at this important point by an article of faith, and therefore ultimately by an ecclesial construct. There seems to be no point in Sobrino's theology where spirituality can be asserted as a general human quality – as Hick argues – named in the Christian religion as the Holy Spirit, because for Sobrino the ecclesial doctrine of the Holy Spirit is always normative.

A problem here for Sobrino is that his hands are tied by his practical reason for writing theology, namely his desire to say something which will change society and culture in Latin America towards an explicitly Christian goal, which in turn has so influenced his choice of key New Testament themes and concepts. Eschatology, hope, kingdom of God, historical Jesus, the *topia* of the revelation of God's graceful will to liberate: none of these ideas makes any sense as a genuinely Biblical concept if it is divorced from the activity and power of the Holy Spirit, because it is the Holy Spirit who makes the kingdom the kingdom, hope hope, eschatology eschatology, and the historical Jesus the historical Jesus. Sobrino's theology functions as a Christian theology, making sense of the earliest Christian texts, by acknowledging

[17] I am pleased to have been able to confirm this impression in conversation with John Hick, and want to acknowledge the relevance of his work for my own argument, here and also in chapter 6.

one of the most important 'limit concepts' (see chapter 5 below) of those texts: the Holy Spirit with which the earliest gospel begins (Mark 1:10).[18]

What all of this means for Sobrino's understanding of the mystery of God, and its place in theology, is that he has drawn a very tight connection between that mystery in his thought, and the way his theology functions as rhetoric; a very tight connection drawn between spirituality and the need of the theologian to communicate socially and culturally which Sobrino, apparently willingly, enters as soon as he starts writing. For the internal coherence of Sobrino's theology this does not matter; such a tight connection is perfectly acceptable, because Sobrino is writing for an audience which seems as willing to accept the doctrine of the Holy Spirit as it is to accept the kingdom of God. For that theology's lessons for theology in general, however, there are clear difficulties. Primarily, Sobrino's theology throws a straitjacket over its own rhetorical abilities at that point where it most wants to communicate socially and culturally – spirituality. Because Sobrino's understanding of divine mystery is tied directly to the Third Person of the Trinity (*pace* the New Testament), his rhetoric and communication is curtailed; dialogue becomes one-sided, resulting in a self-perpetuating circle of liberation theology which simply replaces the previous self-perpetuating circle of Eurocentric ecclesial authority.

This raises a thorny dilemma for my understanding of critical theology. Granted that it wants to steer away from a certain strand of theological idealism, in which the mystery of God has the apparent status of the Hegelian *Begriff*, it must also steer away from restrictive Christian doctrine where it most wants to enter into open social and cultural dialogue, namely the rhetorical. Thus, if a critical theology wants to continue speaking of spirituality as the basis of speaking about divine mystery and by extension humanity itself, it may have to divorce the doctrine of the Holy Spirit from its definition of spirituality.[19]

The future of Christology

The contemporary viability of objectivism In *Christology at the Crossroads*, Sobrino writes: 'it is the faith of Jesus that provides us

[18] See Myers 1988, pp. 127–31: this is why critical theology is theological rather than sociological reflection. That Sobrino's narrative touches no base outside the explicity Christian tradition is consistent with the Rahnerian/Barthian tradition which was so important in his theological education.

[19] I will return to this problem in chapter 6 – the Holy Spirit as a named Person cannot be the only way of speaking of human spirituality if one wishes to enter into interfaith dialogue.

with the key to understanding what constitutes his divinity in the concrete' (1978, p. 81). Sobrino is equally clear that: '[Jesus'] most fundamental gesture is taking sides with human beings in a concrete situation where the existing politico-religious structure has dehumanised people' (p. 92). In short, Sobrino feels confident enough in his theology to be able to conclude:

> In concrete terms, the faith of Jesus can be summed up in his attitude of exclusive confidence in the Father (vertical relationship) and his total obedience to his mission of proclaiming and making present the kingdom (horizontal relationship). This twofold attitude makes explicit the unique faith of Jesus (p. 103).

Sobrino is thus happy speaking of the faith of Jesus in objective terms; happy to speak ultimately about what Jesus felt, wanted, experienced, believed. Indeed, this is the theological-epistemological foundation of everything he wants to achieve rhetorically, because mystery and event are named in the sending of the Holy Spirit to Jesus of Nazareth, and thereby eschatologically.

Sobrino goes on to affirm an ethical/social duty on the basis of this insight into Jesus' own beliefs:

> The most radical and most orthodox affirmation of *faith in Jesus* is affirming that the *faith of Jesus* is the correct way to draw nearer to God and realise his kingdom, and then acting accordingly (p. 108).

Leaving aside here the vexed question of Sobrino's slide away from theology towards social and cultural praxis (which was considered above), the pertinent issue at this point centres upon what Sobrino's methodology means for Christology. What are the implications for Christology of Sobrino's theological epistemology, which rest upon an objectivist reading of the New Testament?

First, Sobrino's objectivism requires absolute trust in the criteria of rational inquiry, the ability of cognitive science to establish with an acceptable degree of certainty insights into the historical Jesus (in this instance). For Sobrino this means being able to speak of Jesus' faith, primarily, but also his intentions in a whole range of circumstances. Remove the reliability of these criteria – something which has certainly occurred this century – and it becomes impossible to accept Sobrino's Christological 'insights' objectively. They become what they always were, subjective impressions (albeit informed by tradition, knowledge of Biblical texts and criticism, etc.), although ones which are socially as valid as any others.[20]

Second, and despite postmodernism's imaginative work in redefining the status of a fact, the effective reduction of the life of Jesus, however critically examined, to one datum from which other data are to be drawn (rather as one requisitions material from a storeroom) inevitably diminishes the status of Jesus Christ. Granted that liberation theology in general and Jon Sobrino in particular do not *want* thus to diminish Jesus Christ, nevertheless this is the effect of their methodology. In short, Sobrino's real concern is with the present situation in Latin America. What he wants to do is demonstrate that the kingdom of God, *he and many others believe*, is the only effective solution to that situation, as the definitive way of alleviating its oppression. This is why Sobrino turns to Christology: to support and establish in acceptable doctrine – certainly in good faith – a particular vision of society and culture, and a particular message for its change and improvement. It is in this sense that he notes in his preface to *Christology at the Crossroads*:

> To put it concretely, it [Sobrino's Christology] seeks to provide the Christological underpinnings for all that Latin American theology of liberation has to say about the nature of ecclesial theory and activity (1978, p. xx).

Sobrino's goal, therefore, is really the material transformation of society and culture, by Church, and hopefully (in a non-pejorative sense) in the power of the Holy Spirit.

What one finds in *Christology at the Crossroads*, then, is a very pragmatic image of Jesus presented as factual; it serves a function, before retiring gracefully and being replaced by an incipient – and socially coercive – divine rule. And this is the problem with objectivism: people – theologians especially – turn towards it when they want a form of modern authority to underpin a specific programme or course of action. The difficulty in theology is that this not only provokes a series of discrete images of Jesus, which are not open to any genuine hermeneutic engagement; it also generates the wrong sense of security. Surely, the pressing concern in theology is not what one should actually do; it is, as it always has been, *who is Jesus Christ*? (*pace* Bonhoeffer). The task of contemporary theology is to establish whether or not – and if yes, how – this question can still find a place between the eternal sense and experience of mystery in the world, which is

[20] I have been influenced here by John D. Caputo's 'Openness to the Mystery' (1987, pp. 268–94). Although this essay is not concerned with Christology, his comments about relativity are directly relevant to my point.

shared by countless people in many different religious contexts, and the rhetorical constructions – both positive and negative – which contemporary society and culture generates. Ultimately, Sobrino's Christology does not even enter this debate, which is why it should be followed as a model only with great care. It is a classic piece of modern theology; but is it flexible enough for the contemporary situation?

The turn to pluralism This obvious criticism of the contemporary viability of objectivism is the one overriding reason why the issue of pluralism has found its way into Christology. As David Tracy has advanced the cause of pluralism in this area over the last twenty years, and as the next chapter is devoted to an interpretation of Tracy's *Blessed Rage for Order*, comments here can be fairly limited, although one or two points must be made.

The turn to pluralism in Christology signals the end of the dictatorship of Biblical criticism over systematic theology in the twentieth century, something inaugurated by Karl Barth's *Romans* I and II but which really found its feet in the post-war work of such Protestant theologians as Fuchs and Ebeling, Moltmann and Pannenberg. Today hermeneutic sophistication – which certainly brings its own problems – means that theology accepts the relative insecurity of a plurality of meanings (in this case, images of Jesus Christ) because of the truth of the methodological case, that objective certainty is a house built of straw. What this means for contemporary Christology is that there is no longer believed to be one single way of speaking accurately of the historical Jesus. Instead there is simply a range of images, some of which have more mileage in them than others.

Obviously, this does not mean that there are now no criteria for discerning one image of Jesus from another. One can say categorically, for example, that there are certain images of Jesus which are bad, and which should no longer be advanced. Moreover, one can happily argue that there are *better* images of Jesus, that one can draw better pictures of Jesus because of familiarity with the fruits of historical inquiry into the world in which Jesus lived (see Crossan 1991). No one, after all, wishes to rule out entirely the notion of historical sensibility and its place in imaginative, constructive theology. That, however, is not the real point, which is that no normative, absolute status can be granted to any one image of Jesus, no matter how persuasive it may seem, no matter how aware of historical sensibility it may claim to be.[21]

In contemporary theology, the study of iconography and iconolatry

[21] Biblical exegetes seem to understand this now, but too many still speak of 'eisegesis' when what they really mean is interpretation.

has become intimately related to Christology at this juncture, explicitly in the work of Dorothee Sölle (1978). The iconoclastic nature of the Christ event is held to shake the foundations of any image of Jesus – famously, the objectively drawn image of the historical Jesus – thereby making it impossible to speak definitively of any one image of this figure. This is the effective doctrinal or systematic outcome of the insurgence of pluralism into Christology. Its implications for how one now goes on to speak of the Christ event – how, for example, methodological questions impinge upon the construction of an image, how one relates an image to the historical figure who must be accounted for *somehow*, how such event *theories* are related to theological understandings of mystery and rhetoric – will be considered at length in chapter 7. Here it is enough to note that the acknowledgement of this point relativizes the Christology one finds in Jon Sobrino's work, with considerable consequences for how one views liberation theology.

The priority of rhetoric This means that Sobrino's theology, rather than functioning as an articulation of the fundamental message of the Christian faith, functions as rhetoric, as persuasive address towards a particular goal, from a specific point of view. Though it never claims to be rhetoric, this is not actually a problem for Sobrino; for every theology, every human expression long or short, is ultimately rhetorical. The real question, and one which contemporary theology has so far failed to address, is that of the double-sided nature of rhetoric. This is the subject of the remainder of this chapter, and will be considered at greater length in chapter 8.

There is a strong sense in which every Christian proclamation, from Peter's confession of faith at Caesarea Philippi onwards, was and is rhetorical and thereby aimed at being persuasive in the sense outlined above. Methodologically, however, the modern concern with rhetoric goes much further, away from questions of intent in rhetoric, and towards the idea of the free-floating, generated independence of rhetorical statements once they have been made. The place of rhetoric in contemporary theology, and the interest shown in it, thus has a great deal to do with modern forms of literary and critical, cultural and historical, theory. Rhetoric in theology functions as the dangerous science of the possible, for the sake of the inexpressible, in the hands of the hopeful. It has, therefore, an eschatological quality.[22]

[22] The Ricoeurian background here is explored more fully in Part II, in which both Ricoeur's work and Heidegger's are influential. On the eschatological character of all rhetoric, see Bourgeois 1990, pp. 132–49, van Leeuwen 1981, and Vanhoozer 1990, pp. 243–7. Vanhoozer writes: 'The eschatological vision of the world thus pertains to one's ability to see hopeful, though yet unrealized, possibilities in the midst of the evil present' (p. 244).

Whether or not one regards that last statement as too strong depends very largely upon the naivety with which one comes to the definition of rhetoric. That advanced in my Introduction above – that rhetoric is the real stage at which social and cultural concerns can and should come into theology – means that rhetoric in theology is always intentional; it is always directed towards a particular situation. Such is the general working out of the axiom that theology is undertaken because of the practical need to be theoretical (as in Sobrino's work).

Modern critical theory teaches people, however, that once rhetoric has been loosed off into the ether of society and culture, once it has been released into the public domain, it tends to take on a life of its own. There is no way, consequently, in which a rhetorical expression's intent can serve as a limit concept of any kind, to direct and channel that expression's interpretation and effects down a particular path. On the contrary, any rhetoric, even the Christian faith's, can generate as many dark meanings as light, as many negative side-effects as positive. There is no guarantee that the rhetorical task of theology can be undertaken at all well or usefully (though it must be attempted).

This is the difficulty that Sobrino's theology encounters. Ostensibly, *Christology at the Crossroads* is straightforwardly an attempt to find the necessary Christological foundations for liberation theology's view of the world, what it wants to see being done in that world, and the goal – the kingdom of God – towards which it wants the world to move. Sobrino is addressing a particular society and culture – primarily, as original recipient audience, Latin America, but also by implication the West as the originator of oppression – in a rhetoric which gives particular utterance to his Catholic understanding of mystery and event. Leaving aside the question of the philosophical and theological frameworks within which that rhetoric is shaped and transmitted, one can see and acknowledge that this is the general drift of Sobrino's text.

Sobrino's problem, however, is that his rhetoric, which is founded upon the Christian principle of love, does not need to be read that way; in fact, its implicitly aggressive stance towards various elements in Latin American society – the well-to-do, the multinational corporations, government – can communicate precisely the opposite of his rhetoric's intent.

Nor is this admittedly simplistic point the most important one; of far greater significance is that Sobrino's image of Jesus expresses *as objective fact* the argument that Jesus' faith and proclamation of the kingdom of God is inherently exclusivist. Whilst it would probably be fair to say that Sobrino would not expect anyone to interpret his words and arguments in this way, and certainly would not wish to direct an attack upon any members of society, nevertheless as rhetoric these are some of the important implications of his theology. Overcoming this problem would entail Sobrino giving up those criteria of objectivity – and therefore accepting the implications of pluralism – which establish his own image of Jesus – for liberation theology – as normative; and that is something which he simply cannot do if his theology is to continue to claim to be the contemporary pronouncement of the gospel. Like Barth and Harnack before him, Sobrino cannot abandon his basic criteria, the motors which drive forward his rhetoric; if he does, then his theology collapses like a pack of cards. It is possible that Sobrino will do what Barth did in 1924 and onwards, changing his theological criteria and methodology – but his work since the 1970s does not suggest such a development (but see Sobrino, 1985, pp. 19–54, where he begins by considering the question of eschatological realism in Christology).

Addressing liberation

The argument in this chapter should not be interpreted as an outright negative criticism of Sobrino's theology in particular, and liberation theology in general; that is not my intention. Rather, and as with the previous chapters, I have tried to recognize a centrally important development in modern theology, and to advance the general cause and course of this book as a whole. In this sense the present chapter has generated some important points which should be recognized before the start of the next chapter.

Primarily, the present chapter's interpretation of Sobrino's *Christology at the Crossroads* has highlighted the way in which contemporary thought has moved away from traditional understandings of the mystery of God, towards a return to Biblical Christology, in the case of liberation theology, and the explicit problems of rhetoric, in the case of postmodern or more methodological theologies. Specifically, Sobrino rejects the old idealist conceptions of God's mystery – still prevalent in Barth, Bonhoeffer and even Moltmann – in favour of a renewed interest in spirituality. This low-key understanding of the mystery of God – which, though Trinitarian, like Rahner's ultimately collapses into theological anthropology – is fading into the background, so that the way is clear for Sobrino's strong interpretation of the Christ event to dominate the entire structure of his thought, even at the expense of explicit reflection upon his rhetoric (which is the ultimate goal and purpose of his writing). Even more than a theologian like Moltmann, therefore – for whom Christology is only one part, albeit major, of an all-enveloping theological worldview – Sobrino's theology is unbalanced; and that, finally, is where it is weakest, and where it allows in the searching criticisms of theological pluralism.

The way forward, therefore (and in this book), is straightforward: finally, the precise role and nature of rhetoric in an internally coherent, socially and culturally relevant theology must be established. This will entail not only thought about rhetoric itself, but also an understanding of how it relates to both mystery and event, the other motors of critical theology. The purpose of the next chapter is to ascertain, via an engagement with David Tracy's *Blessed Rage for Order*, how far contemporary theology has travelled in its appreciation of these matters, before turning, in Part II, to my own constructive inquiries into the relationship between faith and society and its interpretation by critical theology.

5

Tracy: Halting the Postmodernist Slide

If you continue in my word, you are truly my disciples, and you will know the truth, and the truth will set you free (John 8:31–2)

The first four chapters of this book have argued for a certain understanding of twentieth-century theology, the way its themes are structured, and the way in which its logic has developed in line with the engagement between what I have named mystery, event and rhetoric. In doing so, the writings of Moltmann, Sobrino and Rahner have been considered; but what I want to do now is to bring Part I directly into the field of contemporary hermeneutic and theoretical issues. In this area the work of the Roman Catholic theologian David Tracy is preeminent.[1] Here I want to consider in particular Tracy's *Blessed Rage for Order: The New Pluralism in Theology* (1975). Although Tracy developed his ideas more fully in *The Analogical Imagination: Christian Theology and the Culture of Pluralism* (1981), the earlier text is a manifesto of how theology should work in the contemporary world and as such remains informative and articulate, arguably Tracy's most important contribution to the development of method in modern theology.

The reference here to methodology is timely, because *Blessed Rage for Order* is overwhelmingly concerned with this question. In it Tracy concentrates upon how theology must address certain key questions in the contemporary historical and social context (rhetoric), without referring to either the religious background (mystery) or Christology (event) which informs that address. Indeed, one might almost say that

[1] Tracy's major works are his books of 1975, 1981, 1987 and 1990. He has also contributed to the following (of varying relevance for his general theological position): Tracy, Küng and Metz 1978 (short opening address); Tracy and Cobb 1983; Tracy and Grant 1984b, pp. 151–87; Tracy and Schüssler-Fiorenza 1984a (joint editorial); Tracy and Küng 1989, pp. 34–62, 461–71. On Tracy's theology, see Ray 1987, pp. 77–145, and Cunningham 1991, pp. 63–8.

Blessed Rage for Order has nothing to say about what I have termed mystery and event, so concerned is it with rhetoric.[2]

At the end of this chapter I will consider some of the difficulties of adopting this very abstract approach to theology, as part of a wider retrospective of the analyses of Part I and also as a way of looking ahead towards Part II. In terms of the consistency with which he approaches his explicitly methodological concerns, however, Tracy cannot be faulted. As Tracy himself writes: 'A widely accepted dictum in contemporary theology is the need to develop certain basic models or types for understanding the specific task of the contemporary theologian' (1975, p. 22). Such is the task of Tracy's book, and such is the level upon which this chapter will engage with his ideas.[3]

The sequence of chapters in *Blessed Rage for Order* construct a number of theological models, each one of which is returned to two cardinal principles; for, as Tracy argues, 'contemporary Christian theology is best understood as philosophical reflection upon the meanings present in common human experience and the meanings present in the Christian tradition' (1975, p. 34). Theology has to concern itself with experience and tradition, therefore. Tracy's reference to 'meanings' in the plural reveals something of his own intellectual world, because it is openness to the possibility of more than one meaning which establishes the foundations of his own hermeneutic position (see Tracy 1981, p. 3). Tracy thus sounds his own warning against those who would adhere to the general epistemology which characterized much earlier theology, preferring instead, as a matter of urgency, to acknowledge the *pluralistic* nature of any form of dialogue and interpretation. He writes:

> Most Christians now recognise that much of the traditional Christian manner of understanding the cognitive claims made in the Christian scriptures should be rejected by the findings of history and of the natural and human sciences (1975, p. 5).

There is no single answer to what Christian theology, and its resources, actually means; there is solely the task of interpreting it according to certain guiding principles. Fundamentally, what Tracy sets out to accomplish in *Blessed Rage for Order* is the identification and organization of these principles, in the shape of his own model of revisionist theology. The extent to which he has been successful is indi-

[2] Cunningham (1991, pp. 66–7) has some pertinent criticisms to make of Tracy's style in this respect.

[3] I hope that my criticisms in this chapter will be read as constructively as I intend them; see Frei 1992, pp. 30–4, for the kind of analogy I am seeking.

cated by the nature of his influence, and the debates in which he now participates.[4]

Tracy's book therefore represents an essay in typology, similar in style if not substance to that advanced by Hans Frei in his posthumous *Types of Christian Theology* (1992), which is typical of a certain school in contemporary North American theology. Its concerns with methodology mark it out as inherently conservative, as does Tracy's apparent unwillingness to speak of specifics within human experience or the Christian tradition, preferring instead to concentrate upon the mechanics of model-building. What Tracy seeks is consensus rather than the more precarious business of establishing a particular theological position, a claim substantiated by Tracy himself:

> In principle, the fundamental loyalty of the theologian *qua* theologian is to that morality of scientific knowledge which he shares with his colleagues, the philosophers, historians, and social scientists (1975, p. 7).

This loyalty characterizes *Blessed Rage for Order* throughout.

What one finds in Tracy's text, consequently, is a neat balance of two apparently conflicting influences: on the one hand the traditional, almost classical concerns of systematic theology, namely to discuss questions of method; on the other, the contemporary agenda of postmodernism, the clearest sign of which in Tracy's work is his adherence to the principle of pluralism. His movement towards important, hermeneutic questions, a movement against what one might term cognitive absolutism, is thereby checked by his location within a classical paradigm of the activity of the theologian. It is thus justified to speak of the hidden agenda of Tracy's *Blessed Rage for Order* as being 'to halt the postmodernist slide', by establishing certain methodological parameters beyond which theology should not go.[5]

This is the point at which I want to engage with Tracy's early work. Simply, the question here is: what checks can and should be placed on the development of theology's understanding of its rhetorical task, given the current hermeneutic climate? In answering this, chapter 5

[4] Apart from Tracy's obvious pre-eminence as a theologian in North America, I am thinking here specifically of his involvement in the Christian-Buddhist dialogue; see Tracy 1990.

[5] What I mean is that Tracy is ultimately sincere to the integrity and limitations of theology as a specific discourse and discipline, in a way that many other contemporary theologians are not. Indeed, I want to argue that the extravagance of postmodern theologies – of the kind advance by Taylor (1987) and G. Ward (1992b) – poses the greatest possible threat to this discipline, because they misunderstand the genuinely rhetorical character of theology. One cannot simply abandon traditional theology to the vicissitudes of media and communication, as some would like.

will define the goals of Part II, as well as providing one interpretation of how Tracy's work relates to that of the figures discussed in chapters 1–4.

Tracy's basic position: revisionist theology

In his second chapter, 'Five Basic Models in Contemporary Theology', Tracy reiterates his claim that: 'Any contemporary Christian theological position will consider itself obliged to interpret two basic phenomena: the Christian tradition and contemporary understandings of human existence' (1975, p. 23). Later in the same chapter, summarizing what he has said so far, Tracy writes:

> In short, the revisionist theologian is committed to what seems clearly to be the central task of contemporary Christian theology: the dramatic confrontation, the mutual illuminations and corrections, the possible basic reconciliation between the principal values, cognitive claims, and existential faiths of both a reinterpreted postmodern consciousness and a reinterpreted Christianity (p. 32).

The key identification is between Tracy's use of the appellation 'revisionist' and his emphasis upon the 'reinterpreted' status of both postmodern consciousness and Christianity, because what Tracy sees himself doing is bringing together consciousness and Christian faith in the light of postmodern concerns. 'Revisionism' in theology, therefore, is a *theoria*, a way of looking at recurring problems and questions, which informs the methological decisions which contemporary theology has to make.

There is more to Tracy's understanding of revisionism than this, however; for if revisionism were simply the accommodation by contemporary theology of certain recent developments, then it would be far less significant than it actually is. Rather, the key emphasis here should be upon revisionism as *a* way of looking, i.e. one amongst many. What is being rejected here is far more important than what is being affirmed (which can be summarized as religious and methodological pluralism in systematic theology), because what is being rejected is the notion that there can be an inexorable progression from scripture and experience, through reflection and on to expression, which functions with perfect knowledge and one sole meaning. Tracy rejects any conviction that one can move seamlessly from mystery to event to rhetoric, with those developments facilitated by an underlying principle (reason?). There is no such principle, argues Tracy, and so there can be no such facile progression. Instead, what one finds is a hermeneutic circle in which mystery, event and rhetoric are narrated simultaneously.[6]

Tracy therefore cuts the umbilical cord connecting theology as expression and communication with its subject matter in experience and tradition. Henceforth, if theology wants to speak about mystery and event it must realize that it addresses them as do other forms of discourse, with no privileged access or position. Tracy regards this theology as revisionist because it does not seek a status which it cannot sustain or justify, nor does it claim to have any unique cognitive powers which allow it to bypass the normative procedures of the reflective sciences. Again, one returns here to Tracy's definition of revisionist theology: it is straightforwardly a question of reinterpretation, both of postmodern social experience and the Christian tradition. A revisionist theology is contemporary and catholic, scientific and doctrinal, practical and theoretical, simultaneously; anything else, Tracy argues, would simply perpetuate the stagnant dilemmas into which previous modern theologies collapsed. It becomes a question – *pace* Bonhoeffer – of allowing social context to establish theology's agenda, at least in its narrated form.

This raises an important potential criticism of Tracy's definition of revisionist theology, namely whether or not it relegates substantive difficulties to a lower status than methodological ones (something which is particularly relevant for Tracy's understanding of eschatology). At this stage, however, I want to concentrate upon developing Tracy's own argument rather than addressing such overt difficulties.

Tracy moves on rapidly to identify five theses for a revisionist model of contemporary theology:

(1) the two principal sources for theology are Christian texts and common human experience and language (1975, p. 43);
(2) the theological task will involve a critical correlation of the results of the investigations of the two sources of theology (p. 45);
(3) the principal method of investigation of the source 'common human experience and language' can be described as a phenomeno-

[6] This is a important point: the ability to distinguish between mystery, event and rhetoric is a function of theology's character as second-order discourse, which obviously relates to the specific audience to which theology as rhetoric is directed (see Cunningham 1991, pp. 66–7 on Tracy on audience). The difficulty, however, is that as the nature of the audience changes, and theology is itself altered in turn, theology must be rhetorical in ways other than the boringly conventional ones. Unfortunately, writers like Tracy and Cunningham do not seem to have appreciated this fact, which makes their reflections upon the character and audience of theology curiously restrictive.

logy of the 'religious dimension' present in everyday and scientific experience and language (p. 47);

(4) the principal method of investigation of the source 'the Christian tradition' can be described as an historical and hermeneutical investigation of classical Christian texts (p. 49);

(5) to determine the truth status of the results of one's investigations into the meaning of both common human experience and Christian texts, the theologian should employ an explicitly transcendental or metaphysical mode of reflection. (p. 52).

Certain key themes in these theses must be elaborated. First, theses (1) and (2) have been covered by the preceding examination of Tracy's definition of revisionist theology; not much more need be said here, because they establish the parameters of the theologian's task as Tracy understands it. The extent to which one successfully accomplishes this task is something which for Tracy each theologian must discover as she goes about the business of being revisionist. Second, thesis (4) appears to be rather tame, involving little more than a sensitive, hermeneutically aware reading of the Christian tradition. Clearly, Tracy means more here than simply the Bible; he wants to include a much wider range of 'classical Christian texts'. But he does not want to be more specific, and he does not want to become involved with it himself. Nevertheless, Tracy would appear to be on very safe ground in this thesis, with no one really disagreeing with him (by definition, those who would appeal to immediate experience of the divine would reject 'the Christian tradition', and therefore Tracy himself, rather than actually arguing with him).

Further, thesis (5) raises an important question, because Tracy appears to want to give the criteria of judgement of any revisionist theology transcendental status, which is notoriously difficult to establish (even theoretically) and which, even if established, gives the appearance of being entirely abstract and unrelated to everyday life. Granted the alternative – metaphysical status – criteria of judgement of the truth of a revisionist theology can at least be established in a practical sense, simply by making such concepts as 'change', 'liberation' and 'development', one's criteria. Something very much like this is done in liberation theology, even, now, with the attempt to return such metaphysics to the realm of classical western philosophy (see Gutierrez 1991). As Tracy leaves it here, however, the claim is far too nebulous to be accepted on face value; it requires considerable further elaboration (see below).

Last and most interestingly, thesis (3) makes two important moves which are integral to everything that Tracy wants to say in *Blessed Rage for Order*. First, Tracy stakes a claim for phenomenology as the scientific means by which revisionist theology identifies and processes the 'raw data' of human experience which it wants to consider. Tracy thus carefully avoids the usual tiger-traps of epistemological critique which are so often strewn in the path of theological method. Tracy will have other problems to contend with – for example, how to establish the status of history in his interpretation of human experience – but at least he is clear that he wants to operate on the level of historical reflection.[7]

Tracy begins to speak, second, of the 'religious dimension' to everyday life, which at this stage seems to mean that everything in everyday life has the potential to mediate 'the Other' (see Gunn 1979 and Theunissen 1984). Here Tracy does not seem too clear as to what he means by the 'religious dimension': in the text Tracy appeals consecutively to Scheler, Gilkey, Sartre, Merleau-Ponty, Heidegger, Ricoeur, Whitehead and Tillich, each of whom, it seems safe to say, was operating on a different conceptual level to the others. Granted that at this stage Tracy is effectively 'throwing ideas' at what is a very fundamental problem, namely the transcendental dimension (if there is one) of immanent existence, the style of the debate at this point is extremely vague. Tracy is clearly speaking of mystery. But what is 'mystery'?

Tracy seems to be saying that the context in which human experience needs to be interpreted and understood has something about it which simply cannot be 'explained away' by rational and scientific means, but rather which must be left as something fundamentally unknown. Tracy gives it the name 'religious dimension', thereby appealing to a range of thought worlds, moving from Schleiermacher and Otto through to Husserl and Lonergan; but what he seems to want to say is that there is something which is beyond the potential of reason to explain, and which therefore can only be encountered. Phenomenology can help the revisionist theologian 'feel her way' around and towards this unknown area, but even phenomenology can go no further. Ultimately, humanity runs up against a limiting, unknown yet encountered, brick wall.[8]

[7] 'Historical reflection' is used in the sense elaborated by Paul Veyne (1984, pp. 66–70). Tracy (1987) expounds on his own position here, which is heavily dependent upon Veyne's thought.

[8] The real question here, of course, is whether one speaks of this position as being anti-rationalist, or expands one's definition of reason itself to include the intentional appearances that one wishes to discuss.

This is the basic point which the first half of *Blessed Rage for Order* wants to communicate. Tracy, borrowing heavily from other disciplines, refers to the conceptual status of this 'religious dimension' and 'limit', claiming thereby that it functions as the parameter of human discourse in everyday life:

> the concept 'limit' can be used as a key (but not exhaustive) category for describing certain signal characteristics peculiar to any language or experience with a properly religious dimension (1975, p. 93).

This means that what Tracy calls the religious dimension is somehow fundamental to human existence; and though he cannot give a specific name to this religious dimension – such as 'God', 'the Other', 'Spirit' or 'the Absolute' – he knows that it is really there, because his phenomenological analysis of human existence reveals this fact. Again reflecting on what 'limit' actually means, Tracy thus writes:

> All genuine limit-situations refer to those experiences, both positive and negative, wherein we both experience our own human limits (limit-to) as our own as well as recognise, however haltingly, some disclosure of a limit-of our experience (1975, p. 105).

This is precisely what I meant when I spoke of theology's 'rough edges', of the impossibility of accurate description and analysis within a systematic context, in my Introduction.

The way in which Tracy approaches this problem is very significant. Obviously, Tracy is working towards a discussion of something central to the Catholic tradition, namely mystery. And clearly, again, he does not want to leave this discussion solely in the domain of a straightforwardly denominational reference. Consequently, Tracy speaks in the general terms found in these quotations, preferring to avoid traditional solutions to this vagueness – such as naming mystery as the doctrine of the Trinity – so as to maintain what one might call 'ideological balance'. In this sense, *Blessed Rage for Order* is entirely concerned with agenda: what it wants to do is identify a level, and a terminology, which will appeal to lots of different Christian theologians, and also to lots of different religious groups. Once this general preparatory work is achieved then, argues Tracy, a revisionist theologian can go on and establish her own position. But the agenda of Tracy's 1975 text is to identify the market-place.[9]

Tracy is working with this same theme when he writes:

[9] The metaphor is most apt for postmodern theology's concern with what is fashionable; see Sölle 1985 and Rahner 1966e.

However helpful a later metaphysical language may be, all authentic limit-language seems to be initially and irretrievably a symbolic and metaphorical one (1975, p. 108).[10]

This is what Tracy means when he argues that human experience and understanding is pushing up against a disclosure of its actual status, without in any way being able to conceptualize or describe it accurately; for the basic quality of such metaphorical and symbolic languages is that they work indirectly; i.e. by approximating perceived meaning to reality as it is encountered (and because meaning is always approximate). Importantly, therefore, Tracy wants to nominate a negative theology, one which is always aware of its own limitations but which wants to speak in a positive way about limitation *per se*.[11]

This sounds a lot like Schleiermacher, and Tracy's explicit reliance upon the 'religious dimension' of human existence, as the limit-language of how people actually live, echoes quite closely the anthropological prolegomenon of *The Christian Faith* (Schleiermacher 1928).[12] This becomes evident when Tracy, after arguing that God is the ground of all human language and experience, writes:

If this is the case, the proper set of questions for fundamental theology become: first, the question of the 'limit' meaning and existential relevance of a religious dimension to our common lives; second, the question of the meaning and relevance of explicitly Christian language as limit-language; third, the question of the referential-as-theistic-meaning and truth of religious language (1975, p. 109).

What this implies is that Christian speech about God, as a subset of all speech conditioned by 'the religious', occurs within a context of general, theistic anthropology. Tracy is thus able to achieve three important things: first, to develop a sophisticated use of literary and hermeneutic theory, sure in the knowledge (argument?) that ultimately these find their basis in theism; second, to elaborate the question of Christianity's own forms of theological reflection in the certainty of Christianity's necessary religiosity (because it is human); third, to respond to the demands of contemporary society with respect to such

[10] On the philosophical background here, see Ricoeur 1976, pp. 45–69, and on Ricoeur see Thompson 1981, pp. 36–70. See also chapter 6 below.

[11] The important point is that one's talk about limitation is translated theologically into an understanding of the necessity of concealment as being fundamental to truth, and the methodological implications this entails for critical theology; see chapter 7 and Conclusion below.

[12] See Tracy 1975, pp. 26–7, 92–3. An example from literary theory of a similar, though unsuccessful treatment of this same sentiment is found in Steiner 1989.

questions as religious pluralism, because if there is such a thing as 'the religious dimension' which is given general anthropological status, then no religion can be discrete. This latter development has remained an integral part of Tracy's methodology to the present day. Tracy summarizes his philosophical position as follows: 'The reality of God, for the Christian, is a reality which either necessarily touches all our experience or necessarily does not exist' (1975, p. 205). With this, the foundations of Tracy's revisionist theology are complete.

Christology and revisionist theology

A great deal of the subject matter of David Tracy's propaedeutic will find echoes in chapter 6 of this book, particularly the way in which Tracy seeks to relate properly catholic concerns with the apophatic mystery of God with questions of human language and historical existence. Similarly, what one might call Tracy's ideological position, namely that religion – or something akin to his 'religious dimension' – underpins all human existence, will also find echoes in what follows in Part II. This fact notwithstanding, however, there are still important questions to be resolved by Tracy which I now want to consider: where does Christology fit into Tracy's theological analysis?; what parameters are set around theological discourse within religious – all – language?; and how does one move from such theoretical speculations towards the practical situation of Christian communities?

It is initially informative to answer these questions in relation to the theologians who have been considered in chapter 1–4. Thus, Tracy's inherently liberal concern with human religiosity, one can be sure, would have found a sympathetic listener in Adolf von Harnack. Karl Rahner, too, would have been able to identify his own transcendental anthropology with Tracy's intentions, in fundamentals if not particulars. By contrast, however, Barth, Bonhoeffer and Moltmann would all have argued long and hard against the idea that one could identify such a religious basis for human existence, and that this hypothesis should be the starting-point of Christian theology. For Barth, rather – speaking for all three at this point – the divine Yes must come before the divine No; Christology before anything as vague as spirituality or personal 'religion'. On this examination, Tracy finds himself quite clearly in the camp of those who want to make general truth claims – of varying cognitive status, certainly – about the way people really live. Sobrino's theology, with its heavily materialistic bias, is a perfect example of such a phenomenon in contemporary theology.

The question of the relationship between theological and general language, which Tracy highlights so clearly, finds very mixed reactions in modern theology. Barth, understandably, Bonhoeffer perhaps surprisingly, and Moltmann immediately, all seem to want to accord theology a special status because it possesses very clear parameters, defining it as something extraordinary in a world of ordinary languages. In contrast, both Harnack and Rahner locate theological discourse within the purview of other disciplines; in Sobrino's case, one might almost speak of the collapse of general theology into socio-political analysis, with the proviso that it is all earthed in Christology. The clear question here is how these areas are related: what is the nature of the slide between the two, and how much slippage is there? Tracy gives a very clear answer, but it remains to be judged how satisfactory it is in the long run.

Finally, although Tracy's theological model appears to function upon the level of theory – whatever its acknowledgement of there being no real distinction between theory and practice in terms of discourse – it is still true that Tracy works by abstracting back from reality itself, towards universal concepts; the way forward towards praxis is clarified in his final chapter.[13] *Blessed Rage for Order* thus functions as a programme for yet-to-be-revealed activity, and Tracy seems convinced that it is possible to produce such a text in the academic world without stating its practical implications.

What one finds on this analysis, then, is that the most pressing question addressed to Tracy's revisionist theology – granted its open disagreement with others on the question of a religious foundation, and agreement on the question of praxis – is how its structure meshes with the concerns of Christology. Or better: where does Jesus Christ fit into such a revisionist theology? Consistent with his basic approach, Tracy answers this question in terms of discourse and language:

> For Christians, Christological language suffices because it fulfils certain factual understandings of human and divine reality: the fact that our lives are, in reality, meaningful; that we really do live in the presence of a loving God; that the final word about our lives is gracious and the final power is love (1975, p. 223).

What Tracy seems to be saying is that Christology functions for Christians as a subset of religious language, so that, whilst it is neces-

[13] Tracy (1975, p. 240) agrees, however, that he is simply anticipating what must be said elsewhere.

sary for people in general to be religious – this is what Tracy's anthropology tells him – because it is religion which informs everything in reality, people can choose to be Christian, or be chosen, either by the Spirit (God) or because they like what they find in Christianity; and what they find there, as revealed in the principal vocabulary of Christianity (Christology), is grace and love. Once again, therefore, one perceives the market-led nature of Tracy's model of revisionist theology: the way one apparently moves from religion *per se* to the Christian faith *per accidens* is choice (although 'freewill' might be a more traditionally Roman Catholic way of expressing it).

In Tracy's own terms, therefore, Christology is the limit-language of being a Christian. What one learns from the New Testament about the general field in which Christology operates – Tracy's chapter on this question focuses upon the language of 'kingdom' and 'eschatology', relating it to mystery – demonstrates that the fundamentals of following Christ – discipleship – involve qualities which are really to do with how people actually live: faith, hope and love. On Tracy's model, the exegesis and interpretation one needs to make of the New Testament is quite severely limited, because whatever brushstrokes one leaves upon the canvas its basic colours always remain the same. This goes a long way towards explaining why, when he came to write *The Analogical Imagination*, Tracy did not feel it necessary to cite specific passages; for one always operates upon the level of more general enquiries.

It is instructive to compare Tracy's position here with Rahner's Christology, because the former is clearly indebted to the latter. As chapter 3 demonstrated, Rahner constructs what one might term a 'general event theory Christology', one which acknowledges the significance of Christ in transcendental terms. Particular images of Jesus do not really concern Rahner; they simply fit inside his umbrella definition of Christ's significance. Moltmann's Christology is thus not really incompatible with Rahner's; the former simply fits within the latter, which is operating on an entirely different level of sophistication from *The Crucified God*.

By analogy one can now make an important point about Tracy's revisionist theology. Whereas Rahner's Christology accommodated a wide variety of different images of Jesus, because of its structure, Tracy's theology accommodates a wide variety of different doctrinal concerns, again because of its structure. Whereas, therefore, the shift in Rahner is from a general theory of Christ towards particular images of Jesus (in this instant), the shift in Tracy is from a general theory of religion towards particular doctrines ('images'?) of what people actually believe and do. For Tracy the limit-language of being a Christian is Christology, established in New Testament interpretation; but it is at least theoretically possible, on Tracy's model, that a different believing community could adopt a different limit-language yet still be Christian (for example the church of Jesus Christ of Latter-Day Saints, better known as the Mormon church, or the Hutterian Brethren, or the Society of Friends). Tracy must accept this possibility because it is fundamental to his entire ideological stance on the question of pluralism. By anchoring pluralism on the level of a general theory of religion, an anthropology, Tracy has slipped the moorings of doctrinal theology. The result is that (almost) anything goes in the world of self-defining communal limit-language; and Christology is reduced to the status of one amongst many.[14]

The shape of theology in Tracy's world

In theory, therefore, Tracy can write:

> The Christian theologian stands in service both to that community of inquiry exemplified but surely not exhausted by the contemporary academy and to that community of religious and moral discourse exemplified but surely not exhausted by his own Church tradition (1975, p. 239).

This seems entirely reasonable: theology, after all, should always be conscious of its own inherently Janus-faced character. Moreover, earlier in *Blessed Rage for Order* Tracy emphasized the way in which this service character of theology means that it is always experimental:

> the meanings discovered as adequate to our common human experience must be compared to the meanings disclosed as appropriate to the Christian tradition in order to discover how similar, different, or identical the former meanings are in relationship to the latter (1975, p. 79).

The task of the theologian, consequently, is both very simple yet very complex: simple, because all she really has to do is to challenge social and traditional perceptions of 'reality' with each other, in the ideological conviction that thereby, somehow, 'meaning' will arise like

[14] See Lindbeck 1984. On Lindbeck, see Marshall 1990, particularly Hans Frei's contribution, pp. 275–82.

sparks from a fire;[15] complex, because this process of challenge, assimilation and/or defeat (implicit in Tracy's model?), is ever-renewing – it is, hermeneutically, the endless story of Christian self-reflection.

Now, there is certainly nothing wrong with Tracy's position, at least conceptually. His adherence to the basics of hermeneutic theory ensures that, as he writes: 'the present understanding of the task of interpretation insists that the meaning of the text is fixed in the text as ideal and not as a psychic event of the author' (1975, p. 76); and although hermeneutic theory has advanced since 1975 in certain respects, as Tracy and others have acknowledged, and although as a consequence of postmodernism the ideal *status* of meaning – whatever that might be – has been challenged, Tracy's position here remains a respectable and respected one (see Jeanrond 1991). A problem arises, however, when one considers what one might call the philosophical bases of Tracy's position, i.e. what underpins his hermeneutics. It is here, if anywhere, that I want to question Tracy's model of how theology operates in the contemporary world.

Undoubtedly, given his commitment to the principle of pluralism in contemporary theology, Tracy would not want to impose one specific model of how theology works upon the discipline as a whole. On the contrary, as he argues everywhere, Tracy's real concern is to acknowledge meaningfully the way in which many different theologians, working in many different contexts, can all say Christian things about God. At the same time, however, there is a side to Tracy's work, most clearly seen in *Blessed Rage for Order* in his revisionist model, which *does* want to establish some parameters for the mechanics of theology, even if they are simply very general. Tracy thus wants, like Schleiermacher before him, to speak of the religiosity of human existence as a limit upon human self-understanding; and it is with this concept of limit, as Tracy acknowledges, that one encounters the specific point at which he wants to say something general and universal about the way in which one does theology. Here, although Tracy is a pluralist, he is also an ambitious seeker after unifying principles, and although he chooses to locate them upon the level of methodology rather than substance (like Rahner), he clearly believes that in the concepts of limit (universal) and religiosity (particular) he has identified something very important for the way in which theology functions today. Tracy writes, decisively in this context: 'the only real choice is between a self-conscious and explicit metaphysics or an unconscious yet operative

[15] I am reminded here of Walter Benjamin's beautiful notion of 'rubbing history against the grain' (1968, p. 259). On Benjamin and Christian theology, see Wohlmuth 1990a and Jones 1990b. On Benjamin on history, see Roberts 1982, pp. 196–225.

one' (1975, p. 68). Given this choice, revisionist theology, as its name suggests, opts for an explicit, methodological metaphysics (see Green 1989, pp. 119–22).

All of this is entirely acceptable: not only does it make sense, but it is also clearly right, if by 'right' one means that it fits the conceptual parameters that modernity and postmodernity impose upon the way in which a reflective science operates. The question which arises here, however, is more substantial than the one that asks merely whether revisionist theology is right. The question is: is revisionist theology, and its metaphysical foundation, *true*? Whatever sense Tracy's model makes theoretically, and even with respect to the practical circumstances in which theologians often find themselves socially, does it actually say anything, or better, does it actually make it possible for a wide range of theologies to say anything, *true* about the Christian faith? If theology is faith seeking understanding, with what understanding of faith does revisionist theology provide theologies in general?

Tracy acknowledges that this is the crucial question when he writes, of any human experience or language:

> It is 'true' when transcendental or metaphysical analysis shows its 'adequacy to experience' by explicating how a particular concept (e.g., time, space, self, or God) functions as a fundamental 'belief' or 'condition of possibility' of all our experience (1975, p. 71).

Transcendental reflection – of which genre revisionist theology is Tracy's most pressing example – thus 'works on' the raw data of experience and language, subjecting it to the classic epistemological critique – asking if it has good reasons for the particular beliefs it holds – and at the same time so ordering that experience and language against the limit concept, human religiosity. This is how theology works on Tracy's model, so that one might say, cautiously, that the shape of theology in Tracy's world, whatever acknowledgements towards pluralism that he makes, is still western, mental and universalist; it is still, like Rahner's, a general theory in search of a specific image of Jesus and the Christian faith to confess (see Ray 1987, p. 100). Clearly, the word that Tracy is searching for here is 'fundamental', because what his revisionist model wants to establish is a way of speaking about God, so that all specific instances of this process become subsets of one universal principle (see Tracy 1975, p. 43). To be fair to Tracy, therefore, criticisms which focus upon his theology's seeming inability to articulate any practical message for contemporary belief are, at least initially, wide of the mark. It is not the task of fundamental theology to address specific issues of social or ecclesial concern, but rather to provide a frame of reference within which such difficulties can then be addressed.[16]

This does not mean, however, that the question of where society fits into Tracy's revisionist theology, as it is meant to be genuinely fundamental, has been answered, i.e. where and how Tracy's work pivots towards the real world in which people actually live. As was seen in each of the preceding chapters, this is the point at which any theology – whatever its apparently fundamental agenda – must stop prevaricating and adopt a position. Tracy does offer at least some definition of the place of mystery in human existence – his understanding of religiosity as its limit concept – and he also gives some definition to the event which lies at the heart of Christian faith – the way in which, for Christianity, religiosity is defined Christologically. But to what extent is he able to articulate the material and potential rhetoric of Christian faith, its ability to focus a message of change and movement, of *testimony*, in terms which make sense and are therefore (in Tracy's language) *true* for everyday society? This would seem to be the requirement which Tracy's revisionist theology, and everyone who follows him, must satisfy (see Valdes 1991).

Tracy does not really answer this question in *Blessed Rage for Order* (but see the conclusion to this chapter); nor does it occupy a major place in any of his impressive subsequent publications. By comparison with the other theologians considered in Part I, however, it is possible to make some observations about how Tracy's theology should make the said move.

Initially, a comparison with the obvious candidates, Rahner and Bonhoeffer, is fruitful. Both of these, like Tracy, are producing agendas, frames of reference which will function to shape and constrain (albeit constructively) future reflection and articulation. A case can also be made, however, for an important family resemblance to Harnack's liberal theology, because both Tracy and Harnack share the same concern for society as it finds cultural expression. Given that Tracy does not share Harnack's own political commitments, still his liberalism guides him towards the thought world of this strand of Protestantism, a point made earlier in relation to Tracy's Schleiermacher-like understanding of religion (and the same comparison can be made between Tracy's Christology and that of liberal Protestantism).

Unsurprisingly, Tracy's is not so similar to the theologies of Moltmann and Sobrino who, as they explicitly acknowledge, are at-

[16] In this sense it is probably fair to observe that the correct pigeonhole for Tracy's methodological engine is labelled 'Thomism', albeit an odd creation called 'historical Thomism'.

tempting to present clear images of Jesus and the Christian faith. Although one might call The *Crucified God* and *Christology at the Crossroads* 'agenda books', therefore, they are clearly not concerned with methodological agendas, as Tracy is in *Blessed Rage for Order*.

What is more surprising, however, particularly given Tracy's explicit appeal to his authority at various points, is the lack of similarity between Tracy's revisionist theology and Barth's critical one (see Tracy 1975, p. 27). One has to acknowledge here that Barth's early work, culminating in the exchange of 1923 with Harnack, is clearly not a theological agenda. It is, rather, a prophetic message, one which has the explicit character of eschatological testimony. This character of eschatological testimony, moreover, which one finds nowhere in Tracy's work to this day, effectively crushes the explicitly liberal concerns of *Blessed Rage for Order*; for, as Barth (1982b) made clear in his 1923–4 lectures on Schleiermacher, it is the pluralistic and liberalizing tendencies of this strain of theological reflection which drain the Christian faith's eschatological realism of its motive force. Since it is this motive force which gives definition to Christianity's understanding of the mysterious relationship between God, humanity and the world, then consequently any theology which does not attend to eschatology, whatever its methological agenda, will be inadequate in some respect (Barth would have said unChristian, even sinful). Is this as sweeping a condemnation of Tracy's argument in *Blessed Rage for Order* as it seems?

Theology as rhetoric

Certainly, the entire question of eschatology, and of any critical theology's necessarily eschatological character, is something which Tracy does not really consider. Here, apparently, one runs up against the view, found for example in the work of Rudolf Bultmann, that the seemingly objectivist, reified understanding of the relationship between this world and the beyond which one finds, say, in the New Testament, is inoperable for modern humanity. Rationally (so this argument goes), eschatology is something which has to be shed if theology is going to live up to the methodological (and thereby ontological) criteria of modernity and now postmodernity. Here, whatever his explicit intellectual debt to Heidegger and the thinking of historical phenomenology, Tracy reveals himself to be a modern rationalist, so that if people today are going to adduce a meaningful understanding of how they live in the world, in the sight of their belief in God, then for

Tracy it is going to be in terms of historical narrative, conceptual understanding and encounted experience, rather than any eschatologically real conviction. Or at least: the avenue down which Tracy ultimately wants to go, and for which he is concerned to elaborate a map and compass, does not seem to lead to an objective future (in contrast to Rahner 1966d, p. 326).

The positive way around this problem is to assert that Tracy is concerned with what Donald MacKinnon and Fergus Kerr have termed 'the philosophy of theology', that Tracy is really interested solely in elucidating the conditions of possibility of *any* future theology. In support of this analysis, Tracy writes:

> In its briefest expression, the revisionist model holds that a contemporary fundamental Christian theology can best be described as philosophical reflection upon the meanings present in common human experience and language, and upon the meanings present in the Christian fact (1975, p. 43).

But as Tracy's final chapter makes clear, he is not ultimately concerned to leave the argument at this, preliminary, stage:

> Just as the historical theologian's principal aim is an adequately reconstructed *historia* and the fundamental and systematic theologian's principal attempts are to formulate an appropriately constructed contemporary *theoria*, so the practical theologian's task becomes the rigorous investigation of the possibilities of *praxis* which a reconstructed *historia* and a newly constructed *theoria* may allow (1975, p. 240).

There is meant to be a very definite juncture at which theory ends and praxis begins. There is thus a clear halt to the postmodernist slide, and it comes at that point where theology has always been most effective if it is genuinely critical, namely at the collision of faith and society. This is where theology must find its purchase (see Metz 1980, p. 3).

What one finds in Tracy's revisionist theology then is a very careful series of distinctions, marking out the territory of revisionist/fundamental/systematic (these names are interchangeable in this context) theology into discrete packets of information and subsequently tasks. Those packets are history, theory and practical matters, and although Tracy is not entirely clear about how these three packets connect to each other, he is convinced they do and that this is very important for how theology should work. The conditions of possibility of any contemporary theology should work to relate the history of the Christian religion, theoretical constructs and models about it, and the jobs it has to do in society and the world. They thus articulate an interpretation of mystery, event and rhetoric.

What all of this amounts to is that Tracy's revisionist theology sets itself certain very clear parameters. It is not historical, and it is not practical; but as theory it functions as a form of rhetoric, as address and persuasion. It is a form of address which is intended to persuade other theologians to continue their studies in Tracy's fashion. As such it is neither empty (the pejorative definition of 'rhetoric'), nor is it simply oratory, such as Socrates attacked in Plato's *Gorgias*. On the contrary, Tracy really does seem to want his model to function as an elaboration of the conditions of possibility of speaking about God in the postmodern world, and so his model is to all intents and purposes solely hypothetical. This is what rhetoric means in Tracy's theology: it is straightforward hypothesis, given a positive value by Tracy's philosophical rubric.[17]

It is tempting, then, to speak of Tracy's revisionist theology as a blueprint for future work, and most secondary commentators, even those who are quite critical of Tracy, note this intent behind *Blessed Rage for Order*. After all, there is a long and clear tradition in Roman Catholic theology, originating with Thomas Aquinas' *Summa Theologiae*, of people trying to map out the conceptual territory of theology. It is entirely in keeping with the basic thrust of a faith seeking understanding for Tracy to want to address his readership with rhetorical questions, particularly in an era which has raised rhetoric itself to an honourable philosophical/theoretical status.

It is here, however, that Tracy's model demonstrates its most fundamental weakness, because it is unclear what *Blessed Rage for Order* wants to be rhetorical *about*. Tracy's revisionist theology is ably theoretical, and Tracy establishes – lucidly – the line or avenue by which it will move towards being practical; but there is no evidence of the practical situation from which his theoretical model arose. There is no sense in Tracy's model in which one can speak of the material which his theory flourishes rhetorically. Indeed, there is no strong sense in Tracy of what the Christian faith is at all.

Certainly, Tracy presents a very clear account of what it is for a model to seek understanding in a pluralistic environment, and on this level there is a great deal in *Blessed Rage for Order* with which one would want to agree. There is no real sense at all of the faith which is actively seeking understanding, however, or indeed any apparent re-

[17] Tracy's subdivision of theology's publics into society, academy and Church consequently has little real meaning, because his notion of *address* is entirely hypothetical; see Cunningham 1991, p. 64.

flection upon what it means for faith to undertake the activity which Tracy elaborates in great detail. Given this, it is uncanny the way in which Tracy's understanding of the religious limit-language of human existence draws the same fire, from the Barthian perspective, as Harnack's theological liberalism; for at bottom it seems to be an inadequate representation of what it means to receive grace and then to speak about God. Theology may indeed function as rhetoric in the contemporary world; but what is the point, if it has nothing to be rhetorical about? Instead it collapses into its own carefully demarcated world, neither historical nor practical, within which it simply atrophies.

It is this problem which generated the definition of theology as rhetoric which I gave in my Introduction: theology is rhetoric in so far as rhetoric is sacramental narrative, the address to faith and society of a particular understanding of God's mystery and event, for entirely eschatological, graceful and therefore material reasons. In this sense I agree with Tracy that any contemporary theology has to be hermeneutic, i.e. that it has to interpret texts and events historically. Additionally, I agree with Tracy that any such hermeneutic theology constructs models which then have to be tested to see if they produce meaning for people in their everyday lives. I disagree with Tracy, however, when he argues that the foundation (limit) of this process is the religious sense of human existence. Here I would endorse Barth's complaint against Harnack and theological liberalism, namely that it speaks of the cultural values of a particular human era, rather than the Biblical witness of God's action in Christ. If a theology wants to be genuinely critical then it has to result in a sacramental narrative which addresses the Biblical and traditional understanding of mystery and event to contemporary faith and society. Despite his nod in the direction of the New Testament, Tracy's understanding of religion is the same one that western liberalism has been operating with for the past two centuries, and as such it cannot be the foundation of a critical theology today.

Where to begin and end?

This analysis has generated a number of issues which now lead directly into Part II, in which this understanding of mystery, event and rhetoric must be elaborated at greater length. Before that, however, I want to draw some conclusions out of the present chapter in relation to what is to come in Part II.

It is important that the criticisms of the last few pages do not cloud what I intended to be a very positive interpretation of *Tracy's Blessed Rage for Order*, because Tracy comes closer than anyone to articulating the genuine conditions of possibility of critical theology in modernity and postmodernity. Tracy himself, however, identifies the point at which his enterprise goes awry:

> The reflective discipline needed to decide upon the cognitive claims of religion and theism will itself have to be able to account not merely for some particular dimension of experience but *all experience* as such (1975, p. 55).

This is one of Tracy's most significant remarks; and yet ultimately it judges his entire theological enterprise, because it raises the question whether or not his understanding of religion as the most basic limit-language of human existence is tenable. In this sense the above statement serves perfectly as a postmodern epistemological critique of any theological activity (as Tracy no doubt intended): any theological model must have as its philosophical foundation an understanding of human existence which does justice to the existence *per se*, and not simply the Christian Church *per accidens*. Of course this is an exceedingly tall order, and one which, as Rahner understood, any theology will find extremely difficult to fulfil; but if a theology is to be genuinely critical, rather than simply parochial, then it has to accept this challenge. Failure to do so is failure to take seriously the world beyond the churches, which is not without redemption and which is full of hidden (prevenient?) grace.

Tracy's words, therefore, hang over any effort to speak about God in anything like a general (universal) sense: 'The reflective discipline needed to decide upon the cognitive claims of religion and theism will itself have to be able to account not merely for some particular dimension of experience but for *all experience* as such'. The aim of chapter 6 is to be able to settle this account in the chosen terms of an interpretation of the spiritual primacy of immanence. This achieved, the particular dynamics of the doctrine of the Christ event – missing from Tracy's model – will be developed and considered in chapter 7, before finally the perspectival and sacramental narrative of this mystery and event is considered in chapter 8. Tracy's *Blessed Rage for Order* thus establishes the agenda of Part II of the present study, which has to answer the questions this chapter has raised about theological methodology in general.

The way forward, then, is clear. The task of a critical theology is to steer between general structure devoid of detail on the one hand, and rootless particularity on the other, in order to arrive at a form of address/rhetoric to one's historical context which serves both traditional and current understandings of reality. The first stage of this process, to identify a structure to theology which originates in particularity and leads ultimately back to it, is the object of the next chapter, in which I want to move away from the interpretative work of Part I towards the elaboration of my own understanding of what constitutes critical theology in the contemporary situation.

Part II

The Scope and Task of Critical Theology

6

Mystery: The Spiritual Primacy of Immanence

The wind blows where it wills, and you hear the sound of it, but you do not know whence it comes or whither it goes; so it is with every one who is born of the Spirit (John 3:8)

'Mystery' is a term used in many different ways in many different theological discourses; often it is ill-defined, confusing to the reader, and impossible to interpret in any meaningful fashion. It is as well, then, to be entirely clear about how 'mystery' and 'mystery language' are being used in this chapter. In keeping with my Introduction, 'mystery' is defined as the first principle by means of which one understands the presence and absence of God with/from the world. Further, 'mystery' is defined philosophically as the principle by means of which human understanding and discussion of the present and absent God is structured. 'Mystery' is, consequently, a term employed theistically to establish the level upon which one wishes to speak of God. That level is paradoxical and ironic: God is near and yet far, present and yet absent, transcendent and yet immanent, revealed and yet concealed. God, finally, *is* mystery.[1]

The first sections of this chapter will be devoted to an analysis of some of the different levels upon which one can examine this definition, and to an identification of the particular status I want to give to mystery. Initially, however, I want to make the following observations about the language used to interpret the place of mystery in critical theology. Words like 'first principles', 'structure', 'status' and 'establish' imply the primacy of such a discussion of mystery within critical theology; they signal to the reader that he or she is involved in something which will become a frame of reference for any later treatment of specific revelation or interpretations of ways in which mystery might

[1] See Rahner 1966f, Louth 1983, Lash 1988, pp. 231–42, and see also Wiles 1982; for a particularly important treatment of the role of mystery language in contemporary theology, see Thornhill 1992.

be mediated. Mystery language is thus an attempt to provide a general foundation, upon which one can then go on to construct more specific arguments. Speaking of God as mystery means making a universal claim about the world in which one lives and that which is beyond it. In this sense, arguing that God is the mystery of the world means, religiously, adopting a position similar to Tracy's.[2]

Given this, it is right to acknowledge the ambitions of mystery language; the goal here, after all, is simply to identify a universal principle within which one can speak of the particulars of the Christian faith. In terms of the theologians considered in Part I, moreover, one can argue that this quest for a universal principle has been more or less constant in twentieth-century theology. One thinks, for example, of Harnack (1957) and his 'kernel' of the Christian religion, but also of Tracy (1975) and his 'limit-language' of religion, which has continued to be influential for all of his subsequent work. One could make the same case for the other theologians considered in Part I, but the point is clear: modern theology has ambitions to speak of *the* basis of theological method (see Sykes 1984). This is what I want to address in this chapter, elaborating a particular response as a way into the subsequent discussion of both the Christ event (chapter 7) and the sacramental narrative of the Christian community (chapter 8).

Here, I want to develop Tracy's position as found in *Blessed Rage for Order*, namely the question of religion and the natural 'limit' or 'framework' within which a discussion of the relationship between God and the world can occur. I am concerned with the question of parameters, which itself is one of theological method: what religious boundaries – if any – can one identify for theology before one moves on to Christology proper?; how do these boundaries function?; what status can one give them?; what benefits accrue? The terminology employed in this chapter – mystery and its analogues – is designed to answer these questions by identifying the terrain upon which both contemporary society and the tradition want to discuss the relationship between God and the world. I want to establish, therefore, the first principle by means of which faith and society engage to discuss and address the question of the present and absent God (see Bochmuehl 1988a).

The twin notions of absence and presence point towards the fundamental premises of spirituality, of the tension between the apophatic

[2] In a Christian sense, I think it also means adopting a position similar to that of Jüngel (1983), though acknowledging religious and methodological pluralism; see chapter 7 below.

and the katophatic in faith and reflection. Indeed, one of the arguments of this chapter will be that critical theology should originate in a constructive relationship with spirituality (see 'Time and mystery' below). Further to this basic point, however, one can argue that the idea of absence and presence, when 'translated' into the terminology of modernity, reduces to the question of atheism or the denial of the existence of God. Philosophically, the battle between theology and modernity has been fought out over this question of theism versus atheism, which itself can be reduced to the question of immanence, i.e. to what extent one can speak of the meaningful presence of anything 'other than' this world and the sphere of historical experience. In this sense the subtitle of this chapter, 'the spiritual primacy of immanence', develops this question of absence and presence, atheism and theism, and considers it in terms of the general agenda of this book as a whole – discussing theological method in relation to Christian truth. The subject matter of this chapter, therefore, within my general agenda, is to identify a criterion by means of which it becomes possible to mediate theistically between the antitheses of atheism and fundamentalism, i.e. total certainty in either direction. This is the plane upon which discussion of the mystery of God occurs: mediation between absolute denial of God's presence, and absolute denial of God's absence. This world of mediation is the world of immanent spirituality (see Williams 2/1990).

The reason why this agenda has to be considered once again, despite the major efforts of such theologians as Harnack, Barth, Bonhoeffer, Rahner, Moltmann, Sobrino and Tracy, is that they have failed to address sufficiently the social requirement of theological method and its terminology to engage with issues of change and development, the lesser mystery of *time* against which all theology occurs. One of my central theses – that truth is temporal because its *locus* of encounter is constituted in human existence – has been largely ignored by such theologians as those considered in Part I. Consequently, the integral relationship between Parts I and II of this book needs to be reiterated, but understood now in terms of the positive relationship between truth in time and theological method. My goal, then, is clear: to understand mystery in such a way that it functions socially and methodologically as the level of discourse upon which one can locate a general treatment of the question of change and development. Paradoxically but importantly, this is intimately related to the question of structure and its place in human reflection. The theologians considered in Part I do not make this move from structure to change and back again, necessitating this discussion.

Some rejected definitions of mystery

The purpose of this section is not to claim that the following understandings of mystery are wrong, because that agenda would contravene the pluralistic attitude which one finds in Tracy's *Blessed Rage for Order*, and with which I concur. Rather, what I want to do here is to demonstrate why I think these three ways of understanding mystery are too limited for my purposes, and why I want to offer an alternative. It is, then, a necessary prolegomenon to the more constructive reflections considered under the heading 'Time and mystery' below, clearing the ground upon which I want to build a different theological model.

Given this rubric what I want to do here is to discuss three twentieth-century theological explorations of mystery and the philosophical problem of the relationship between transcendence and immanence which establishes it. These are: Karl Barth's defence of the autonomy of the Word, first articulated in *Romans* I of 1919, but then central to his entire theological career; Karl Rahner's shift towards transcendental anthropology as the epistemological basis for any discussion of divine mystery, found in various writings but specifically his famous essay on the place of mystery in Catholic theology; and David Tracy's attempt to identify a linguistic-cultural basis for how human beings understand mystery in a broadly postmodern world, an argument found in *Blessed Rage for Order* and, subsequently, in *The Analogical Imagination* and *Plurality and Ambiguity*. The first section of chapter 6 is therefore deliberately continuous with the final chapter of Part I, forming an important link in the development of my argument as a whole.

Barth: the truth claims of eschatological realism

As I argued in chapter 1, the debate between Barth and Harnack in 1923 was about methodology; but it was also about more fundamental theological claims on reality, its nature and how one might name it. For Barth such questions reduce to Christian truth, and in particular to the truth of the gospel, revealed in Jesus Christ. In so far as this gospel was and is eschatological, consequently, one is justified in calling Barth an eschatological realist.

What, however, is 'eschatological realism'? In his brilliant essay on Barth, Ingolf Dalferth (1989) argues that Barth's theological position is realist, in a philosophical sense, because: (a) Barth speaks ontologically of a genuine reality external to human thought and society; (b) he speaks semantically of the truth of Christian doctrine solely in relation to Christian understanding of this mysterious reality; and (c) Barth speaks epistemologically by claiming that human beings have real knowledge of the object of faith (although the object is determinative of knowledge). Dalferth argues that Barth's theological position is *eschatologically* realist because for Barth:

> the reality with which theology must deal ... is the reality of the resurrection in which the eschatological kingdom of God became manifest and which, in the proclamation of the gospel, continually represents itself by the power of the Spirit (Dalferth 1989, p. 20).

This means, argues Dalferth, that Barth is not beholden to any philosophical understanding of the conditions of possibility of anything. On the contrary, it is the Risen Word of God which is solely and entirely normative for Barth's interpretation of the relationship between God and the world, and therefore the relationship between transcendence and immanence.

In terms of a Christian understanding of mystery one can make a number of important points about Barth's position. First, it is established in strong doctrinal concerns, unlike Schleiermacher's, where theology and anthropology elide in one single conceptuality (a criticism also levelled at Karl Rahner; see below). These are Christological and relate to the absolute significance of the incarnation in the economy of salvation. Barth holds up this doctrine for glorification and profession because Christian speech about God can begin only with the expression of God's will to save. For Barth, therefore, being an eschatological realist means identifying the economic revelation of God with the immanent being of God.

Second, Barth has a strong understanding of divine grace because it is in, by and through grace in Jesus Christ that human beings come to know God. Barth's theology thus leads to a definite understanding of God's revelation and will to save acting in the world as a result of his eschatological realism: the point of any such realism is to establish theology's relevance for the understanding of faith within society, and to address a definite alternative to society (which is for Barth the theologian's prophetic mission). Unlike Schleiermacher, therefore, who works more with an *a priori* conceptualization of humanity in terms of consciousness, Barth locates theology firmly in the midst of the world. This is what grace means, argues Barth.

Third, Barth's authority for making this move is not an *a priori* appeal to the social processes of historical change and development, as in Marx's inversion of Hegel's phenomenology (although there are aspects of this in Barth's *Romans* I).[3] Rather, it is his understanding of the Bible, which is shaped by a distinctively Christomonistic hermeneutic. For Barth the Bible relates the story of God's eschatologically real action in Jesus Christ, this being its 'meaning'. What one finds, consequently, is that Barth's theology assumes the Biblical witness within itself. For Barth one speaks, theologically, in synchronicity with the Word of God as it is revealed in the Bible.

Fourth, and finally, Barth maintains a theological understanding of mystery over against human conceptions of misunderstanding. For Barth faith is not a matter of intelligibility but of acceptance: mystery demands a reorientation of the human will which can only be achieved by the grace of God, but which nevertheless involves the whole being of the individual as she lives in society. This dynamic interpretation of the mystery of faith focuses Barth's theology upon its mediation, the eschatologically real event Jesus Christ. Mystery is thus related to event at the level of eternal truth, not human God-consciousness (as in Schleiermacher), cognition or any other philosophical system.

What are the advantages and disadvantages of Barth's position? Barth's theology is attractive because it emphasizes the conviction that the mystery of God is the mystery of *God*, a genuinely divine, eternal, other reality, of which humans can speak, in specifically doctrinal and Biblical terms, solely by way of the saving event of the incarnation. Barth thereby centres theology upon historical reality which, certainly, entails its own methodological problems, but which simultaneously maintains the practical significance of theological discussion. Structure and dynamic in Barth's theology combine fruitfully to identify Christology as the foundation of all systematic theology, and eschatological realism as the basis of all theological methodology. For Barth, truth and method are not opposed, but rather identified.

Against Barth's theology, however, is the fact that it is exclusivist, because there is no level upon which one can speak of God's fundamentally mysterious relationship with the world other than the Christological. Instead, mystery is effectively reduced to event, so that in terms of human experience and language – which are themselves part of the theological understanding of mystery – Barth can maintain that 'wrestling with the mystery', for theology, means simply talking about Jesus Christ.

[3] On Barth in 1919, see Hood 1985, pp. 45–54. On Hegel and Marx, see Habermas 1987, pp. 25–42.

Barth's view has profound implications for many of the questions confronting theology today, such as interfaith dialogue, because if there is no way to speak of divine mystery other than Christologically, how does this admit the truth claims of other religious traditions? Moreover, given Barth's understanding of eschatological realism, how does this admit of any other way of speaking about Jesus Christ? Granted the truth that Christ is indeed God's eschatological event, yet it must also remain true that this event is open to a variety of meaningful, imaginative interpretations: that is what eschatology means. (This is the point made in chapter 4, quoting Vanhoozer about eschatology in Ricoeur's philosophy.) Without such an argument, theology devolves into a question of right and wrong, invoking historical-critical research and doctrinal correspondence as the arbiters of theological meaning.

Rahner: the shift to theological anthropology

Whereas for Barth the foundation of Christian theology was eschatogical realism and therefore, importantly, *time*, for Karl Rahner theology's foundation was philosophical and more specifically transcendental. The story of Rahner's theology is thus the story of a twentieth-century theological metaphysics which grows from nineteenth-century philosophy to embrace the agenda of interfaith dialogue in the 1960s in the shape of Rahner's notion of the 'anonymous Christian'. Crucially, however, that story, because of its very metaphysical nature, is simultaneously the story of a Christian understanding of mystery. This brings my argument back to the tension between exclusivism and inclusivism which I identified in Barth.

To understand Rahner's theology I want to turn to his interpretation of the doctrine of the Trinity, in which one recognizes what Rahner means by the mystery of God. Rahner argues that the immanent Trinity – the true, threefold being of God, indivisibly one as the Persons Father, Son and Holy Spirit – is *the same as* the economic Trinity – the one revealed in history through the story of Jesus Christ. Rahner thereby escapes from the dilemma of speaking about a real mediation between the transcendent and the temporal by replacing a Barthian dialectic of difference with a Thomistic metaphysics of identity. Rahner consequently argues that the true task of theology is to locate and rationalize the correct language by means of which people can speak of the identical mystery of God, without lapsing into particulars, but by considering universals in terms of being and matter, namely ontology. Theologically, what Rahner wants to avoid is the danger of collapsing grace, and thereby mystery, into historical relativism. Metaphysically, the way he achieves this is by speaking of unity and identity in terms of the transcendental conditions of the possibility of knowing God.

This is not as difficult as it first appears, because what Rahner is actually doing is short-circuiting the whole problem of speaking meaningfully about mystery in terms of a relationship with the Christ event. If transcendence *is* immanence, if what theologians speak of is not paradox but identity, then the real question about mystery is not when or in whom it is revealed, as with Protestantism, but how people know what it actually *is*. Rahner, therefore, must proceed by arguing for the possibility of transcendental knowledge; for it is only transcendental knowledge which can know itself as identity, and therefore know itself before grace. Since grace is God to all human intents and purposes, self-knowledge is transcendent (and thereby truly immanent) to the extent that it knows itself to be in fundamental identity with God, as grace. This is the basis of Rahner's theology of mystery (see Rahner 1966f).

Translating this into Barth's terminology for a moment – 'wrestling with the mystery' – one can see that for Rahner such a bout is gnoseological; it is knowledge alone which is the genuine home of any understanding of what mystery is. For Rahner, therefore, it is difficult to see how witnessing to the mystery of God can be anything testimonial, in the Barthian sense of an eschatologically real encounter which transforms the individual's (and community's) historical existence. Rather, Rahner's transcendental anthropology seems actually to preclude such an encounter. Instead, what one has is *knowledge of identity*. This is what Rahner is searching for in *Spirit in the World* (1968), and this is what he means when he writes of 'hearing the Word' (1963). It is a profoundly different hearing, and some would say a profoundly different Word, to Barth's.[4]

Stepping back for a moment from metaphysics, what does all of this mean? It means that there is something about the relationship between nature and grace in humanity which is identical with the nature of God as grace; or at least, that is the most that humanity can know and understand. What *this* means, for Rahner, is that God as Creator, and human beings as creatures, are intimately if indirectly related upon the level of transcendental knowledge. This relationship Rahner categorizes in terms of his well-known concepts, the 'presence-to-self', which defines human being in identity with divine Being, and the 'supernatural existential', or 'agency' of God in humanity as

[4] On Barth and Rahner together, see Marshall 1987.

grace. When these two things engage with each other, in the individual as transcendental knowledge, then there occurs the *possibility*, but only the possibility, of what Rahner refers to as 'conversion to the phantasm'. That this actually occurs as knowledge, however, is dependent upon an encounter with Jesus Christ, although even here Rahner's real emphasis seems to be upon possibility, understood metaphysically, rather than actuality, understood historically.

Rahner's work achieves a great deal. He claims as territory for theology the realms of spirituality, existence and transcendental knowledge, intimately related upon the level of possibility, and 'divinizes' this process by means of his understanding of nature and grace. The question which remains, however, is to what extent this does justice to a Christian understanding of mystery.

Rahner's notion of the anonymous Christian, mentioned above, helps to explain his basic distinction further (see Rahner 1979). For Rahner, being an anonymous Christian means being 'implicitly religious', i.e. having the potential, as nature and grace, to have transcendental knowledge of God's will to save. Grace empowers grace, so that the real question is not whether or not one achieves this potential (for it is God who achieves it), but rather whether Catholic theology, on the basis of its philosophical understanding of human being in relation to divine Being, asserts an eternal identity (in the will of the immanent Trinity) which establishes the universal foundations of human existence. If this is achieved, Rahner argues, then the theologian can go on to speak of the beautiful and truthful particularities of the Christian faith, which believers hold to be God's unique revelation. If it is not, however, if unity and identity are not asserted on a transcendental level, then one is left without any foundation to speak of God's action in the world.

What Rahner achieves is an identity of transcendence and immanence which ensures that theology is methodologically on certain ground when it wants to make absolute truth claims about its faith. For Rahner, *absolute* truth claims are in fact claims about *transcendence*, which is accessible to humanity via *knowledge*. The question, therefore, of anonymous Christianity simply demonstrates one of Rahner's most central methodological principles, namely that talk of inclusivity must precede talk of exclusivity.[5]

The most attractive feature of Rahner's theology, particularly in contrast to Barth's, is this inclusivity. Is it achieved at too great a Christological price, however, reducing *Jesus* Christ as it does to an

[5] This I would take to be the essential point of Rahner's transcendental methodology, particularly with reference to the questions at issue here; see Sheehan 1987.

icon of the invisible God (cf. Colossians 1:15)? Granted that Rahner's methodology gains some important ground for modern theology, at least in terms of ontology, is this achievement not too expensive? For the present study, the answer to this question must be a reluctant 'yes', because if nothing else Barth warns theology in the twentieth century that one forgets Christology at the cost, ultimately, of everything. Theology must maintain a strong sense of eschatological realism in its methodology. The real question then is how to relate eschatological realism to the need for inclusive philosophical foundations. If Rahner's ontology cannot be accepted, where does one turn for a genuinely transcendental ground of human existence?

Tracy: The priority of narrative

In modern Roman Catholic theology since Rahner, David Tracy provides one answer to this question. Tracy, giving particular weight to the developed understanding of modern theology's pluralistic context and the concomitant swing away from unique and definitive answers to methodological questions, argues for the place of language and narrative at the heart of theology's attempts to speak intelligibly of God. Tracy has related these overtly methodological problems to what he regards as the inherent ambiguity of contextualized discourse, facilitating such questions as interreligious dialogue and intrafaith discussion. This emphasis upon media and communication is typical of postmodernism.

If one pushes this argument to see where it impinges upon the way modern theology works, things are quickly reduced to two main points: inclusivity is moved away from the plane of transcendental knowledge and understanding, as in Rahner, and placed upon the level of dialogue, discourse and communication (i.e. language); language itself is considered in terms of narrative and imputed movement towards meaning and understanding. I want to consider these separately.

First, probably very few people in contemporary theology would disagree with Tracy on the question of the importance of language for how people understand theological methodology. His publications, particularly *The Analogical Imagination*, changed the theological landscape in the 1980s, making people much more aware of what they were doing when they appealed to various forms of non-linguistic, non-cultural authority. Similarly, Tracy's obvious regard for Rahner (and Lonergan) helped people to view his work as a development of the older man's orthodox position. Hence Tracy, it has been argued, is not really disagreeing with Rahner and the natural, Roman Catholic concern for order and dogmatic stability. Rather, he is working out Rahner's insights in terms of current understandings of the relationship between faith and society. This is why, so the argument runs, Tracy moves towards such things as language and meaning, understanding and ambiguity, rather than pursuing Rahner's somewhat reified interest in transcendental knowledge. In short, Tracy is more sensitive to the true nature of social and cultural discourse as it occurs.

Despite the fact that Tracy has moved away from Rahner's clear interest in transcendental knowledge, however, Tracy himself is still obviously concerned with questions of universal validity; hence his assertions in *Blessed Rage for Order*, when he writes of the 'limit', linguistic and religious, of human existence, and the way in which this parameter 'shapes' the social and cultural forms in which people live. Whatever the shifts that have occurred between Rahner and Tracy, one is still dealing here with a Catholic interest in what one might term 'the ground of being'; one still observes with Tracy a profound interest in what is fundamental in theology.

Second, this concern with fundamental theology manifests itself in Tracy's commitment to questions of meaning and understanding – that, whatever one says about the ambiguous nature of modern and postmodern human existence, the theologian's task is still to mediate towards a sense of why things happen the way they do, and what this means for a Christian understanding of the relationship between God and the world. Tracy's best articulation of what this sense actually is – Christ – comes in *The Analogical Imagination*, but his position was clear as early as *Blessed Rage for Order*.

If one attempts to synthesize these two factors in Tracy's position the following occurs: questions of Christology become the *grammar* or *syntax* of more general theological discourse, which itself becomes recognizably social communication. Importantly, Tracy is thereby able to maintain two central tenets: Christology is still crucial to theology, but the question now is what *status* does one give to the Christ *event*?; and theology in a general sense is *still* anthropology, as in Rahner, but the effective 'measurement' of theology's anthropological character has shifted away from epistemology in Rahner towards cultural phenomenology in Tracy.

For a theological understanding of mystery, Tracy's developments are brilliant, because they reflect contemporary ideas of what understanding, meaning, plurality and ambiguity actually are, and because Tracy's theology addresses the concerns of his western philosophical context. Mystery, therefore, obviously can be interpreted in terms not of human knowledge, as with Rahner, but of appropriated cultural sense, so that 'the mystery of God' becomes a conditioned statement. Tracy is correct to sense this shift in modern theology towards narrative as the basis not only of description, but also of analysis, and his methodology elaborates an intellectual framework within which people can speak of God as the mystery of human existence.

There are, however, certain question-marks which hang over Tracy's position. First, his concern to give sufficient attention to the linguistic character of contemporary reality, which is fully justified, means that when it comes to understanding faith it is unclear what it is that Christians believe *in*. Tracy's theology gives tremendous attention to the nature of mediation in society and culture, and considers at length the difficulties of communicating meaning in language; but there is little attention hitherto given to what it is that is mediated. Tracy thus speaks at length about the linguistic foundations of immanence and how it is understood and interpreted; but in the process transcendence is effectively reduced to the level of a structuring agent. In itself, of course, there is nothing wrong with this position; a 'critique of pure structure' is required in contemporary thought, and Tracy is right to assume that one simply cannot move directly from the questions of understanding itself (or indeed knowledge) to a statement of what it is that is being understood/known, or what the agent is which enables understanding/knowledge (see Cunningham 1991, pp. 149–64). This cannot mean, however, that in theology one can settle for a discussion which simply recognizes the fact of structure, without going on to state/argue what that structure is believe to be. As Heidegger pointed out in a lecture in 1928 (1976, p. 49), theology is a positive science, and as such must begin by witnessing to a structuring agent which is eschatological – Jesus Christ.

Second, it is insufficient for Tracy simply to state, as he does in *Blessed Rage for Order*, that theology draws certain key concepts from the New Testament/early Church period. Rather, theology must take extremely seriously the tone and intent of religious belief evident in this period, which was overwhelmingly concerned with eschatology. Barth was right, and for the reason that Rahner and Tracy are wrong (on this point): theology must be established broadly in eschatological realism. Granted, there will be implications to this commitment which need to be developed (see below); but without it Christian faith loses one of its fundamental, graceful components – hope.

Third, Tracy's theology is static; there is no room within it for a dynamic of change, the clearest evidence for this being the lack of a developed Christology or doctrine of the Holy Spirit (in addition to the noted lack of eschatological consideration). This means that it is very difficult to estimate where and how Tracy's theology will find any purchase on the world. All one seems to have in Tracy's thought is a strong assertion of the spiritual primacy of transcendence, as in Rahner, but without the prophetic 'rootedness' of Barth's dogmatics. Certainly there is a need for theology to speak of transcendence, and Tracy's limit concept (and even religion) proves successful at keying thought into questioning the finitude of human existence. Without an adequate metaphysics of immanence itself, however, what is the point? This is where one must take leave of Tracy's theology.

Given an acknowledgement that language and narrative must have a role to play in any theology's understanding of mystery, but that it is not possible (with Tracy) to turn language and narrative into mystery, what is the alternative? There are three aspects to this question's answer.

First, there is now a clear understanding of the need for eschatology at the very heart of theological methodology; without this, there is little point in attempting to address the specifics of the Christian faith. Second, it leaves theology looking for a suitable plane upon which to locate a discussion of that which establishes Christian discourse about eschatological events. Theological methods which turn towards some form of transcendence, as in Rahner and Tracy, are rejected because they desiccate the practical questions of how theology understands everyday reality. Third, it leaves theology wanting to make both exclusive and inclusive claims for Christian faith, but unclear as to the level upon which to place these different agendas. It leaves theology with a methodological crisis that remains too much in evidence.

Granted these factors one thing seems clear: Rahner is right, and there is no mileage in speaking of the difference between transcendence and immanence when everything one wants to assert in theology must be expressed in terms of identity. If Rahner's own programme, however – speaking in terms of transcendental knowledge – is rejected, then this leaves only one methodological route for critical theology. It must speak of the spiritual primacy not of transcendence, as in modern theology, but of immanence itself.

Time and mystery

As stated above, the question of mystery is wrapped up in that of identity and difference, in speaking of God's relationship with humanity, and of God's absence and presence from/in the world, which in modernity is reduced to the tension between theism and atheism. What I want to do in the second half of this chapter is to examine the three main qualities which, I argue, make *time* the most suitable analogy for speaking of mystery. In what follows, therefore, the adequacy of time will be considered, respectively, in terms of its ability to address the ontological, epistemological and semantic problems associated with a theological understanding of mystery. The examination will not be exhaustive, and there will be areas where further questions will be raised which cannot be answered at this stage of my enquiry. If the spiritual primacy of immanence can be established in the methodological primacy of time, however – if truth and method, 'calculation and ecstasy' (Glenn Gould), can be combined – then a way forward towards such matters as Christology (chapter 7) and sacramental narrative (chapter 8) will have been found in accord with my definition of critical theology.

Time/past: ontology and the question of completeness

Initially, the customary distinction in thought between past, present and future offers a tripartite model by which to interpret mystery. Indeed, one can go as far as to say that this model is inherently 'Trinitarian', and that the tripartite division of time mirrors, though very indirectly, something of God's own being. The difficulty with this argument, however, is that it is unconvincing because impressionistic, when what is required is an understanding of time which communicates something of the meaning of mystery analogically. What I want to identify, therefore, is a way in which time/past language can be employed to answer, analogically, the ontological questions which 'being' language has traditionally handled. This centres upon the idea of completeness.

Most simply, 'the past' is generally regarded as *history*, the repository of data which can be indexed to previous events (where by 'indexed' I understand here a causal relationship). The past is history because it 'belongs to' certain series of time and space which have gone before the present and which cannot be materially recalled. Such events 'exist', therefore, solely in the imagination of people and the research of historians – that and the effects they instigate which can be measured. Thus, and irrespective of their material causes, past events as 'texts' – things to be interpreted – can take on the status and power of symbol, in so far as they possess the integrity to generate meaning which can then be interpreted. An example of such an event is the

French Revolution, which Tracy cites in *Plurality and Ambiguity*. This process allows past texts to structure the interpretation and understanding of the present, and one's expectations for the future. It is a quality which inheres to the past in general and to past texts in particular.

I noted the structuring power of symbols in my Introduction and subsequently with respect to the theologians considered in Part I. In terms of the past, however, as one of the three elements of time as a means to interpret mystery and thereby as the basis of human reflection upon the God/world relationship, this structuring power takes on a further, important quality. If one can say that the past is itself a symbol it is because one can consider 'the past' ideally, i.e. as something which conveys meaning to the present and thereby has a power beyond material cause and effect. And if one can understand the past itself as an idea, albeit one which is inherently purposive, then one is justified in speaking of the completeness of the past; for ideas are complete if they are anything.

Philosophically, if the past as symbol is ideally complete, and contains within it texts – such as the French Revolution – then it follows that such texts can be spoken of analogically to answer ontological questions, because ontology itself is a science which wants to speak of completeness.[6] An identity can thereby be made between the past, completeness and ontology, because of the past's ideal, symbolic status. Without such an identity one or other of these elements is consigned to speaking not of completeness, but incompleteness. And since it makes no sense to speak of being, the past or a symbol as incomplete, this identity is secured for argument.

What this achieves is a form of discourse which circumvents the traditional, 'substantial' difficulties associated with ontological language because, by analogy, ontological statements are now interpreted according to the horizon or plane not of 'being' – understood as some*thing* – but of completeness, which is a function of relationship and therefore of identity and difference. This shift provides the grammar of a new way of speaking of God's being. The vocabulary which is associated with that grammar will depend, of course, upon the specific circumstances of the interpreter engaging with the grammar (and there will be a variety of different vocabularies). The important point, however, is that the grammar of completeness is independent of the

[6] Here I am heavily influenced by Coreth's *Metaphysics* (1968, pp. 120–5), where the same point is made, though in the language of unity.

constraints of the language of substance, and can therefore be used analogically to speak of the mystery of God, which obviously cannot be reduced to the material.

In terms of critical theology's discussion of mystery, the following points need to be made. First, since mystery language wants to speak of an identity between God and the world which necessarily entails a discussion of difference but does not start there, that identity must be secured upon a level open to language and experience, because that is the only way that identity can be understood. To justify this claim, however, mystery language must itself make ontological, epistemological and semantic sense, because questions about being, the conditions of possibility of knowledge, and the communication of meaning, are fundamental to how people use and interpret language and experience.

Second, therefore, mystery language must speak of completeness, incompleteness and potential, because – understood by analogy with time/past/present/future and therefore conceptually tensed – being is complete, knowledge incomplete and meaning potential. Any other allocation of these three qualities makes no analogical sense: one could not, for example, speak of the completeness of knowledge by analogy with time/past (because the past cannot be completely known), nor the potential of meaning by analogy with time/present (because the present is contingent).

The first 'proof' of this argument has been made by considering the past as a complete idea possessing structuring power because, like present and future, it functions symbolically. On this argument time/past is capable of supporting ontological claims in a unique way, because the completeness of being is most meaningfully interpreted not in terms of spatial qualities, but in terms of temporal qualities. This is the only way in which one can speak of being meaningfully. Any other level falls into the trap of incompleteness, which cannot, by definition, be a quality of being. This is the effective argument against expressing ontological questions in terms of matter. There is no perspective from which one can speak analogically of the completeness of matter, and therefore there is no perspective from which 'matter language', as opposed to time/past language, can express the fundamental structuring power of a complete symbol.[7]

[7] One way of understanding this distinction would be by analogy with the difference between something like historical phenomenology (e.g. Veyne 1984) and historicism, i.e. empirically verifiable research. In terms of ontology, my own analogical approach is designed to prevent the unwarranted speculation one finds in much recent theology, where questions about 'being' are asked almost as if people actually believe these questions can be answered! On this, see Gunton 1991, pp. 71–81, as an example of such over-ambitious 'ontologizing'.

An example will illustrate this point. If one wishes to speak of the French Revolution then it makes no sense to speak of its being materially, because there is no viewpoint from which one can speak of its completeness materially, and therefore no viewpoint from which one can answer ontological questions about it. One *might* wish to speak of the French Revolution's effects, which would entail a discussion of the material and how it has been changed by the social, political and economic forces unleashed in 1789. But such a discussion would always be incomplete. Nor could one ever imagine being able to analyse and evaluate *all* of the material effects of the French Revolution, even if – unimaginably – a perspective existed from which one could make such calculations.

The rejection of the material in favour of time/past as a way of answering ontological questions analogically, which is necessary for my discussion of mystery as something complete, illustrates another important aspect of the past, validating its ontological status. The completeness of past events like the French Revolution cannot be diminished. On the contrary, it is renewed each time interpretation engages with it, thereby implicitly confirming its ontological significance. All ontology, consequently, in so far as it is concerned with being and therefore, by analogy, with completeness, is simultaneously concerned with the past as symbol. This is the only way in which ontology can remain a viable mode of discourse in contemporary theology, because any other definition effectively condemns ontology to the self-defeating task of emptying little boxes of matter, which is of no earthly use to anyone.

Certainly, this does not mean that one cannot attempt to speak ontologically of matter; but as critical theology approaches mystery as symbol it is at least clear that the congruence of time/past, completeness and being establishes the claims that the Christian faith wants to make concerning *God's* being and action. Nor could anyone be so crude as to think that this consigns God to the *past* in any linear fashion, because past, present and future, as symbols, do not function on that level. Rather, God is past to all human imagination *because* God is *complete*: that is the only way in which God is universally relevant to any and every interpretation of reality, and thereby to any and every understanding of the relationship between faith and society (which is what Tracy means by 'limit'). Ontological claims about God, therefore, must be made in terms of God's completeness: this is how the mystery of God's being must be interpreted symbolically. That this places God on the same level as, for example, the French Revolution, at least ontologically, only illustrates the inadequacy of ontology *alone* as a way of speaking about God and why it is necessary, methodologically, for critical theology to relate its discussion of God's universal mystery to God's particular event of self-revelation, Jesus Christ. Mystery *as* completeness is unapproachable because there is no viewpoint from which one can find any purchase upon it – intellectually, spiritually, historically. On the contrary, completeness must be mediated as incompleteness, this being the basis of all Christology.

Time, therefore, can sustain ontological debate. Indeed, my argument is that it is only time, as time/past, which adequately answers, analogically, ontology's questions about being as completeness, thereby establishing ontology itself at the heart of critical theology's understanding of mystery. As stated, however, such completeness must be mediated by incompleteness, thereby bringing ontological questions into relation with epistemological ones.

Time present: the temporal context of knowledge

On the rubric established here, if the past is understood as symbol then so is the present and by implication the future, which means that it is necessary to assess the argument that knowledge is involved with critical theology's interpretation of mystery. *How* this is possible is the subject of the present section.

Initially I want to dispel the impression that somehow one *knows* the past, so that one can obtain purchase upon the past which exerts control over it – 'knowledge'. In fact, because the past is complete one cannot know it *per se*; one can only remember it *per accidens*, which means recalling completeness in so far as it gives meaning to one's situation in the present. That this is true both of the individual and society is best illustrated by the selective way in which memory functions as democracy, where past and complete texts are invoked because they facilitate the smooth running of government, an inherently manipulative process (see Peck 1988, p. 37).

That the past is remembered because it is complete and therefore too powerful for anything but partial recollection – as particular event or text – implies that the present is knowable *because* it is incomplete, i.e. that one can have knowledge of something which has not been completed, because it is only the incomplete which is sufficiently weak for knowledge to control it. (Again, the implications of this are witnessed by the day-to-day administration of any government, at any level, where it is always government's control of ongoing situations and legislation which gives it credibility or, in certain cases, destroys its public image.) This has considerable implications for how one defines the present as the context of knowledge (see Habermas 1987, pp. 301ff).

If the present is defined as incomplete, because there is no way in which it can be complete, this implies that one cannot speak ontologically – even by analogy – about the present. Rather, one speaks epistemologically about the present, about knowledge and how it is obtained. Moreover, by extension one can assert that since knowledge pertains to what is incomplete, and what is incomplete is what is present, then one cannot have knowledge of what is complete. Epistemological discourse is thereby understood to be distinct from ontological discourse because of the way critical theology speaks analogically about time and mystery.

Talk about knowledge, consequently, cannot be reduced to the level of transcendence, because when that occurs (as in Rahner) the text of knowledge – whatever it may be – becomes divorced from its *context*, which is always the incomplete present. In terms of my metaphysics of time, the important point with respect to the incomplete present is that, unlike memory, which though formed by context is not dependent upon it alone, knowledge is entirely dependent upon context. When an individual or society remembers the complete past, therefore, it does so dependent upon the being of what is remembered (such as the French Revolution) and thereby upon its completeness. When the same individual or society knows the incomplete present, however, its basis is not being but rather the contingent circumstances of the incomplete present. In this sense the incomplete nature of the present actually establishes the temporary status of knowledge itself, something which real life demonstrates constantly (see Wolff 1983).

To illustrate this point one has only to consider the extent to which anything at all is actually known, for example that newspapers are generally printed in black ink on white paper. One *knows* this because one *sees* black and white newspapers for sale in high street newsagents and because knowledge is dependent upon data and information gathered by sensory perception. Anything that does not depend upon such data and information cannot be the subject of knowledge. It may be *remembered* on the basis of other texts and events – for example, the claim that all newspapers used to be broadsheet in format may well be remembered on the basis of existing documentary evidence – but it cannot be known. People know far less than they actually think – or rather, remember and imagine.[8]

[8] On the implications of this approach to questions of knowledge, memory and imagination – which I want to accept – see Casey 1987, pp. 262–313.

This means that knowledge is dependent upon social construction, which is achieved via culturally determined language and experience. With respect to critical theology's understanding of mystery, its foundations in a metaphysics of time must recognize that knowledge itself is fundamentally insecure because of its own construction by language and experience. In turn this means that any knowledge an individual or society might claim to have concerning mystery – as symbol – must be regarded as incomplete not because of any particular conviction one might have about the nature of mystery itself (which would be methodologically irrelevant), but because knowledge simply does not possess the status of certainty. On this basis theology can happily devote attention both to the ontological claims to completeness understood by analogy with time/past and to the epistemological claims to incompleteness involved in time/present, certain in the knowledge that they do not contradict each other. On the contrary, completeness and incompleteness, being and knowledge, are complementary discourses which must be addressed to any understanding of mystery by analogy with time.

If it is not possible to speak of knowledge as *certainty*, however, what status can one give to knowledge? The answer to this question is intimately related to the concomitant question regarding the status of memories with respect to the completed past, which is ideal, i.e. they function as ideas which inform any understanding of human existence. Because of the symbolic status of time/past and the status of its events and texts as completed ideas, therefore, the status of memories ensures that they shape any human understanding of reality. People remember and subsequently imagine; that is how they live, and that is how time/past as symbol invades and structures human existence.

The status of knowledge, by contrast, is contingent: it depends upon the specific circumstances or socio-cultural context in which the knowing individual/society finds itself. As such it would be wrong to imply that knowledge, because of its very incompleteness within the present, could actually be normative for any understanding of reality. It is not, because when any claim of knowledge forgets its incompleteness and attempts to assert itself normatively, it effectively shifts itself to the level of social memory. When this occurs, as, for example, with Darwin's hypothesis concerning evolution and the origin of species by natural selection, it means that theory is being reified to the level of *complete* and therefore *past* being: ontological claims are made for some part of knowledge as that knowledge becomes generally accepted. On this analysis the testing of ontological claims is often something which occurs because an individual or society has sought special status for a piece of knowledge. The results of that testing are, of course, open to debate. What cannot occur, however, is that knowledge simply elides into being; for incompleteness does not become complete simply because, by analogy with time, present becomes past. That would make no sense theologically: one would not want to argue that something which happens in Church today simply *is* identical with the Word of God, unless one were rejecting the entire basis of interpretation in which my argument is established.[9]

Time as a way of understanding mystery analogically thus preserves two important qualities. First, with respect to time/past it preserves the ontological priority of completeness as the structural power of time's symbolism. Time/past becomes the realm not of *superseded* events (that would be to maintain a crudely indexical notion of past, present and future, rather than a symbolic one) but of meaningful ones, i.e. events and ideas – texts – which, via interpretation, address something of continuing significance to the human understanding of reality. The mystery of God, on this reading, shares in this symbolic structural power of time/past: it has ontological meaning for humanity because it is complete. As such, however, without any particular revelation, it remains simply part of the conceptual baggage which humanity carries around with itself. This is the point at which limit-language – as in Tracy or Hick – leaves the argument: precisely where as a Christian theologian one needs to start considering incarnation.

Second, and in terms of time/present, mystery interpreted by analogy with time establishes the incompleteness of knowledge because of the social and temporary construction of language and experience, thereby securing for mystery the impossibility of its complete appropriation by knowledge. This is crucial for critical theology's understanding of mystery, because if mystery as a question were open to simple cognitional verification or falsification, then no such thing as revelation would be required, and thereby mystery would remain in the realm of universal symbols. Clearly, if mystery is to migrate from the plane of completed ideas, which are important to human understanding but which are not in themselves part of the contingent world, to the plane of human action and knowledge – and if faith wants to assert a *real* movement between the two – then an event needs to occur which mediates between the two states of completeness and incompleteness. In critical theology this methodological task is undertaken

[9] People who reject this hermeneutic approach overwhelmingly have at the centre of their agenda another claim for authority, often either charismatic or Biblical fundamentalism. Ultimately, one is speaking here of 'Church building', which inevitably leads to questions of power, how it is wielded, by whom, and on what basis; see chapter 8 below.

by eschatology, thereby identifying truth and method (see Ratzinger 1988).

The structural power of the two symbols past and present indicates how critical theology's understanding of the completeness and incompleteness of mystery is fundamental to the way in which religious people and communities exist in the world.[10] Moreover, the mediation between past and present, between completeness and incompleteness, points towards an event of revelation in which the two symbols are joined in one understanding. This clearly directs Christian attention towards the question of Christology, the subject of the next chapter.

Simultaneously, however, there remains the question of the future: to what extent is it too a symbol, and how can individuals and societies interpret it? This is the subject of the final part of this section.

Time/future: meaning and change

Here it is important to recapitulate the procedure by which these questions have been approached. First, I argued – on the basis of the studies undertaken in Part I – that talk about mystery is talk about the first principles of critical theology. Second, however, because mystery is *mysterious* and therefore closed to knowledge, it has to be understood as symbol and, because symbols possess integrity as ideas, mystery is a symbol which has to be interpreted *analogically*. Third, therefore, the analogy which I have employed to interpret mystery is time, rather than the other procedures discussed and rejected in the first section of this chapter.

In terms of that process of interpretation, three questions are directed at time and thereby mystery as symbol: ontology – how is mystery understood to be complete?; epistemology – how is knowledge of mystery incomplete?; semantics – how is mystery's meaning open to future interpretation? Having answered the first two questions and thereby defined two tensed responses of interpretation to mystery as complete and incomplete, it is now necessary to consider the third question, which is concerned with mystery's potential. Answering this

[10] This would seem to me to be the basis of unity and diversity in religious pluralism, which I acknowledge has to be taken seriously by systematic theology. On this question, see D'Costa 1992: although I agree with the very general point being made here, I cannot accept the tendentious language or the conclusions offered. One must tackle the question of the reality of mystery and those who claim to name it. Without such an acknowledgement, talk of the 'end' of systematic theology abandons its integrity as a way of doing systematic theology.

question completes the framework within which I want to name mystery from the viewpoint of Christian faith.

Time/future is the realm of the possible because it is where possible meaning 'resides'. If one therefore wants to speak of the various possibilities of meaning which might exist for any symbol, and which might be made relevant to the way in which people think about that symbol, one must do so by analogy with time/future; for whereas both time/past and time/present refer to the status of a symbol and how it is known (or not known), time/future is concerned with what it is possible to say about that symbol. Meaning is something which develops, consequently, not from the complete and incomplete status of mystery as symbol, but rather from the responses of human understanding *to* that symbol. In the case of mystery as critical theology seeks to understand it, one can say that meaning always lies *ahead* of it rather than *within* it (where it would not be accessible) or by knowing it (when it would not be intelligible). On this analogy the most basic quality which one can predicate of mystery, in terms of its potential meaning, is its future.

The production of meaning is a process of change, and in so far as change implies development and the realization of potential meanings, one can say that mystery is always in the process of being realized for Christianity in the life of faith and of Church (see chapter 8; this understanding makes mystery relational). This works well with traditional notions of mystery, such as one finds in Christianity, where what is complete and yet incomplete about human understanding of mystery is yet open to the continuing development of both Church and religious experience. It is also true, however, of the contemporary theological situation, where the question of pluralism dominates a certain area of debate and where many different theologies appeal, ultimately, to the one mystery of faith. In relation to this pluralism of applied theologies, the task of critical theology is to elaborate their methodological foundations (see Gilkey 1991, pp. 21–47).

The following point can be made about the question of identity and difference in critical theology's interpretation of mystery. Whereas the completeness of mystery is clearly a quality of identity, and its incompleteness is concerned with the impossibility of knowing identity *as* identity, mystery's potential to change and develop meaning is a quality of difference, because it is a function of the way in which mystery becomes interpreted into human existence. This is not a question of whether or not mystery can change in itself; for clearly that question, which depends for its intelligibility upon verification, is what remains incomplete in human understanding. This would apply whatever analogy one deployed to interpret mystery theologically; but the fact that I have chosen time highlights the dangers of speaking too substantively of inherent change, when what one actually means is change in interpretation and thereby the production of different meanings.[11]

This question is socially relevant because on any interpretation issues of change and development, of the production of meaning, inevitably involve matters of social construction, and therefore involve the use of the imagination to move beyond existing forms (see Casey 1979, pp. 38–60). The development of meaning thus occurs to the extent that the social imagination plays upon the circumstances in which mystery (or any other symbol) is interpreted, thereby resulting in the renewed application of theology to its specific context.[12]

Certainly, this emphasis upon the social imagination sounds potentially dangerous, as if change and development were ends in themselves (a danger with which postmodernism has yet to grapple). Again, however, this is simply the process one witnesses today in, for example, liberation theology, or feminist theology, or green theology. As long as theology reflects critically upon mystery the question of change and development will be evidenced as one of interpretation and therefore different responses to the one symbol, rather than fundamental alterations to 'the thing in itself' (as might be required if other analogies, such as matter, were employed instead of time).

Together, these three notions of completeness, incompleteness and potential return the question of first principles in theology to the arena of immanence, the direct result of answering fundamental questions about mystery by analogy with time. Simultaneously they bring centre-stage the question of human existence and its role in applying understanding to the historical contexts in which people live. Mystery is to be understood both as the basis of theological method and human existence and therefore as the most appropriate level upon which to discuss the issues which apply universally to society in general. Mystery is indeed a symbol, therefore; but it is also *the* symbol, because it reflects the temporal qualities of human existence.[13]

[11] N.B. the Kantianism of all modern theology in this respect. See also Lindbeck 1984 for the way in which this affects our understanding of doctrine, and the final section of chapter 8 below for the application of this process to a specific doctrine (the cross).

[12] Some of these ideas were developed at a meeting of the Birmingham Philosophy Society (1993), in my paper 'Nietzsche's Animals'. I would like to thank my colleagues at that society – particularly Sebastian Odiari, Nick Dent, Barry Falk, Joss Walker and Chris Hookway – for their comments and criticisms.

[13] I acknowledge that there is a slide here between the deployment of an explicitly religious symbol – mystery – and a general theory of symbols established finally in a wider understanding of mystery which can be appropriated by secular reflection (although I would

Metaphysically, this interpretation of mystery by analogy with time offers definite results. It remains to be demonstrated, however, how these general insights can best be related to the particular concerns of the Christian faith in Jesus Christ. That is – and here Barth is a guide – having provided a general analysis which suggests for time what Schleiermacher achieved for consciousness, and what Rahner advocated for transcendental knowledge, I still have to find a way of relating these insights to Christian questions of faith and hope. The obvious solution to this question, as in Barth and Rahner, is to appeal to grace; but how is grace to be related to mystery, understood by analogy with time?

The rest of this chapter is concerned with answering this question, thereby linking with the next chapter's examination of Christology. Simply, what I am going to attempt to provide is a way in which the three qualities of mystery understood by analogy with time – completeness, incompleteness and potential – can be related to three areas of theological concern which are fundamental to how Christianity understands grace. In this way what I hope to provide is an understanding of the relationship between mystery and grace which will establish the basis for a more detailed consideration of the *event* of grace itself, Jesus Christ. Thus, the theology of the symbol which is the result of the present chapter's concentration upon mystery, becomes in chapter 7 a theology of the *image* of Jesus Christ.[14]

The three parts of the final section of this chapter, therefore – Spirit, kingdom and the Trinity – are intended to correspond to completeness, incompleteness and potential, as mystery and by extension human existence are understood by analogy with time and thereby named for the Christian faith. As with everything in chapter 6, however, it is important to remember that there are no easy distinctions between these different parts, so that one might straightforwardly equate, for example, Spirit solely with a past/complete understanding of mystery.

---

argue that this slide is also the basis of Heidegger's late event theory). The point I want to make, however, is that because mystery sustains interpretation by analogy with time, thereby becoming open to appropriation by any individual or group which exists in time (the human race), then it can function as the fundamental limit (in Tracy's sense) of any understanding of human existence. 'Mystery', then, is something of an umbrella definition; but I want to argue that the idea it denotes is sound with respect to the way in which people actually live. The question, whether or not one gives objective definition to meaning, remains open.

[14] The shift here is from a universal or general level of symbol theory – albeit centred upon the explicitly Christian symbol mystery – towards the production of particular images of Jesus Christ as they occur in specific contexts (see Dulles 1992, pp. 17–39). Although I do not agree with Dulles' 'postcritical' approach to theology, I believe that his argument is moving creatively towards the real business of theology – contextual address and interpretation.

That way lies the reification which I criticized. On the contrary, what I want to provide here is a methodological bridge by means of which critical theology can conceptualize both what makes it one with other forms of reflection upon mystery, and the named event which distinguishes it entirely.

Grace and time: theology's witness to mystery

The position of this chapter, therefore, is quite clear. Mystery is the fundamental symbol of religion, and the most meaningful analogy by which to interpret that symbol is time. For Christianity the possibility of interpreting mystery meaningfully, of naming it and thereby appropriating it for human existence, is by grace. One must thus speak of the integral relationship between grace and time for Christianity and therefore for theology as faith seeking understanding, because this is how grace is understood to be effective in human existence. In this way it makes sense to speak of the gracefulness of temporal existence, meaning that the basis for any human understanding of its relationship with God comes through being in time. This much is revealed by the incarnation of the Son.[15]

Since time in this sense is intended to be the general basis to human existence *per se*, rather than a peculiarly 'theological' or 'religious' existence (neither of which would make any sense), it follows that time is the basis of any understanding of society because the narrative of society is one of past, present and future – completeness, incompleteness and potential. Faith and society are thus intimately related, as Metz argues in *Faith in History and Society* (1980); but that which distinguishes them is faith's acknowledgement of grace. This means that the connection between faith and society can be established on the level of the analogical interpretation of symbols, and that consequently there is no need to look towards Christology in itself to provide such a connection. Instead, Christology, as the next chapter will demonstrate, must be left to the particular task of representing, without pause, Jesus Christ as the confessed image of mystery.

This means that the question about what it is to be religious, and what it is to be human – fundamental to the relationship between faith

[15] The point here is that both truth and method have to reflect the fact that God mediates through all time in general because of God's participation in time in one particular event, namely the incarnation and ascension. A metaphysics of time, consequently, is far more fruitful than one of space, which has an implicitly limiting effect upon the analogies one can employ to speak of divine love and action.

and society – can only be answered *in general* in terms of an interpretation of mystery as symbol. It is, as Tracy argued, a question of how one limits discourse and understanding, so that one can speak meaningfully of a relationship between all people and all societies. Christology cannot do this, because Christology is not about applying general limits to discourse and the possibility of meaning. On the contrary, Christology is the specifically Christian naming and appropriation of mystery.[16] Acknowledging mystery as the limit of all discourse and understanding about religion and society, therefore, is something which witnesses to the pluralistic tendencies in the contemporary world and allows critical theology to make general claims about what it is to be both human and religious. This is the genuine foundation of interfaith dialogue, and as such must be included as a stage of reflection in theological methodology – because it argues for the truth of mystery's primary status – before theology turns in faith to a consideration of the event which makes a specific revelation of mystery. Discourse about the Christ event itself cannot sustain this level of interpretation, because it has an entirely separate agenda, namely witnessing to belief in the grace of the Son.

What I want to do now is specify the three 'names' by means of which Christian theology appropriates the more generally religious discussion of mystery which has so far occupied this chapter. These three names are Spirit, kingdom and Trinity, and with them I want to move away from the general, towards the particulars of Christian discourse, in preparation for my consideration of the Christ event in the next chapter.

Spirit

The basic point to be made here is very straightforward. Since the Biblical witness to faith argues for the pivotal role of Spirit in creation (cf. Genesis 1:1), any philosophical idea of completeness must be theologically intelligible in terms of Spirit itself. The statement that 'God is Spirit' thus makes even clearer sense of the ontological status of completeness, because if God is not to be the basis of completeness then it is difficult to imagine what God can be in Godself. On this analogy, rather, an appeal to Spirit as the most appropriate theological name to give to completeness emphasizes the power of cohesion which must –

[16] Ultimately, the naming and appropriation of mystery is the basis of all religions, an axiom which has to be accommodated in everything critical theology wants to say about both truth and method.

on the same principle – bring faith and society together, because God is the ultimate originator of both faith and society.

Ingeniously, this is the meaning one finds given to Spirit or *Geist* in Hegel's *Phenomenology of Spirit* (1977b), which has been so influential for modern theology and which Rahner attempted to synthesize with Aquinas and Heidegger in *Spirit in the World* (1968). Evoking Hegel, however, highlights the problem with this shift from philosophy to theology, because the question which then occurs is: 'What status can one give to "Spirit" language in theology?' Hegel's answer – that Spirit functions on the level of pure concepts which find expression phenomenally – makes a certain sense of the development of humanity and society, teleologically (see Findlay 1970, pp. 131–47). Teleology in theology, however, would undermine the clear relationship between Spirit and completeness which I have made in this chapter. What one requires, therefore, is a way of naming Spirit which maintains its complete status without reducing it to the level of pure concepts, a way of naming Spirit which reverses Hegel's shift from the phenomenal to the speculative.

For critical theology this means naming Spirit the *Holy* Spirit. Moreover, it means making the Holy Spirit the complete foundation of both faith and society – as grace – because the inversion of Hegel's slide from the phenomenal to the speculative means that the naming process – of moving from idea to person – occurs immanently in the world. The Holy Spirit therefore not only gives a temporal interpretation to mystery on the level of naming and movement from symbol to immanence, it also establishes the spiritual primacy of immanence itself within critical theology via a specific doctrine.

Kingdom

The same should be argued for 'kingdom' language, which for critical theology must always be eschatological. The point which needs to be made here is that the kingdom can be understood by analogy with time because of its emphasis upon the incompleteness of time/present and this world. This means that in the interpretation of mystery as the religious symbol, the quality of incompleteness which is predicated of epistemological discourse about mystery finds theological expression via the doctrine of the kingdom. This is because eschatology, as a form of apocalyptic, argues that present knowledge of the heavenly secrets – mystery – is incomplete and must await the end of time itself before being satisfied. Kingdom discourse is thereby addressed not so much towards humanity's ontological questions as towards its epistemological questions, because the time/eternity problematic is concerned with the rupture of identity between ontology and teleology which is so often found in philosophical theology (see Swinburne 1991, pp. 133–51).

Given this one can argue that the notion of the kingdom, understood eschatologically as that which ruptures human attempts to understand the world and its development as complete, signals the dependence of incompleteness upon completeness – methodologically – and therefore the truth of the claim that faith and society are intimately related because God is the foundation of all existence. (This at least is the interpretation one arrives at when mystery is interpreted by analogy with time.) Developing this argument further, however, one can argue that the methodological priority of time over matter reflects the theological argument that the relationship between nature and grace must always be interpreted in terms of the priority of grace over nature, because it is grace which completely reveals the incompleteness of human existence. The relationship between nature and grace thereby becomes a question of the necessarily immanent relationship between the Holy Spirit and the kingdom, because that is the medium – for Christianity – by which God's being as the mystery of the world is revealed.

Trinity

Because questions about the completeness and incompleteness of reality are understood theologically by analogy with time, so that one can speak of God's being as the mystery of the world in terms of time/past and time/present, it follows that the same procedure must be applied to time/future and the possibilities of existence towards which the world is moving, and within which humanity must find its own realization. For critical theology the only true answer to this question of the realization of meaning in human existence finds expression through the doctrine of the Trinity, because *being with* the Trinity is the perfect future of the world, beyond which there is nothing greater (see Gunton 1986).

One can, like Boff (1988), interpret this perfect future by analogy with the temporal existence of society, and speak in terms of non-hierarchical equality as the most fundamental model of human relationships. Or, like Barth, one can speak in eschatologically real terms of the Trinity as the true goal revealed in Christ towards which all human existence is moving. Or one can adopt other models and interpretations (e.g. Scharlemann 1985). Which model one adopts, however, is less important than acknowledging the appropriateness of speaking of the Trinity in this way. The incarnation reveals that the most important way of speaking of God as the mystery of the world – the way most easily named and thereby appropriated by people – is by addressing God's Word to what the world, and therefore society, can become; without this emphasis upon dynamic, no amount of structural reflection upon mystery will make meaningful sense for the way in which people live their lives. This is why critical theology wants to speak of identity and difference when it comes to describe the Christ event and address it to the society in which it operates.

Mystery and Trinity

In this chapter I have therefore moved towards a very traditional and apparently conservative position, namely that the Holy Trinity is the Christian understanding of mystery. To achieve this understanding, however, I have made certain moves and employed certain ideas which have marked out my interpretation from other attempts to make the Trinity the centre of their reflection, such as the theologians considered in the first part of this chapter. The point of all of this has been to establish mystery, the key religious symbol, both as the basis of human existence as interpreted by analogy with time, and as the motor behind such names as Spirit, kingdom and Trinity itself. There is, therefore, an important continuity running throughout this chapter which, I want to argue, establishes the pattern of the following considerations of event and rhetoric, namely the image of Christ and the address of Church to its historical context.

The character of this continuity is secured by the notion of structure, the philosophical significance of which was argued in my Introduction. Mystery as that which structures all critical theology, consequently – in so far as mystery structures all human existence – functions by being the first principle of religion and therefore the religious symbol. Unlike signs, which function to the extent that they point towards the existence of something else, such a symbol has independence and autonomy; a symbol is, and as such structures the way in which humanity responds to its personal and social existence. On this interpretation, humanity is bound primarily to interpret symbols, religious or otherwise; that is its fundamental limit (to employ Tracy's expression). It is the defining point of existence to engage with this process and responsibility, and to abdicate from it is either to remove oneself (or one's community) from society at large, or to move into an entirely separate realm of symbols, such as the retreat to nature envisaged (and occasionally undertaken) by isolationists.[17]

It is against this background of the interpretation of symbols, and mystery in particular, with its basis firmly in human existence understood by analogy with time, that I now want to turn and consider the Christ event; for it is this image of the divine which signals in faith the true qualities of mystery, and which thereby provides the necessary dynamic for critical theology's appropriation of structure. Mystery and its names – Spirit, kingdom, Trinity – all find their clearest expression in the problems of Christology.

Obviously, on one important level this will involve a consideration of the question of the historical Jesus and thereby the question of the incarnation in time of mystery itself. This, however, can only be the necessary but preliminary stage to the most important methodological question of Christology, namely: 'How "big" does one make one's image of Jesus?' The real problem for Christology thus is not establishing a foundation in the historical Jesus, because the whole question of 'establishment' has been achieved in this interpretation of mystery. Rather, it is in tackling the fundamental predicament of scale which confronts all modern and contemporary Christology.[18] This is the subject of the next chapter.

[17] Examples of this would be the Jonestown massacre in Guyana in 1978 or the Branch Davidian crisis in Waco, Texas in February–April 1993.

[18] I first worked out this notion in conversation with Alison Griffin, who went on to develop its more general methodological implications in an essay on global issues in theology (unpublished). My thanks to her for permission to use the expression now in an explicitly Christological context.

7
Event: Christ and the Predicament of Scale

And the Word became flesh and dwelt among us, full of grace and truth (John 1:14)

As I have already argued, the environment in which theology finds itself today is inherently pluralistic, both within Christianity and in the wider context of the world. It is no longer possible for theology simply to collapse mystery and event into each other – as was done until quite recently – in the belief that there is only one way of speaking about God's revelation in the world, namely Jesus Christ. Instead, and taking seriously the argument that God as the mystery of the world can be named and appropriated with validity by different religious traditions, theology must accept that its efforts now have relative, rather than normative, status within the world as a whole (although they will be confessionally normative within a given community or church). An acceptance of this point guided the writing of the last chapter, which at heart was an attempt to find a method by which one could accommodate pluralism and yet leave the door open for a specifically Christian understanding of mystery.

For Christology this has certain obvious implications. First – and whatever realist claims that faith might want to make about God's revelation in Jesus of Nazareth, and its truth – any theology which seeks understanding in a pluralist world must accept that speaking of the Christ event has the status of one form of discourse amongst others, and that consequently it is governed by the same grammar of mystery – completeness, incompleteness and potential – which I identified in chapter 6. Second, Christology cannot claim normative ontological, epistemological or semantic status, because each of these questions to mystery must be answered analogically, as with any other discourse about mystery. Third, Christology is ultimately about creating images of mystery – God – from the viewpoint of communities which believe that God has been revealed in a certain individual, Jesus of Nazareth. These are the restrictions placed upon theology by religious pluralism.

The present chapter must therefore be understood within the context of chapter 6, so that questions of truth and method in Christology are governed by questions of truth and method in the naming and appropriation of mystery itself. This, I want to argue, should not prove difficult for a discipline which claims as one of its principal ideas that of *kenosis* (cf. below) – but it is easy to forget how quickly imperialistic tendencies can arise in Christology, and difficult to guard against them successfully.[1]

In what follows I will assume this context and concentrate exclusively upon the Christian business of naming and appropriating mystery from within a specific tradition and with the needs of specific communities in mind. I will be concerned not with elaborating a framework within which the possibility of different discourses about mystery are given equal weight and significance, but rather with the particular claims about reality that Christianity wants to make on behalf of the Christ event, and which Christian communities seek to communicate socially. Certain of the key themes involved in this process – Spirit, kingdom, Trinity – have already been raised but will now be analysed in greater depth, showing that they are at the basis of how Christology functions within critical theology.

To achieve this the present chapter is divided into three main sections. First, I will identify what I want to speak of as the central concern of contemporary Christology. Second, I will identify the principal aspect of this concern as the task of constructing a specific image of Jesus Christ as the representation of mystery. Third, I will establish this image in a theory of the dynamic event of encountering Jesus Christ as the real future of creation. In this way, finally, my argument will lead into a further discussion of the specific duties of Church as it seeks to address rhetorically and therefore sacramentally the relationship between faith and society. The question, then, is how Christology actually works, within a more general situation of addressing certain beliefs to peoples' religious experience.

[1] The position I want to move towards here is a confessional theory of truth. Though I would accept that this cannot be the entire story within theological metaphysics, my argument is that such an understanding of truth – confessed because interpreted as revealed and concealed – together with the notion of language games drawn from Wittgenstein, preserves specifically Christian truth claims whilst acknowledging the validity of other such claims to name mystery authoritatively. The implications of this position are explored in this chapter.

Mapping grace: the dynamic character of Christology

This question is both straightforward and yet complex: straightforward, because its concern is simply to understand how Christology and mystery relate to each other; complex, because this will involve a thorough analysis of the predicament of scale, which has afflicted modern Christology to the extent of creating within it a fundamental division. The present section will thus consider in much closer detail the constituent elements in the ability of event to mediate beyond the methodological dilemma found in modern Christology.

To define the relationship between mystery and event I want to use the expression 'mapping grace', by which I mean the way in which the event of Jesus Christ particularly maps or delineates mystery, which in Christianity is named grace.[2] The event of Jesus Christ maps or formats mystery, giving it specific content and, from a Christian viewpoint, making it accessible to human approach and understanding. The notion of mapping grace thus forms the interpretative bridge between mystery and event; without it the two definitions would separate entirely, which would make about as much sense as having an hourglass without a neck. Mapping grace reveals the purposiveness of the Christ event. It is intentional, and draws its meaning from the general analysis of mystery which is common to all human religiosity, and which is so fundamental to Christian spirituality.[3]

There remains, however, the question of how this event's purposiveness is to be interpreted and understood, because without a clear sense of the ways in which event renders mystery intelligible, the relationship between truth and method which critical theology seeks to establish remains obscure. To answer this question I will return to the three modes of reflection – ontology, epistemology and semantics – which were employed in the previous chapter to name mystery's qualities. I will also continue to use the analogy of time, arguing that if this is most appropriate and meaningful for understanding mystery, it

[2] If one makes mystery the level upon which one attempts interfaith dialogue, then one must accept the argument that grace is simply Christianity's name for mystery. Other religions will have other names.

[3] I am conscious that I have not demonstrated this claim via a detailed analysis of the world's religions, although I would claim that an authority like John Hick has revealed as much in his various writings on comparative religion (e.g. 1989). I hope, however, that it is not a contentious claim, and that it causes no offence to any individual who might read this book; it is not meant to be a reductive argument, but rather acknowledgement of the integrity of every world religion.

remains doubly so for understanding the Christ event. I want to interpret this event as that which maps grace and therefore bridges the gap (in faith) to mystery, in terms of past, present and future, which, in line with chapter 6, raises for discussion the three qualities of completeness, incompleteness and potential. The questions which have to be considered before I can discuss the 'size' and encounterability of the Christ event, therefore, are: how is this event complete?; how is it incomplete?; and how does it have future potential?

Ontology: the completed event

The first important point to note here is that this ontological reflection, and the ensuing claim that being implies completeness, means that one is speaking here of uniqueness, i.e. independence, integrity and self-sufficiency. This was seen with respect to the status of mystery as a symbol (and by extension to symbols *per se*), so that a connection between the religious symbol mystery and the more general interpretation of symbols *in toto* was advanced: interpreting symbols is one of the things people *do* socially, and therefore 'being religious' in this sense of interpreting mystery can be claimed to be specifically social (see Ricoeur 1974, p. 289).

The same claims can be made with respect to event, namely that a general theory of events, to the extent that they are similar though independent and discrete and therefore self-sufficient *as* events, is possible. Such an event theory is found in Heidegger's later philosophy, for example, and informs Rudolf Bultmann's Christology (see Jones 1991, pp. 15–62). Though less fundamental (metaphysically) than a general theory of symbols, and arguably dependent upon it, such a general theory of events makes considerable sense of the way in which human beings encounter and experience reality.[4]

The problem, however, is whether such a general theory of events is actually of use to theology, which seeks to understand questions of truth and method via the central theme of Christology, and therefore of one event in particular. There is a parallel between the constructive isolation of mystery away from other symbols in chapter 6 and the

[4] These are ideas I developed in my 'Nietzsche's Animals' paper for the Birmingham Philosophy Society (1993). There is a fascinating question here regarding the relation between Heidegger and Wittgenstein. Arguably, the key to understanding Heidegger's event theory is to understand its establishment in an acknowledgement of mystery (see Caputo 1987, p. 268; but see also Caputo 1982 on Heidegger and Aquinas), which is of course an area where Wittgenstein, though still equivocal, had some very meaningful things to say. On Wittgenstein and Heidegger together, see Mulhall 1990, pp. 160–77.

constructive isolation of the Christ event here, which is complete and discrete and which is claimed to be of ontological significance by the Christian faith and those who seek to understand it. The Christ event, therefore, *must* be unique; for if it is not unique then it cannot be complete, and therefore can have no ontological significance.

In one important aspect of the relationship between faith and society, this moves to the very heart of critical theology's treatment of questions of truth and method. In a weak sense, the ontological claims here for the Christ event, and in chapter 6 for mystery, apply solely to the Christian faith, i.e. they are ontological solely if one believes in the truth of God's revelation in Jesus of Nazareth at a certain moment in time. If one wants to speak of these claims in a strong sense, however – that they are universally relevant and should be acknowledged as such – one is on very difficult terrain. Arguably, one might be able to claim that mystery is the most fundamental symbol to all human existence; that mystery, which one might name 'life', 'death' or whatever (there is certainly no necessity to name it 'Spirit' on this level), really is the strongest ontological category or condition of which reflection can speak, and that consequently there is a way in which religion is fundamental to all human existence and therefore society (Tracy argues for this in *Blessed Rage for Order*). It is difficult to see, however, how this can be true of the Christ event ahead of any other event (the 'Big Bang', perhaps). On the contrary, the Christ event is divisive: it cannot be used to speak objectively of *all* peoples when all peoples have not and cannot know of that Christ event.[5] One must acknowledge, against any such attempt at universalizing the Christ event as the only vehicle of God's revelation and therefore as the sole mediation of mystery, that it is one event amongst others when understood in this way. To argue differently is to evacuate Christology of its specifically historical context, and thereby Christianity of its humanity.

None of this means, however, that one cannot make ontological truth claims about the Christ event, in so far as one wants to argue that it is complete in itself as an event of revelation (because truth *is* revelation). But it does mean that this claim must be acknowledged as being made *in faith*, and that one of the primary qualities of faith is the humility to acknowledge its own inadequacy. To reject this argument is to abandon Christ to the level or plane of abstraction, which is precisely where this particular event cannot be located if it is to mean anything as the historical origin of the Christian faith. The Christ event cannot simply be equated with mystery *per se*, and mapping grace as a

[5] The fundamentals of this debate were hammered out by Rahner and von Balthasar in the 1960s; see Williams 1986a.

relationship is not simply a process of identification, because the claims of faith to absoluteness have to be qualified theologically when it seeks understanding.

Epistemology: the incomplete event

Ontological truth claims can be made about the Christ event, therefore; but they must be made against the background of certain methodological conditions, which apply specifically to the relationship between faith and society, and which necessarily demarcate certain limits, or terrain, beyond which theology cannot assert its own power without seriously compromising its integrity, at least in the eyes of society (something which various churches, particularly the Church of England, have taken an inordinate amount of time to realize). It is this situation which establishes the importance of acknowledging the Christ event's *incompleteness*, at least epistemologically, because there is something incomplete about theology's knowledge of the Christ event which bears directly upon the ontological question considered above. How is this intelligible? The Chalcedonian Definition offers a way forward here. The worst mistake with respect to Chalcedon is to misread the definition of the relationship between the two natures of Christ, understanding it as an attempt to define the precise and immanent being of Christ as the Second Person of the Trinity. Certainly, the language of Chalcedon is ontological, reflecting the intellectual context in which the definition was written. Its intent, however, is concerned with the incomplete knowledge which I have established as one of the basic qualities of a theological interpretation of mystery, and therefore of event. The point of the Chalcedonian Definition is to acknowledge the incompleteness of human knowledge with respect to Christ, but to assert something fundamental about the nature of identity, interpreted theologically.

What is this assertion about identity? It is the strongest relationship between God and humanity, so faith believes, occurring in Jesus Christ as an identity of two natures, i.e. both together but not mixed, in one person, Jesus Christ. Chalcedon is making an ontological truth claim about the Christ event on the basis of faith; but it is doing so through the imprecise and therefore incomplete language of identity and nature, because that is the only route open to it. The truth to which Chalcedon looks forward, beyond the limits of language and understanding, is eschatological. That is the basis of Chalcedon's equally important assertions about the resurrection and the Last Judgement, which are too often forgotten in the rush to condemn the Christological Definition.[6]

The Chalcedonian Definition about the Christ event, consequently, is all about mapping grace; it is all about establishing what it means to say that God acted in a human being, and to push out the boundaries of this idea as far as possible to make the strongest possible claim about the true identify of God and humanity which faith believes to be the basis of salvation.[7] The true task of the Chalcedonian Definition – at least in terms of this analysis of questions of truth and method – is to find a way to speak of mystery as complete symbol which relates to the historical story of Jesus of Nazareth. No one should really argue, therefore, that Chalcedon is making irrational claims about the 'real' nature or substance of grace, where it is located, of what it is made, and so on; for Chalcedon is attempting to avoid such questions by making a more fundamental identity, one which works solely because at the deepest level it is incomplete.

This means that for theology's understanding of the person and work of Jesus Christ, its characteristic feature is incompleteness. This is central to any theological language and critique which might be offered to substantiate faith's claim that in Jesus mystery found its definitive revelation. When speaking of the person and work of Jesus Christ as event, therefore, the next thing one must say (after one has argued for the ability of event to carry the weight of communicating the completeness of mystery as Spirit) is that this event is not concluded. On the contrary, there is more to come, in the literal sense of this event's having a real present and a real future to which theology must give complete attention, and against which the very concept 'event' must be measured. The Christ event is not one which can be isolated in the dim and distant past; *because* it is the *complete* event of Spirit's immanence in the world in Jesus Christ, it is the *incomplete* and therefore *eschatological* event of the present world's predicament. The two questions which then arise – how 'big' is this event, and how does one encounter it? – are consequent to event's eschatological character.

[6] This lack of awareness leads to many of the most embarrassing misjudgements of the debate about the 'myth of God incarnate'; see Frances Young's article 'A Cloud of Witnesses' (in Hick 1977), where she writes of Chalcedon: 'This so-called definition defines only in a negative sense, by excluding the extremes of both Christological approaches, without being able to offer positive Christological understanding' (p. 28). Needless to say, I reject this attitude towards Chalcedon, preferring the more sensitive reflections of Rahner. It should be noted that Young has substantially modified her position (e.g. 1991, p. 79).

[7] God loves so much that he becomes identical with us – that is the highest form of love we can specify and encounter. But it is something which will only be fully understood in the future, and therefore eschatologically. This is the tension which establishes theological ethics.

One of the advantages of this way of defining the person and work of Christ, as Bultmann recognized, is that it accords with the New Testament's understanding of the eschatological significance of Jesus, particularly that found in the Fourth Gospel. There is no sense in which the concept 'event' reduces Jesus Christ to the level of historical data or information; 'facts' are insignificant when set alongside eschatological meaning, something which is doubly true given my definition of mystery as symbol. The question which remains, however, is: granted the completeness and incompleteness of event as it names mystery in the world, as Jesus Christ, and granted the fact that completeness and incompleteness say something very important about the nature of faith and how theology maps the grace which substantiates faith, how can theology speak of the *potential* of the event?

Semantics: the future meaning of event

Again, the initial, metaphysical answer to this question is to employ the analogy of time, thereby pointing towards the *perfect future* of event, 'fleshing out' this idea theologically with the name Trinity: the Trinity is the perfect future of the Christ event, because the Trinity is the real potential of the eschatological event of Spirit's immanence which occurred, historically at least, nearly 2000 years ago. This statement, however, needs breaking down into more manageable pieces. I want to achieve this by working through three stages, each of which says something important about the way in which this understanding of event works in theology, and each of which says something important about the way in which truth and method come together in this particular concept.

First, the point of the Christ event, theologically understood – and in terms of faith – as something which occurred nearly 2000 years ago in space and time, is ultimately (and therefore eschatologically) to say something, however imprecise, about the goal of human existence in God. There is, consequently, something teleological about the Christ event; it points towards something which faith believes is real, and which may even be assured in Christ's cross and resurrection, but which in the fullest terms is yet to come. This raises a question about the *real* future of human existence.

Second, in the Christian faith the name which theology gives to this goal is 'being with the Trinity'; this is the fundamental and spiritual mystery which faith believes rests before all human existence. For the

Christ event to point towards anything, therefore, it must point towards the Trinity; hence the naming of this aspect of mystery *as* Trinity in the previous chapter. Without this naming process the dynamic here is too general and too loosely connected to human reality; without this establishment in the particulars of faith, it simply floats away on the wind.

Third, and final, however, theology can approach this question of the perfect future and potential of the event as Trinity only in terms of a semantic critique, its meaning and how this can be interpreted. Though faith wants to speak of the real future of human existence in the Christ event as the Trinity, and though theology can address the claims to real completeness and incompleteness of this event ontologically and epistemologically, theology must understand the potential of event semantically. To do anything else would be to abandon theology's intellectual credentials, which would be quickly unrewarding in the relationship between faith and society. Today more than ever, with all of the awareness it has gained from modernity and postmodernity, theology must recognize that the level upon which it can *discuss* things is different from the level upon which believers *assert* things. This much is axiomatic for critical theology, and in its fullest implication means that there can be no facile identification methodologically of what faith takes to be self-evidently true, namely that Christ is the mystery of the world. All theology operates under this constraint of the tense relationship between truth and method.

There is, consequently, a logical progression from completeness to incompleteness to potential, which is mirrored by the names Holy Spirit, kingdom and Trinity, and which gives identity to the way in which mystery (God) is mediated and revealed via event (Christ). There is a logical progression, too, in the way in which theology addresses such ontological, epistemological and semantic questions, moving gradually but consistently though the realms of faith's *certainty* about revelation, its witness to revelation's *presence* in the midst of the community, and its hope for the *reality* of God's Trinitarian being as the true home of humanity. Event has to carry the weight of all three of these realms, and there are considerable difficulties associated with each; but establishing the genuine credentials of the perfect future of the Christ event can be the most difficult of them all, because it is most open to misinterpretation.

Why should this be the case? Because it allows into the frame the widest possible range of different models of representation and argument, *rhetoric* as I will call it in the next chapter, which makes it very difficult for Church, in its relationship with society, to articulate precisely what it wants to say about the nature of this perfect future. This, after all, is the most direct implication of naming the perfect future of the event as 'potential': sheer potential admits of endless variety, which in turn means that what it will actually be like when God's being as Trinity is fully revealed to humanity is open to endless different images and descriptions.[8]

Certainly, this is a theoretical analysis of the problem; in practice, as the next chapter will argue, the rhetorical address to society, which must occur in terms of certain definite colours and shapes, will always be far narrower than pure potential might admit logically. The task of any church or community, after all, is simply to paint a specific picture and to be loyal to it; witnessing to what one thinks is the truth is all one can ask of anyone. Moreover, both in theory and practice this rhetorical activity on the part of Church should always be informed by the reflection upon mystery and event which Part II has been concerned to interpret and understand. If the event is something like a moving image, therefore, then the actual face it presents to the public is only going to be the latest stage of a process of construction and development which will involve both universally spiritual and Christological reflection upon the completeness and incompleteness of the event itself.

Methodologically, however, the truth is that both ontological and epistemological reflection in theology are established in history and tradition, because there is a history of Jesus of Nazareth, and a tradition of spirituality when discussing mystery, which help to shape and define the event about which theology wants to theorize. With potential or perfect future, however, this is not the case. Rather, simply because it *is* future, meaning can be interpreted semantically only within very broad guidelines. One may want to say something very specific about what it will be like to be with God as Trinity, consequently, and one may wish to base this upon certain very clear convictions and arguments about Spirit and eschatology; but the fact is that at this point truth cannot be contained in small vessels. On the contrary, as modern hermeneutics has amply demonstrated, meaning lacks the closure which faith demands of its event, which is something which faith *seeking understanding* must learn to accept in all humility.

[8] This is why theology speaks of mystery, though as I will say in the next chapter the true task of any church is to identify one particular vision to pursue, to articulate it in its social context, and then to follow it to the end. The problem is that any such vision must be guided by considerations of the relationship between mystery and event as one of naming and appropriation, which is so often not the case.

Event: the triumph of method over truth?

Recapitulating how my understanding of event arrives at this stage reveals a number of important points. First, the fact that the event is entirely related to mystery means that it is always the event *of* mystery, i.e. it is always dependent upon mystery for its real definition. Even when theology wants to speak of the event as complete, therefore, even when theology wants to make ontological claims about the event, it must do so against this background of mystery as complete, incomplete and potential, which means that even complete claims about the Christ event contain within them the seeds of incompleteness and potential, named in the Christian faith as kingdom and Trinity. Without this important proviso Christology can become dangerously reified as, arguably, one finds in the later work of Bonhoeffer and the early work of Moltmann.

Second, this would appear to mean that, Christologically, the epistemological and semantic critiques of mystery, which result in the acknowledgement of its incompleteness and future potential, tilt the balance over in favour of method against truth. Thus, even when incompleteness and future potential are named as kingdom and Trinity, the real emphasis is upon the methodological limits placed upon Christology and therefore theology rather than upon the truth of the event itself. If this is genuinely the case, then it would imply that Christology derives its power solely from the truth claims of the analysis of mystery as symbol which, since they do not necessarily imply any specific reality to symbol itself, probably means that Christology becomes reduced to an intellectual game. If this is the case, then methodology has effectively won the day over the search for truth.[9]

That this cannot be the case, however, is guaranteed by the premise with which this entire study began, namely that theology is faith seeking understanding. The analysis of mystery as symbol is itself established in the *a priori* argument that the turn towards mystery is the primary response of faith towards the divine, and is therefore something inherently graceful. Thus, if one wants to speak of real things like faith, grace and truth as themselves all 'true' in a religious and

[9] Such might be the case if theology could be reduced to aesthetics, whereby talk about 'God' became the same kind of art or technique as painting or sculpture, with the proviso that its raw material were symbols rather than pigment or stone. The reductive drift of much contemporary, postmodern theology would seem to indicate that such an aesthetic understanding of theological discourse is gaining ground at the moment, arguably necessitating a return to Barth's prophetic call to arms of 1919. On the links between aestheticism in postmodernity and consumerism, see Callinicos 1989, pp. 162–71.

hence an absolute sense, then to do so is rightly to be understood as necessarily *prior* to the business of theology proper.

This means, third, that in critical theology one must speak of the 'triumph' of method over truth, because truth has 'triumphed' in a prior sense as the real ground in which theology as 'seeking understanding' is established. It is thus correct to argue that mystery as symbol in *theology* does not have to be given specific existential identity; it can simply function *qua* symbol. Similarly, the Christ event can be given over to methodological constraints because it has already been acknowledged and accepted *a priori* by faith *as* grace and truth. Event does not need to establish the grace and truth of a person, Jesus of Nazareth, which is experienced for itself by the individual and community as God's Word. Rather, the question this analysis of event is really attempting to understand is how theology can make truth and method claims about faith which are communicable and therefore effective in the world of society and culture. For if not this, what else is theology to do? (see Lash 1986).

The thrust of the conceptual division between mystery, event and rhetoric, therefore, as my general Introduction argued and as I have emphasized at various stages, is to move from the truth claims of faith towards a meaningful statement of the relationship between faith and society. The ultimate stage of this process, the rhetorical address of the community to its context, is the explicit concern of the next chapter. Before that, however, and developing this argument about the way in which the Christ event maps grace, I want to address the questions about the 'size' of the Christ event and how it can be encountered.

Naming mystery: the terrain of the event

The moving image

Functioning upon this level of analysis, event and mystery are related in theology as Jesus and grace are related in faith. One can legitimately speak, therefore, of faith seeking understanding upon this methodological level as a question of truth *and* method. The criteria of philosophical hermeneutics are thereby honoured, whilst at the same time one acknowledges that these criteria are here at least in the service of the specific truth claims of a particular religious tradition. This much reiterates critical theology's important, conservative tendency.

The description of the Christ event as a 'moving image' appeals to this tendency, as well as simultaneously affirming the dynamic nature of Christology in its relationship to mystery. Thus, in the same way that the theory of symbols (and specifically mystery) in chapter 6 structured its understanding of reality, so this description of event as image provides the dynamic quality or motor which drives Christology along. As image the Christ event provides a picture of Jesus, thereby bringing theology full circle to its origin in faith's graceful experience of this individual.

To this stage, therefore, my argument cannot be reduced to the level of philosophical necessity, as can Hegel's in his *Faith and Knowledge*, where the reduction to the level of the 'speculative Good Friday' constitutes the necessary affirmation of pure concepts as the fundamental level of reflection. On the contrary – and in this respect I am closer to Barth's Christology – my argument begins with faith's experience of Jesus, so that *this* Christological reflection upon the event is always informed by *that* appeal to a specific historical individual.[10] This is why the event is described as a moving image. The task of Christology is to give conceptual life and meaning as well as descriptive colour to the Jesus story, but always informed by the understanding of mystery which has preceded it. The real concern of this section is thus to 'flesh out' the parameters and features of the Christ event, in relation to Jesus, in order to facilitate the relationship between mystery and event which is constituted in grace. The issue tackled here, consequently, is the predicament of scale.

It is significant that the three 'labels' or names given in chapter 6 to the qualities of mystery – completeness, incompleteness and potential – are drawn from early Christianity, because their key task is to engage Christology with the Jesus story which originates in the historical individual, Jesus of Nazareth. Spirit, kingdom and Trinity, as completeness, incompleteness and potential, constitute the point of entry into the current task – giving meaning to the Christ event – so that: (a) it can be claimed as explicitly Christian (rather than simply conceptual); and (b) the point of encountering this event is revealed.

[10] The insertion of mystery as a stage of reflection between Jesus and Christology allows theology to address such questions as general spirituality and thereby interreligious dialogue. It also allows theology to affirm the possibility of a non-explicit understanding of the meaning of the Jesus experience, something which will be important in the last section of this chapter and the next chapter *in toto*.

Spirit, kingdom and Trinity: some basic qualities

As the moving image starts to take shape, therefore, certain of its key features need to be delineated, a process of creation in which Biblical studies offer considerable assistance to theology. The first evidence of that assistance is provided by establishing the credentials of the three names, Spirit, kingdom and Trinity, with respect to the New Testament evidence about Jesus; for the validity of these three names as the legitimate correspondents to completeness, incompleteness and potential depends upon their historicity within the Jesus story. If they are not established at the heart of that story, then they are simply inappropriate names, and Christology must look elsewhere.[11]

Historicity At least in terms of Spirit and kingdom this process is straightforward, because the earliest stage of the tradition, as far as historical-critical research can identify, speaks of both the reality of Spirit and the presence of the kingdom with respect to the historical person of Jesus. The most obvious reference as evidence for this argument is Mark's Gospel, where the first chapter explicitly links the Spirit and kingdom of God to Jesus of Nazareth, as the origin of the 'good news' or gospel (cf. Mark 1:10–15). Though clearly the Markan account is theological, all the most reliable evidence in the New Testament suggests that Jesus appealed to the Spirit and kingdom as the real authority for the proclamation of his message of God's judgement of this world, redemption for those who repent, and damnation for those who do not. Jesus' message, therefore, is one of dramatic and dynamic social and personal change, the power for the ultimate success of which comes from God in the form of Spirit and kingdom. This argument, and the appeal to historical evidence, is found in the theologians considered in Part I.

In the case of the Trinity, however, the argument is less easily won. Whilst it is readily apparent that Jesus appeals to the Spirit as the *complete* being of mystery, so that it is the Spirit which establishes everything (which is presumably why the proclamation of the gospel in Mark originates in Jesus' baptism by the Spirit), and that Jesus names the kingdom as that reality which is in the process of breaking in and which is therefore *incomplete* to human knowledge and understanding (even to apocalyptic visionaries), it is less apparent that Jesus points

[11] Biblical criticism, consequently, can help theology to create 'better pictures' of the historical individual with which it is ultimate concerned; but that does not mean that the historical-critical method can be allowed to exercise any dictatorship over what theology says or does not say in any given situation – a dictatorship which has dominated much of modern theology.

towards the Trinity *per se* as the perfect future of God's being which is the ultimate goal of human existence. On the contrary, one might almost say that the Christian notion or doctrine of the Trinity, whatever its merits and appropriateness, is entirely opposite to the powerful rule which Jesus seems to have had in mind when he proclaimed the gospel and died in its name.

The point at issue here, however, is not whether Jesus himself explicitly looked towards the Trinity as the perfect future of human existence, but whether the early Christian Church did in its experiences of Jesus. Here the three vital extra ingredients over and above the proclamation of the historical Jesus are resurrection, Pentecost and parousia. From the viewpoint of the early Church these three new things become bound up with the historical Jesus, so that his proclamation of the kingdom in the power of the Spirit has added to it a new goal: being with God. Resurrection, Pentecost and the expected parousia, consequently, *change* things; they make people think theologically about Jesus of Nazareth. The evidence is that when they do this in the New Testament, and when they start to think about what the real future of their belief and hope actually will be, they think in terms not of two powers in Heaven, but three identified in one eschatological will to save (but see Segal 1977).

The most obvious evidence for this is to be found in the words at the end of Matthew's Gospel, the blessing in Paul's letter to the Corinthians, various other minor epistles, and of course the Fourth Gospel, where arguably one finds the deepest theological reflection in the New Testament upon the Trinitarian being of God.[12] The most important point here is not whether the Three Persons are subordinate or not, or whether they share the same substance, as some have argued, thereby translating back into the New Testament the misguided attempts at understanding of some post-Chalcedon theologians. It is, rather, whether one can speak of an *identity* of purpose in the being of Father, Son and Holy Spirit. On this there can be no real argument: the New Testament is agreed that in the light of the resurrection and Pentecost and in anticipation of the parousia of Christ, there is a genuine Trinitarian identity of Father, Son and Holy Spirit which is the light of salvation revealed through the cross of Jesus.

There is no point, therefore, in attempting to destroy the evidence for the Trinity in the New Testament (implicit as it might sometimes be) by arguing that the New Testament's language does not corres-

[12] Ashton (1991, pp. 420–5), however, finds no evidence that the Spirit in the Fourth Gospel implies any Trinitarianism. My own theological argument is of course different, but I recognize the strength of Ashton's exegetical case.

pond to that employed in later periods, as some critics do; for the genuine link between Spirit, kingdom and Trinity with respect to the story of Jesus, and thereby the genuine link between completeness, incompleteness and potential, is established soteriologically. In the New Testament this language of salvation is not substantial, or conceptual, or logical, as it can be in later theologies; rather, it is eschatological. The question of salvation in the New Testament, which forms the thread connecting Spirit, kingdom and Trinity, is itself thus established in the identity of time and eternity which for Christian faith occurs as revelation in the Christ event, which itself is established in the early Church's convictions about the true fate of Jesus of Nazareth.

Eschatology This said, there is little more to add about the role of eschatology in the early Church, and therefore in the present understanding of the Christ event; for eschatology is so central, and so important, that with Barth all should assert that without it theology is not genuinely Christian. Jesus' baptism by Spirit which begins the proclamation of the gospel, the kingdom itself, which forms the heart of that proclamation, and the Trinity, which is identified by the early Church as the true destiny of Christ's divine being, are all eschatological in nature. They are all defined theologically in terms of the identity of time and eternity in the particularity of the Christ event. This is the still, silent centre of all theology.

On the basis of this eschatological identity the following point must be made about the relationship between mystery and event. Faith's claim is that Jesus is of eternal significance for human existence. Hence, the description which is given to what lies behind this eternal significance is mystery. In terms of human existence it is appropriate that the analogy used to interpret eternity as mystery is time. Reflection thus returns its consideration of the truth claims about Jesus to the world of its own experience, though now employing the categorial description of symbol as completeness, incompleteness and potential to interpret faith. Eschatology is present throughout this process because the motor behind the conceptual reduction to the level of symbol is the attempt to understand the relationship between time and eternity, which has become pertinent in this case because of the starting-point, the Jesus story. Subsequently, any attempt to construct an image of the Christ event as the conjunction of time and eternity, on the level of the categorial description of symbol, becomes a moving image, i.e. a dynamic 'picture', drawing people within its boundaries of perception. Finally, the pronouncement and description of this image, in line with the level of symbol and image itself, must be undertaken on the basis of the human linguistic condition. It becomes a rhetorical task.[13]

The advantages of this approach for theology are enormous. Instead of positing an independent reality to 'eternity' – 'substance', 'matter', 'the Absolute', 'the Other', 'the Noumenal' – which would mean that it was committed to an alien 'thing' as its guiding authority, one can speak of eternity as symbol. One can then locate all subsequent discussion upon the level of this particular conceptuality. Theology is thus able to function fully on the borderlands of faith and society without compromising their independent integrity. Instead, therefore, of becoming hopelessly partial in this fundamental relationship, critical theology moderates between the two positions, thereby becoming a model of *communication*. Certainly, it is one always informed by the time/eternity problematic, and one which always originates with the historical Jesus as a specific individual. In so far as its own operations are concerned, however, theology on this understanding must function independently. This is its special role and responsibility.

The obvious argument against this understanding of theology is that it is essentialist, i.e. it evacuates eschatology of any explicitly *real* content, such as it might originally have in the New Testament, simply in order to fit this analysis of symbol (and it must be acknowledged that this accusation has been levelled before at the two thinkers who have most clearly attempted a similar reduction, Kant and Bultmann, though to very different conceptual levels). But this attack fails to realize that the point of such a reduction is so that a subsequent realization can occur; for the process of reduction/realization – in which the time/eternity truth claims which are made about Jesus become, theologically, methodological arguments about mystery and then the Christ event – is always directed towards the translation of those truth claims *out of* the language of religious absolutism (about which no communication is possible) and *into* the rhetorical discourse of modern human existence.[14] Of course, therefore, there is a reduction occurring here; but the whole point of that reduction will be realized only when the necessary *rhetoric* of Church is considered in full in the next chapter, and on the basis of a more complete understanding of what constitutes the Christ event.

[13] For the background in rhetorical and social theory to this point see Root 1987 and Leith and Myerson 1989. On further literature on rhetoric, see chapter 8 below.

[14] The reduction/realization model is found in Buchdahl (1981) in his brilliant study of Kant. This is influential for my own understanding of the way in which critical theology generally operates to generate and communicate meaning.

The transforming power of spirit, kingdom and Trinity Once the historicity and eschatological validity of Spirit, kingdom and Trinity have been established, both in terms of the historical Jesus and the conceptual scheme of this understanding of theology, the obvious question relates to the purpose of these names with respect to Jesus, so that the question of soteriology becomes of paramount importance. Here the evidence of the New Testament strongly suggests that, rather than being understood as a substantive 'alternative world' to this one, to which people miraculously transfer after death, the rule of God which Jesus proclaims occurs as transforming power, i.e. grace which reconstitutes this world in terms of the will of God. Salvation is not so much the migration of the soul from one world to another, but rather the transformation of the world into the image of God's truth and grace. In so far as Jesus proclaims this transformation by means of the power of Spirit, kingdom and Trinity, one can say that Jesus himself is of definitive importance in this process. The task of theology thus becomes the interpretation of the Christ event in terms of this transforming power, thereby relating the truth questions attached to the historical Jesus by faith to the methodological considerations necessary to render these claims intelligible and actionable in modern society.

Obviously, such an analysis can be found in a wide range of modern theologies. Chapter 4 examined one such, Jon Sobrino's, and others include the later work of Jürgen Moltmann and Edward Schillebeeckx. In this case, however, the problem was, as chapter 4 indicated, that there was no clear philosophical framework within which the shift from Christology to social message could occur. Instead, what one found was a philosophy of history which claimed, implicitly, to be able to move with stealth from the present day, back to the world of first-century Palestine, and then forwards again to the contemporary, in order to validate certain points about the gospel and why it is significant in a world where oppression of the poor by the rich occurs daily. The problem with such a philosophy is that it does not work, because it rests upon the 'time-machine theory', often advocated by writers in the modern era (particularly Biblical scholars) but never sufficiently identified in order to protect it from its critics. This approach can be destroyed in about ten seconds by any reputable philosopher: 'time' is a social construct and therefore something requiring interpretation, rather than an objective reality through which one somehow 'travels', either forwards or back.

By identifying this transforming power, as Spirit, kingdom and Trinity, with the Christ event as moving image, however, two things occur. First, the vagaries of history become meaningless, because what one is now describing are the features of an image, rather than the 'facts' or 'data' which 'prove' an argument 'true'. Second, those features themselves become open to further redescription, as theologians engage with the image and represent it in different contexts and situations. Two important developments are thereby safeguarded by critical theology which otherwise, as in the theologians named, are in danger of falling into disrepute.[15]

First, the transforming power of Spirit, kingdom and Trinity is identified with the Christ event as image in terms of the categories of completeness, incompleteness and potential. The level upon which this occurs is that of symbol interpretation, which itself becomes meaningful when symbols are interpreted by analogy with time. There is no way, therefore, that the problem of historical fact actually becomes relevant to this theology, because the question of historicity simply establishes the validity of speaking of Jesus, as faith wishes, and the Christ event, as theology must, as Spirit, kingdom and Trinity. That this is historically accurate neither faith nor theology doubts; but such historical accuracy does not impinge upon the workings of this theological model. In this way the criticism which attaches to the likes of Sobrino, Moltmann and Schillebeeckx cannot attach to critical theology, because it does not attempt to prove its case by appeal to historical evidence. On the contrary, its appeal to authority and responsibility is directed in entirely the opposite direction.

Second, the obvious implication of this approach is that one now has an image, the clearest features of which are Spirit, kingdom and Trinity, which requires further representation and description to be translated into the vocabularies and contexts of modern society. The image has to be held up to inspection so that people can appropriate it from their own viewpoint, a point which returns here to the philosophical rubric outlined previously: critical theology is about structure (mystery) and dynamic (event) from any consequent viewpoint

[15] I am in no real position here to argue this question with Biblical critics, but it seems to me that this process – whereby necessary theological procedures are sacrificed in order to acquire contextual power and authority – occurred within the communities which produced texts now included in the New Testament (for example, the Johannine literature), and that the production of the canon was itself an extension of this reification of certain favoured images of God's action in Jesus Christ. Similarly, the production of a contemporary 'canon' of images of Jesus is something which must occur through communication and media – dialogue – rather than through imposition from on high. This is why it is the task of theologians – of whatever description – rather than bishops; and this is why the office of the theologian in Church has a different – and lesser – authority to that of the bishop, and why bishops generally make such bad theologians. Of course it is entirely possible that a good theologian makes a good bishop, but even here different authorities generate different priorities, some of which are simply incompatible.

(social representation and interpretation). The problem with establishing one's theology in an appeal to historical evidence is that one is thereby either right or wrong; there is no room for interpretation. Such an argument is actually anti-hermeneutic: it reduces the methodological agenda of theology to the level of forensic science. The worthiest examples of this mistaken approach, such as in liberation theology, at least have the excuse that they are addressing that social evil which the gospel clearly condemns. In other, western examples however, the spectacle is one of theologians claiming to be hermeneutically legitimate, whilst simultaneously and surreptitiously appealing to the authority of evidence as of the earliest quest of the historical Jesus. There is only one way to avoid this disreputable error: maintain theology on a level other than that of historical evidence

This casts theology back onto the task of drawing pictures which, though they are informed by historical-critical research and are thereby better pictures, are still theological constructs, i.e. they are still themselves pictures of the Christ event itself as moving image. The task of theology, subsequently, is to tell stories about that image, attempting thereby to reveal it in its glory and significance to people in their social contexts, on the basis of faith and grace. Whether or not people will thereby encounter Jesus themselves, as the revelation of God's will, is neither here nor there for theology. It may even be the case that the genuine encounter with the Christ event will not occur through the representation of the image, but will occur indirectly through action upon its truth (a possibility examined in the next section). The real question for theology is how one represents the Christ event as image, and where one identifies its boundaries as one enters this process of representation; for the question of boundaries necessarily implies a normative understanding of what is within and what is without which is of paramount importance.

Telling stories about Jesus: the boundaries of the Christ event

There is an important question implicit in this analysis which will have to be confronted at some stage, namely: is it possible to encounter the Christ event without realizing it? The preliminary answer at this stage – 'yes' – will be considered in more detail in the next section, which will examine the two ways in which one can encounter the Christ event both individually and in relation to each other, and their implications for an understanding of the work of Christ. As background to that positive answer, however, I want here to identify the specific boundaries of the Christ event as they are indicated by the preceding understanding and as they are established by my analysis of mystery.

The ultimate, eternal boundaries of the Christ event are established by what I have identified as the Jesus story, namely the belief that in this historical figure something of decisive significance for the relationship between time and eternity occurred. This identification of eternity with the Jesus experience was established theologically in mystery, which was also the point at which both social concern with absolutes, and the religious claims of other faiths, were identifiable in relation to the Christian faith. With the philosophical reduction of mystery to the level of symbol, the conceptual boundaries of the Christ event were established as completeness, incompleteness and potential, corresponding to ontological, epistemological, and semantic critiques. Finally, these conceptual boundaries were named and thereby realized theologically as Spirit, kingdom and Trinity, names which were then established in their historicity, eschatological significance, and transforming power.

In itself, therefore, the Christ event is already an amalgam of fideistic, conceptual and methodological boundaries, all of which, though on very different levels, are operative theologically as one attempts to present this image of God as an effective agent for salvation in the everyday world. Simultaneously, however, there are yet further, social boundaries implicit within the Christ event, which become functional as soon as the image is represented and interpreted from the consequent viewpoint of any particular context. These boundaries are indicated by the identification of Spirit, kingdom and Trinity with transforming power. Liberation theology is therefore correct: the names which theology gives to the conceptual boundaries of mystery as symbol, and which are identified as the necessary link with the Christ event, itself established eschatologically and therefore gracefully as the identity of time and eternity, must themselves be established as the signs of transforming power in real social change. Hence, since the rhetoric of Church is itself established in the Christ event as image of God, it follows that this same address must occur upon the level of transforming power as social change. This is the point which every theologian considered in Part I recognizes and attempts to articulate with varying degrees of success (even those who, like Rahner and Tracy, do not seem to be that involved in socio-political discourse); and this is the point which the present analysis wants to move towards as the real goal of truth in faith, and method in theology.

The only real alternative to this interpretation is to understand the transforming power of Spirit, kingdom and Trinity in individualistic terms, i.e. to regard them as the names given to a process which concerns the individual's salvation, but which cannot be extrapolated to a level of social relevance.[16] There are three major difficulties with this alternative, however, which make it unsuitable for the Christian faith and therefore critical theology.

First, the terminology itself – Spirit, kingdom, Trinity – does not lend itself to individual appropriation, since it is as senseless to speak of an individual's relationship with the Trinity or kingdom as it is to speak of an individual's communication with Spirit *per se*; the terms or names themselves would have to undergo translation into individualistic meanings for this to make sense, something which the criteria of historicity and eschatology (if not explicitly transforming power) render impossible. It might be possible to speak of Jesus' ethical message, as Kant once did, and claim that this spoke to the noumenal meaning implicit in the stories of the New Testament; but even Harnack (1957, p. 91) acknowledged that the historical evidence argues for social morality, not individual.

Second, the three names Spirit, kingdom and Trinity are themselves established theologically in an analysis of mystery as symbol which, as a general theory, is thereby designed to reflect upon the way in which society as well as religion (in this case, Christianity) interprets symbols as a whole. It is not, consequently, a philosophical rubric concerned with the subjective cognition of symbols (which would belong to the philosophy of mind), but rather with the interpretation of symbols by *people* by analogy with *time*.[17] Certainly, one might possibly argue that symbols are cognized subjectively and therefore individually; but then they would cease to be symbols, becoming instead, by direct implication, named objects. On the contrary, a symbol (such as mystery), because of its inherently incomplete status as understood by analogy with time (and therefore in response to an epistemological critique), cannot simply be cognized. It must be interpreted, which is a social activity. To speak of the transforming power of Spirit, kingdom and Trinity, in individual terms, would require their establishment via an entirely different theological conceptuality to the current one.

Third, to speak in individualistic terms of this transforming power would render its goal effectively solipsistic; it would imply subjective

[16] Bultmann has often been accused of this (see Jones 1991, pp. 185–92, where Sölle's attitudes are also discussed); but it remains a possibility which many, including popular evangelical churches, want to advocate. That this is wrong is, I believe, axiomatic for Christianity.

[17] As such, of course, it is very close to Heidegger's mature event theory, on which see Bruns 1989; on historical intentionality, see also Ricoeur 1984–8, vol I, pp. 175–225.

experience searching for subjective conceptuality, searching ultimately for subjective salvation. This might be acceptable to certain religious movements, but there cannot be a case to answer that it represents the eschatological basis of the Christian faith in which, by contrast, the fate of the individual is always related as closely as possible to the fate of the group and therefore society.

The final deterrent against such individualism is the ultimate goal of faith, namely what is the real future of humanity in God, and how does one encounter it in Jesus Christ? If this discussion of image concerns the person of Christ – understood as grace – then its complement is an interpretation of the work of Christ, which must be encountered.

Event: encountering the real future

Theologically, the notion of the future of humanity, at least in terms of the names given to the potential of mystery, is expressed by Trinity, so that one could say that the future of humanity on this model is to be with the Trinity, eternally. This, however, remains on the level of the symbol theory elaborated in chapter 6 which, though a necessary phenomenological reduction for critical theology, nevertheless leaves to one side the question as to the reality of this future. Faith wants to express its conviction that Jesus Christ, as the Son and the second Person of the Trinity, constitutes the real future of humanity, that beyond the past and present and memory and imagination, there lies a future which really exists. For critical theology, such realist claims must be made on the level of Christology, therefore reflection upon the Christ event, and therefore as one way – albeit for Christians *the* way – of naming and appropriating mystery. Critical theology is justified in making absolute claims about the identity of mystery and event within the confines of Christology proper; but it must simultaneously preserve a stage of reflection and appreciation which acknowledges that mystery cannot be named solely and absolutely in one way.[18]

This has certain important implications for theology. First, it means that questions of method in theology effectively 'shadow' questions of truth, approximating to them rather in the way that time approximates to eternity, but ultimately being separate. Theology, consequently,

[18] This is why chapter 6 belongs before chapter 7, even if the alternative might seem more logical on first inspection; this also has important implications for how one understands the incarnation.

cannot articulate 'the truth', because human understanding is not identical with divine will. Second, this implies that when theology wants to argue for a particular position, it has to do so pedagogically. It can teach, but not instruct in any absolute fashion, because it does not have the real authority to do so. If one wants to speak of the point of theology, therefore, one must do so entirely in terms of its educational value (see Jones 1990a); as the next chapter will demonstrate, this is the genuine role of theology in society and Church. Third, this pedagogic role for theology implies that when it wants to speak of the future of humanity and help to educate people as to its meaning in their Christian lives, it can only do so on this level of the image; for the real future of faith is theologically expressible solely by means of the image of God in the Christ event.

Much as people have criticized him, therefore, Bultmann had a point; for when he refused to lapse into the eschatological realism which he found in Barth, he took his stand upon the Kantian distinction between appearance and reality which, through Heidegger's historical phenomenology, Bultmann had come to appreciate as the necessary distinction between existential encounter and the moment of revelation itself. For Bultmann one can confront people with the Risen Lord as Word, Bible and preaching; but whether or not they really encounter Christ is up to God and not, therefore, open to theological analysis or description. The great strength of Bultmann's position is the certainty with which it ensures the priority of faith and ultimately grace. These things are not the business of theology; they are mystery.[19]

All of this is important for this stage of my analysis, because it means that the representation of the Christ event must be guided by the need to move people towards their own encounter with the Risen Lord as the real completeness, incompleteness and potential of that mystery which is the ultimate limit of their lives. To a great extent this is achieved already in the establishment of the parameters of the Christ event in terms of Spirit, kingdom and Trinity, understood historically, eschatologically and as transforming power. One can thus speak of encountering the Christ event *as* Spirit, kingdom and Trinity, because that is how Christology depicts Jesus as the true image of God. The fundamental question then is how one encounters the Christ event not solely explicitly but also implicitly.

[19] It is thus that I would argue that Bultmann has a clearer idea of theology as faith seeking understanding than any other of the individuals considered in Part I, something which makes him the most significant radical yet conservative theologian of modernity.

Encountering the event explicitly

Before moving onto the more difficult aspect of this question, however, I want to pause and consider how one encounters the Christ event explicitly. Primarily – and remembering here that one is not asking, theologically, the question of a *real* encounter with the Risen Lord – this is intimately related to the parameters established as Spirit, kingdom and Trinity, which define the Christ event as genuinely religious man, eschatological prophet and Son. Encountering the Christ event as Christ event, therefore, is going to occur representationally, because what is being considered is the depiction of the Christ event itself.

What one has to look for are the distinctive features of an image as something which draws the individual or community into the event which is being projected (as in the classic inversion of perspective in iconography). The most vital thing here is the idea of being drawn into the image, because if it does not have this power to move and affect, in the very process by which it is witnessed and interpreted, then it will not be successful; it will simply be an imitation. Such imitations can be very pretty, and indeed moving, particularly ones of Jesus. They are different, however, from the notion of the Christ event as moving image which draws people towards a vital understanding of the Christian faith and the way in which it changes their lives. A real encounter with the Risen Lord, therefore, is not part of critical theology's remit; but constructing an image of Jesus Christ which helps such an encounter occur *is*.[20]

The entire business of theological hermeneutics, consequently, is intimately related to aesthetics, so that one must speak of the powers of depiction and their place in theology with a clear recognition of their importance. This does not mean, however, that theological hermeneutics can be reduced to aesthetics *per se*, a point which can be understood more fully if one considers one or two examples from modern theology.

Edward Schillebeeckx's *Jesus in our Western Culture* (1987) presents a very clear image of the Christ event: Jesus is the eschatological prophet of the kingdom in whom theology must affirm the possibility of real change through the actions of faith and grace. This means that the palette of 'colours' which Schillebeeckx employs are themselves social, political and economic categories, so that his image is not a work

[20] The presupposition here is that such 'help' can only be pedagogic *after* God's graceful action – as faith seeking understanding – rather than creating the possibility of 'knowing' God in any Pelagian sense.

of art, but of praxis.[21] Similarly, the image of the Christ event which Rudolf Bultmann presents, for example in *Jesus Christ and Mythology* (1958), is expressed in the language of individual possibilities of existence, the opposite of Schillebeeckx but still a viable alternative for theology, at least in the 1950s.[22] Both examples, Schillebeeckx's and Bultmann's, offer very different palettes for 'painting' their image of the Christ event, each of which works in its own terms.

There is a strong sense, therefore, in which one is well advised to return to Barth's model of the threefold Word in order to identify the ways in which the Christ event can be articulated, recognizing his comments about the Bible as Word and also preaching and acknowledging that, finally, what Schillebeeckx and Bultmann are speaking of are different ways of proclaiming the Christ event and thereby participating in the ancient kerygmatic duty of Church. In this way different books of theology, different statements about the Christ event, indeed different attempts to speak even of the historical Jesus, are all part of this process of proclaiming the Word. It sounds banal and mundane; but encountering the Christ event can be reduced to the different images that theologians, of varying offices and descriptions, produce when they want to speak kerygmatically.

No matter how important theologians think they are, however – and the same must be applied to their close relatives, preachers – it should be acknowledged that other media, such as film, music, drama, literature and the various forms of popular culture, all now carry considerable weight when it comes to the creation of images of the Christ event.[23] Moreover, within the liturgy one can think of two significant instances, the offering of signs of peace and the eucharist itself, where images of Christ are communicated very meaningfully, but not in the format of the spoken or written word. When it comes to creating images of the Christ event, therefore, theology does not have a monopoly on good ideas, even if it does have important authority with which to identify their criteria, as the previous chapter demonstrated.[24]

[21] As is well known, this is the basis of Schillebeeckx's entire Christology; see Hines 1989.
[22] I agree reluctantly with Pannenberg's somewhat cruel answer – 'Bultmann was a luxury we could no longer afford' – to the question why Bultmann's influence had waned in the late 1960s, though this does not mitigate Bultmann's significance in modern theology as a whole. My thanks go to Gene Outka of Yale for this story.
[23] See Pelikan 1985, pp. 1–8. And I entirely agree with Borg (1985), who writes: 'The absence of an image – the most common fruit of biblical scholarship in this century – leaves us with no clear notion of what it means to take Jesus seriously, no notion of what loyalty might entail, no direction for the life of discipline' (p. 200).
[24] The generation of images of Jesus in popular culture – literature, film, stage, art – and the often novel and exciting criteria they demonstrate within their parameters, is something I hope to write about in a later book.

All of this means that when one starts to speak of revelation *as* revelation, so that the Christ event is recognizably the Christ event, there is a wide variety of source material to consider and a large number of different ways in which the individual and the community can both represent and encounter the Christ event. Some of the sheer plurality of such images of Christ is indicated by the way in which modern theology has recently developed, particularly in terms of postmodernism, and particularly with respect to the effective liberation from the perceived authoritarian criteria of historicism. David Tracy's work is a fine example of such theology, exercised with considerable imagination and style (even if Tracy still has not developed a clear Christology, the chapters in *The Analogical Imagination* notwithstanding). Similarly, the different Christologies of Jürgen Moltmann (1974 and 1990), though separated by over fifteen years, indicate the way in which different images perform different functions: both are equally valid, both, like many other such images, posses vitality because of their ability to interact with their socio-political context.

Such image construction is overwhelmingly the business of modern theology; for though it rarely acknowledges the fact, Bultmann was correct, and it is the question of the historical Jesus, *as question*, which dominates contemporary reflection, and which guides theologians all over the world in their attempts to render the gospel as socially relevant as possible (see Jones 1991, p. 15). The only effective constraint against this massive explosion of images is to be found within one's theological framework, which means implicitly one's understanding of mystery; for without the constraints which such a framework provides it becomes possible to say almost anything about Jesus of Nazareth in the name of faith, but without clear relation to the methodological questions specified above. Some might argue that this is entirely permissible; and certainly, there might be criteria other than those named in chapter 6 as Spirit, kingdom and Trinity, and elaborated in this chapter in terms of their historicity, eschatological meaning and transforming power.[25] The important point, however, is that such criteria *are* recognized, elaborated and acted upon in the construction of explicit images of the Christ event, and thereby in the deliberate attempt to draw people within Christianity.

[25] The early Pannenberg, and Moltmann to a certain extent, advocated historical change as itself such a criterion, constructing his theology upon the basis of a metaphysics of historicity (still true today). This certainly allows one to move directly from the Jesus experience to the Christ event; but in the process it means that one is effectively making history itself mysterious. This has a long pedigree in modern theology and philosophy, but it has the same problems as any other theology which derives from Hegel – absolutism. I would still want to argue, therefore, that Kant is the only safe ground here for critical theology.

Encountering event implicitly

I now want to turn to the question of whether and how it is possible to encounter the Christ event implicitly. My initial comments here are guided by the examinations of modern theologians' work carried out in Part I, particularly in the chapters on Barth and Rahner. Barth, clearly, was against the idea of an implicit encounter with Christ. His entire theology is geared towards the verbal expression of the kerygma in preaching, with the consequence that his theology is exclusivist: without an explicit awareness of Christ, Barth cannot really see how any one can be saved. Rahner, by contrast, advances his idea of the 'anonymous Christian', arguing on the grounds of his transcendental analysis of human understanding that, as creature and thereby in part graceful, the individual is given the implicit possibility of knowing Christ indirectly. Barth and Rahner correspond to the two poles of this debate, behind which looms the greater question of pluralism and interfaith dialogue.

Fundamental to this largely unspecified debate is the vexed question of the relationship between nature and grace, which is vital to this section. For the *possibility* of an implicit encounter with the Christ event always asks the question: '*How* does this encounter occur?; on what level does one locate its possibility?' Rahner locates it on the level of the conditions of possibility of transcendental knowledge, arguing that people of their nature possess the potential to know God in Christ. Such transcendental analysis, however, is not open to critical theology, which has not reduced faith phenomenologically to pure conditions, but rather to the level of symbol. If critical theology wants to consider the possibility of an implicit encounter with the Christ event, it must do so in terms of the completeness, incompleteness and potential of mystery as symbol, and therefore in terms of the names theology gives to these qualities: Spirit, kingdom and Trinity.

It is important to be clear about the shift which is being made here, theologically. The question now is the divine intent which theology identifies behind the ideas Spirit, kingdom and Trinity; for even in ideal terms – which are all one can offer at this juncture – the possibility of encountering the Christ event implicitly rests upon the possibility of realizing this ideal intent in one's daily life. It is an existential question: does one realize the intent of the Christ event – to draw people towards a transforming power which will materially change the circumstances of the world – in the way that one conducts one's life? If the answer to this question is 'Yes', then effectively one is already doing what Christ came to reveal, namely the will of God. If the answer is 'No', then this raises for theology the difficult question of how to understand sin and sinners, a doctrinal matter which theology has to consider in line with Church policy. At this point, however, it is most important simply to allow the possibility of the answer 'Yes' and to explore its implications for theology.

Primarily, of course, it is crucial to appreciate that this possibility, if it can be asserted at all, can be asserted for theology only as a possibility. It does not mean, however, that one is free to say that such an implicit encounter with the Christ event is really possible; it may well be, but that is not for theology to know, but rather God alone. The only task that theology can achieve here is to argue that such an encounter *is* possible, because this theological model argues that it is possible; and indeed, that one of the key attractions of this analysis of mystery, as with Rahner's (although on a different level of interpretation), is that it asserts this possibility, which would seem only just from a human viewpoint, and necessary for any understanding of the mercy of God which initiates the Christ event.

In this way it is possible to counter the classic argument advanced by agnostics and protest atheists: 'What happens to all those who have never even heard of Jesus? Are they automatically damned?'. Critical theology's answer to this question is that its model wants to argue for the salvation of all people and that, consequently, it makes the Christ event open to all people by asserting its ideal intent in terms of the socio-political and existential effects of encountering Christ either explicitly or implicitly. Faith alone is insufficient. Rather, faith needs to be manifested in good works, and where there are good works there, recognized or not, is faith of sorts and thereby grace.[26]

This certainly does not mean that the Christ event itself can be reduced simply to the level of a socio-political code, following which allows one to realize the will of God and the divine intent which lies behind the Christ event. That would be to ignore the entire question of the eschatological significance of the Christ event, which cannot be expressed entirely in terms of transforming power. It does mean, however, that the boundaries of the Christ event as image are 'perceptible' in terms of social and individual action; they can be identified deliberately though unconsciously, and can be effective in the behaviour of individuals and groups as they go about their daily lives. To argue against this possibility, and to alter one's theological model so as to exclude it, would mean interpreting the Christian faith in exclusivist

[26] I can see no good reason not to name such grace 'prevenient', as in the Catholic tradition (see Rahner 1979, esp. p. 58)

terms. The Christian faith might well be exclusive, and there is an important degree to which, even within a progressive theological framework, Christology must always be exclusivist. Again, however, a contemporary theology, with all that it has learned from the modern and postmodern analyses of the human condition, simply cannot aspire to the authority required to make that assertion. For better or for worse, the possibility of an implicit encounter with the Christ event must be built into critical theology; that is what its interpretation as image requires.[27]

Obviously, this creates the danger that theological models and Christological images, constructed along these lines, can begin to sound simply like blueprints for social development; that because of their desire to leave open the possibility of speaking of faith and grace through the actions of individuals and groups, such theological models reduce all religious questions to the level of materialism. This criticism has been directed frequently at liberation theology, where – although within a very different theological setting – questions of material change are intimately related to the entire process of redemption, expressed in revolutionary terms. Such a development, so the argument goes, undermines the authority and majesty of God's unique revelation in Christ, as confessed by faith.

Is that revelation, however, not self–undermining?

The kenotic character of revelation

A great deal of literature exists which examines the Christian understanding of God's revelation in Jesus Christ, and the idea of incarnation which accompanies it, from Biblical criticism through to contemporary postmodern theologies. There is, moreover, a significant body of work concerned with the idea of *kenosis* in theology, i.e. the self-emptying of the Second Person of the Trinity in the incarnation of the Son. There is, however, comparatively little work upon the methodological implications for theology of attempting to reflect the kenotic character of God's revelation in Christ. Of the theologians considered in Part I Barth, certainly, recognizes this question in the *Church Dogmatics*, and Rahner, predictably, also considers it briefly in the *Theological Investigations*. Barth and Rahner apart,

[27] Any other theological understanding would effectively throw a straitjacket around God's activity in the world, which – though Christianity names it via Christology – cannot be limited *a priori* to solely one activity.

theologians like Harnack, Moltmann, Sobrino and Tracy, if they reflect upon the kenotic character of revelation at all, gloss over its relevance for theological methodology. This tendency is echoed in almost all other areas of modern theological reflection (see Ayres 1992, pp. 26–7).

Of the theologians in Part I the most considerable exception to this tendency is Dietrich Bonhoeffer, whose letter to Eberhard Bethge of 16 July 1944 can be characterized as straightforwardly a reflection upon the kenotic character of revelation. Thus, the thrusting of God out of the world, on the cross, God's allowing the world 'to come of age', and the sheer 'religionlessness' of contemporary society and existence, all point towards God's willingness to take upon Godself this degree of self-abnegation for the sake of salvation. Bonhoeffer's statements in themselves are faith seeking understanding in that they express a deep conviction about the fate of the world as it is confronted by God's self-sacrificing love.

Simultaneously, the metaphysical language of Bonhoeffer's letter creates significant difficulties of its own which must be confronted by contemporary theology. The point here is that Bonhoeffer's observations are in fact the starting-point for a theological epistemology; they provide the metaphysics within which subsequent theology can go on to develop methodological points about how it actually functions in a 'world come of age'. Unsurprisingly, Bonhoeffer's own text does not go into this problem. What one finds here instead are good reasons for believing that theology must reflect upon the absence of God and this event's significance for methodology, which I now want to elaborate within the scope and language of my understanding of critical theology.

How will this work? First, one must convert Bonhoeffer's metaphysical speculations about God's being into procedural arguments about theological methodology. Bonhoeffer's claim that God is thrust out of the world is thus translated into the methodological inability of theology to describe God's presence in the world. Second, Bonhoeffer's argument for the coming-of-age of society is translated into the methodological primacy of social and cultural context in terms of theology's hermeneutic task. Third, the 'religionlessness' of modern society, expressed speculatively by Bonhoeffer, becomes for critical theology the methodological assertion of mystery's symbolic primacy, with the necessary corollary that mystery itself cannot now be addressed simply in religious terms. It is, rather, a symbol, and as such functions to inform and condition all human existence, which means that mystery can be appropriated in a secular fashion and for secular ends.[28]

This way of understanding the kenotic character of revelation says something very important about how one interprets the Christ event, because the methodological limitedness which this kenosis inserts into theological statements, correctly regarded, necessarily implies that there can be no one interpretation of the Christ event *qua* event which then overrides all other interpretations. Instead, the Christ event, as a theological construct and thereby as the necessary stage of theological depiction which must precede any specific address to a social/cultural context, remains itself something which theology can never articulate perfectly or entirely. It remains, for faith, the revelation of that mystery which faith always maintains is Jesus Christ himself, but for theology is the kenotically limited medium through which all genuinely theological and therefore practical utterances have to be made. Without this qualification, which does not limit faith's perception of its encounter with Jesus but rather theology's representation of the Christ event, there is no real safeguard against the arrogant and unjustifiable appropriation of mystery by one particular religious tradition or denomination, with correspondingly disastrous results for theology's understanding of its task in contemporary society and culture (see Kuschel 1992, p. 23).

The point of Christology, therefore, must be different depending upon the angle from which one approaches it. For faith, Christology is simply the theological-epistemological elucidation of the good reasons why people believe in Jesus Christ as the mystery of the world, and why they come together in Church to worship God as God (a point taken up in the next chapter). For theology, by contrast, Christology is never straightforward. Rather, it is always the business of taking seriously the limitations of theological language and interpretation implicit within the kenotic character of revelation, and which thereby affect the way one attempts to speak of mystery itself. Faith dares to speak its name in grace; but theology must acknowledge the mysterious origin of that grace by acknowledging its own God-given limitations, which even affect the way in which it wants to speak of the Christ event of revelation. That is the paradox of faith; and it is a paradox which, in contemporary theology, must be asserted again and again, and equally repeatedly assessed for its methodological implica-

[28] I think this is one area where postmodernism in all of the reflective arts can be of great assistance to critical theology, making it aware of the way in which many different secular communities and discourses have their own 'eschatologies' and 'mysteries', 'revelations' and 'concealments', every bit as much as Christianity (see Peukert 1992).

tions as never before if theology is to take seriously the true nature of today's pluralistic society and culture.

The dynamics of mystery

Theology today therefore finds itself in a new situation. It must acknowledge the explicit, absolute claims of faith, but in such a way that it also acknowledges the pluralistic and relativistic world in which it seeks to operate. The fact, then, that so many churches and congregations find no use whatsoever for theology in their daily existence is unsurprising: in a world where it is security and certainty which people seek, particularly from their investment in religious belief and practice (and to regard it, somewhat romantically, as *not* an investment, in human terms, would be disastrous), a theology which actually denies these things, in whatever name, is going to be less than popular (see Ritschl 1986, p. 295). One recognizes in this the seeds of theology's present situation, where its most creative practitioners – academic, clerical and lay – are yet being swamped by a tidal wave of suspicion and inertia.

This leads directly to the important questions of Christian self-definition, to which I alluded in my Introduction but which have been held off while I attempted to identify the roots of these questions in twentieth-century theology (Part I) and while I have been mapping out the nature and extent of theology's authority and character, in terms of its understanding of mystery and event, for being genuinely critical and thereby practical (Part II so far). Indeed, the next chapter will be concerned exclusively with those qualities and actions, the constituents of a community's self-awareness, which determine how it is to understand itself and how it is to fulfil the requirements which theological reflection have identified. Before that culminating stage of my argument, however, I want to reconsider some of the important implications for Christian self-definition, in today's society, recognized by chapters 6 and 7.

First, the relationship between mystery and event is one of structure and dynamic, because mystery structures the way people understand the world – in Tracy's term, it 'limits' this understanding – and the Christ event gives a particular and explicit name to that structure, hence dynamizing it. Certainly, this process of naming and appropriation via the Christ event involves a claim upon reality *per se*, and chapter 6 acknowledged the veracity of Barth's eschatological position in this respect (even though it cannot be regarded as exclusively correct). The shift from what one might call methodological reflection upon structure, towards a specifically theological naming of that structure Christologically, necessarily involves a turn towards a claim upon reality which, at least as self-determination, reflects a degree of exclusivism. It is important to recognize, however, that such Christian exclusivism is echoed, as naming, by the great majority of other religious groups, even if it is expressed not in terms of superiority, but rather of an advantageous access to the reality of mystery.[29]

Second, giving a dynamic name to structure involves Christian theology in making an exclusive claim upon the reality of mystery as the name of Christ, i.e. the Word; but this does not mean that the real meaning of mystery, as it is interpreted theologically, is thereby exhausted. Rather, it means that theology itself is thrown back upon the kenotic characters of revelation – incarnation, cross, resurrection and ascension – as themselves dark and mysterious things which conceal as much as they reveal, so that theology, in so far as it attempts to echo or mirror what faith believes occurred in the incarnation, crucifixion and resurrection of God's Son, is necessarily limited by mystery. What theology has to move away from, consequently, is the notion that it is possible perfectly to articulate the graceful nature of faith so that people can understand and communicate it in one uniform manner anywhere in the world. On the contrary, the mysterious nature of the Christ event, and for Christian theology the Christ-shaped nature of mystery, are entirely determinative of the scope and extent of Christian self-definition. For faith, Christians must proclaim the uniqueness of Christ as the revelation of mystery; but for Christ, Christians must acknowledge the partiality of precisely this faith. Any other attitude would betray in human words the divine intent of the Word, and the kenotic character of that Word as it is revealed and concealed in Jesus Christ.

Third, and finally, the way in which this dynamic element engages with the structure of mystery, and the way in which this process must be understood theologically, argues something very important about grace and its ultimate revelation, namely that it lies ahead of everything Christian so that, in faith and in the presence of Christ, Church journeys towards its God. The acknowledgement of this point, in humility, is the beginning of wisdom; but it is also vital to the liberation of the true conditions of Christian self-definition which are the subject of the next chapter. Thus, if theology is part of the staging of the Chris-

[29] It is of course difficult to arrive at one definition which satisfies all religious traditions, but hopefully this approach is less offensive than many.

tian story, articulating the limits of humanity's knowledge of God, then it is a staging which is vindicated by what it has to say about the activity of each and every Christian individual and community. It does this by discussing how they create images of the Christ event in order to articulate their understanding of mystery and their personal (through Christ) relationship with it. Theology has, finally, a character which cannot be justified on the basis of what it says, so much as on the basis of what people *do* on the basis of what it says. This is the subject of my final chapter.

8

Rhetoric: The Necessity of a Sacramental Narrative

When the Spirit of truth comes, he will guide you into all the truth; for he will not speak on his own authority, but whatever he hears he will speak, and he will declare to you the things that are to come (John 16:13)

Chapter 6 was concerned to establish the general religious basis upon which theology could identify the subject matter of reflection, focusing upon mystery as the symbol of all such discourse. Chapter 7 then argued that for critical theology the Christ event gives definitive status to mystery, so that theological reflection itself becomes a matter of constructing images of the Christ event within the context of reflection upon mystery. The present chapter will now consider the medium through which this exercise can be realized – rhetoric, in its various guises – and also the specific duties of Church in its rhetorical address to its members and, as importantly, the socio–cultural world in which it exists.

Chapter 8, therefore, develops the argument of this book as a whole towards its already stated goal: the practical duty of Church and its theologies as it relates faith and society together. My argument – that this practical duty is conducted rhetorically in the many different forms of sacramental narrative – will be elaborated at some length, leading to a detailed consideration of what I want to name as the two main tasks of Church in any of its manifestations: witnessing to the presence of Christ, as Holy Spirit and Sacrament; and relating faith and society together through discourse and address. Each of these tasks, I will argue, has two aspects, so that finally the challenge of this last chapter is to identify the contribution of critical theology to each of these four elements.

To achieve this I want to consider the life of Church, in so far as it is constantly in the business of addressing people, in terms of rhetoric, i.e. the art of persuasion. The goal of Church's rhetoric or persuasive discourse has traditionally been considered by such disciplines as missiology and New Testament studies because the early Church was a kerygmatic institution (see Kinneavy 1987); and certainly this quality of Church's rhetoric, persuading people to be open to the Spirit of Christ so that God might reach them, is integral to Christian self-identity, as well as being a developing social phenomenon. What I want to do, however, is to highlight a different aspect of Church's rhetorical existence, something which depends considerably upon the precise character of rhetoric itself (see Cunningham 1991, pp. 34–8).

In contemporary theology, rhetoric has become a highly fashionable concept.[1] Overwhelmingly, however, it is regarded in an altogether positive light: rhetoric is *a good thing*, with no evidence whatsoever that people understand the darker side of this activity and its background in the literature of classical antiquity.[2] The failure is damaging to any theology which seeks, as many do today, to be rhetorical. Not only does it fail to recognize the ambivalent power of rhetoric to be both good and bad, light and dark, simultaneously, it also seriously compromises the status of the audience for theology's rhetoric. The result of this double failure can be seen in certain contemporary theologies, where 'rhetoric', 'discourse','communication' and 'understanding' are all happily related to each other, sometimes within the purview of modern theological hermeneutics, sometimes within the posited 'differential flux' of postmodernity, but always with scant regard for the integrity of those who would be addressed.[3]

In writing this chapter, consequently, as in writing this entire book, I have kept in mind always the dual nature of persuasion and its arts, specifically with reference to the status of theology's social audience. I want to address the faith which seeks understanding towards society, and I want to understand the means by which it achieves this goal; but simultaneously I want always to remember that society itself must address Church, and that sometimes, perhaps often, it will reject Church's rhetoric as inherently perfidious. On the basis of what I have argued so far, particularly in chapter 7, such rejection must have Christological dimensions; it must be understood, theologically, in terms of both revelation and concealment. The universal background to this,

[1] My own reflections here have been guided by (amongst others): Warner 1990; Leith and Myserson 1989; Edmondson 1984; Podlewski 1982; White 1980; Corcoran 1979; Cherwitz and Hilkins 1986; Mailloux 1989; and Root 1987.

[2] The obvious historical context here is Plato's *Gorgias*, which is concerned with precisely this problem. Though he has over twenty pages on the historical background to rhetoric, Cunningham (1991) fails to cite *Gorgias*, thereby demonstrating my point. (My thanks go to Robert Dodaro O.S.A. for pointing out this aspect of contemporary North American theology.)

[3] Milbank 1991, for example, is guilty of such an omission, and Cunningham's account of the audience (1991, pp. 82–95) seems pietistic rather than genuinely critical. For a better treatment, see Geffré 1987, pp. 159–80, and Jossua 1985.

as chapter 6 argued, is the status one gives to mystery itself, and the possibilities this status opens up for recognizing the integrity of other religions and interfaith dialogue.[4]

The relationship between faith and society is always symbiotic, something which both Church and theology must reflect and reflect upon. As with all true theology, which acknowledges its profound limitations in the face of real mystery, Church must confront the possibility of its own extinction if it is to understand entirely the status of its audience, and the character of the world in which it lives and seeks to do the will of God. Bonhoeffer was right; and if the world has come of age, it may be necessary for Church to grow up and confront the possibility of dying in the name of Christ, for the affirmation and liberation of its audience. In one respect this would simply mean the application to ecclesiology of a principle long recognized in Christology, and discussed explicitly in relation to the doctrine of the cross – kenosis.[5]

This attitude colours everything I want to say in the present chapter, and after that in my more general conclusions concerning revelation and concealment. It is an attitude shaped in encounter with modern theology, particularly with respect to the interpretation and representation of eschatology and the realism which must always be related to it; but it is also an attitude generated by reflection upon the growing influence of postmodernism, and the way in which its theory seeks to influence how people undertake theology and the entire business of communication in contemporary society. Some reflection upon this development is necessary before I can turn and address the more substantive questions involved in the relationship between faith and society, Church's witness to Christ, and the interpretation of this witness in relation to the questions and attitudes of the vast majority of people.

The next section is entitled 'rhetoric and sacramental narrative', and once it has established certain important matters regarding definition and methodology, I will turn to the four, substantive claims that I want to make regarding faith and society, and critical theology's task in mediating that relationship. Those four claims concern: the work of Church in the power of the Holy Spirit; the presence of Christ as Sac-

[4] I am therefore in broad agreement with Gavin D'Costa (1992), although I have many difficulties with the specifics of his argument. The more general point here is that the way one conducts rhetoric has important implications for the way in which one understands mystery and event, because of the priority of what I call 'consequent viewpoint' within theological media and communication.

[5] It is a difficult, perhaps impossible, thing for Church to regard its own extinction with equanimity as evidence of grace; but see Morris 1979 (my thanks to Carole Irwin for bringing this text to my attention).

rament; the production and regulation of doctrine by theology; and interpreting doctrine in dialogue with society's own constructs and tensions.

Rhetoric and sacramental narrative

As stated, contemporary theology is profoundly interested in rhetoric, a situation intimately related to the reduction of questions of reality to the level of discourse alone. One might blame various philosophers for this predicament (Wittgenstein?, Habermas?, Ricoeur?) with varying degrees of justification; but the fact remains that, specifically in terms of the relationship between faith and society, much modern and contemporary theology has been absorbed within a 'movement' which effectively refuses to address the present state of humanity and the claims for reality it makes (in whatever form).[6] Such theology collapses into theory; and, whatever the justification for this phenomenon – intellectual or otherwise – this position and its ideology threatens to dominate today and tomorrow's understanding of what theology is actually about. Paradoxically, therefore, in the name of pluralism (*pace* David Tracy) and the practical situation of the world, contemporary theology is rapidly constructing the most beautiful of ivory towers, and the most elitist form of reflection yet known in the Academies.[7] Certainly, it is impossible to speak here of 'postmodernity' *per se* as it is unjustified to speak entirely negatively of the aims and aspirations of various postmodern theologians (although there is an astonishing range of writers who now claim to be in agreement with this attitude; see Callinicos 1989, p. 1). It is possible to identify some of the most important claims made by a variety of postmodern theologians, however, and to draw some very incontentious conclusions from their own texts.

On the one hand, this produces some wholly predictable results. One thus sees that the employment of discourse, narrative, metaphor and dialogue – all important words for postmodern theology – has resulted in a renewed emphasis upon the question of interfaith dialogue, with some encouraging results with which hardly anyone could

[6] Habermas (1991) is probably the most pertinent influence here. On Habermas, see Honneth and Joas 1991, particularly Charles Taylor's essay 'Language and Society' (pp. 23–35). On critical theory and theology, see Siebert 1985, particularly chapter 3, 'Critical Political Theology'.

[7] In this respect alone, I might well agree with the comments of Bloom (1987) and Steiner (1989) on the state of contemporary reflection, particularly in theology.

disagree. Contributions from Gavin D'Costa (1990), for example, and John Hick (1989), have greatly enhanced this debate, producing sensitive and subtle interpretations of this specific question and the challenges it addresses to systematic theology. Undoubtedly, interfaith dialogue is very important for the future of systematic theology and, as I demonstrated in chapter 6, it has a place in critical theology at the level of understanding mystery, so that one can identify possibilities for dialogue on the basis of religions' common interest in Spirit and eternity and the concomitant interpretation of time and history.

This is all highly acceptable to any form of theology, save the truly recalcitrant. On the other hand, however, is the more dubious claim – made in a wide variety of postmodern theologies – that the question of reality *per se* has effectively collapsed into complete relativism; that, when confronted by the sheer implausibility of any one understanding of reality being correct, and when confronted by the profound degree to which any interpretation of any question or text is culturally determined (often by factors of which one cannot be aware), it is impossible to say anything meaningful about the way people actually live. All that remains is narrative, in one form or another, namely language and discourse. This position has been advanced by some extremely well-known philosophers, and adopted uncritically by a legion of theologians.[8]

The difficulty with this position will be readily apparent. The claim that interpretation is culturally conditioned is now incontestable; but this does not mean that any interpretation is as permissible as any other. On the contrary, the vast majority of human beings, even those in the western world, do not live in something called 'the differential flux' (Milbank 1991); they are not adrift within an endless process called the 'ecology of personhood' (McFadyen 1990); and they do not require an absolute theory of the world's inherent contingency in order to understand their role within a community or analogous social group (Ward 1992a). Rather, they participate in the world according to the *realistic* claims of any one of a wide variety of different religions, attitudes and worldviews. These positions are certainly relative, understood hermeneutically; but this does not alter the fact that they are all making important claims about reality (see Dulles 1992, p. 13).

This is the significant point for critical theology; and I would want to go further, *naming* this situation whereby, for example, Christianity makes realistic truth claims for its beliefs which cut across the absolute relativism of the various postmodern positions. It is, as Dalferth

[8] On this question, see Taylor 1987 (a worst-case scenario?), Jossua 1979, Gill 1980 and Schweiker 1990. On theology and postmodernism in general, see Gilkey 1991.

has recognized with respect to Barth's theology, *eschatological realism*. Eschatological realism is the basis of everything Church, and theology, is able to address meaningfully and religiously to the society with which it must relate. That is the *sine qua non* of faith seeking understanding and therefore of theology.

What does this mean for the relationship between faith and society?: that when faith makes certain claims about its character and significance, when it seeks understanding by speaking theologically, it does so in the name of a certain view of reality. This means that questions of pluralism, correctly stated, cannot be addressed methodologically, but rather must be stated metaphysically; they must be addressed to the way in which that reality is interpreted and the reasons why it is interpreted in a certain way, rather than adopted at the later stage of that interpretation's representation to society at large. Such a pluralism on the level of methodology reduces all understanding to groundless discourse which, though some might regard it as a good thing, is significantly different from the way in which people live communally and socially.

This is why it is wrong to speak theologically either of a general theory of narrative, or a general theory of discourse, or metaphor, or the linguistic nature of human existence; for when a specific set of beliefs, based upon a particular understanding of and claim for reality, is articulated, it is entirely unsatisfactory to start speaking of relativity. Relativity simply does not matter when one group comes to evaluate its address and communication to other groups in society, and society in general. Genuine relativity, rather, has to be established on the more fundamental level of the claims made about reality. This was the aim of chapter 6, and everything said here about the way in which the Christian faith communicates with society is determined by what was said there about *relative* claims that Christianity can make for its named appropriation of mystery. Anything else would misrepresent the nature of the Christian faith as a religion, and unduly compromise the purpose of its self-communication to society.

For theology, therefore, words and expressions like 'discourse', 'narrative', 'metaphor', 'grammar' and indeed 'rhetoric' must be disconnected from the electricity of general theory, and identified in terms of the specific process of appropriation which occurs when the Christian faith, via theology, seeks to address society.[9] Faith and society cannot be regarded as discrete entities, only relating to each other by means

[9] The terminology is Adorno's (1986). I am in complete agreement with Adorno's comments, and seek here to apply the criticisms he made of existentialism to postmodernism in contemporary theology.

of the one, careful, and tidy avenue of discourse and narrative. There is profound slippage between the two, leaky vessels that they are, and many different discourses and narratives are relevant for any understanding of what the Christian faith, in one particular form, wants and is able to say to society, in one particular form. This does not negate the fact, however, that faith's *discourse* is always *faith's* discourse, and that the interpretation and narrative that conducts this discourse is always explicitly theological. Its vocabulary is Christological and eschatological, and its syntax may be social in its basics; but its grammar is explicitly driven by the motor of theology.

When one wants to speak of rhetoric in terms of this relationship between faith and society, a number of important points become readily apparent. First, it is insufficient simply to speak of the nature of discourse as fundamentally rhetorical, as if it is self-evident that social existence *per se* is rhetorical, and therefore every facet of it must similarly be rhetorical. On the contrary – and in line, here, with Wittgenstein's understanding of language games – rhetoric is something very specific, entered under certain clear circumstances, and exercised in certain very clear ways. Rhetoric is always faith's rhetoric, and it is always to be understood explicitly theologically. Without that understanding rhetoric is evacuated of all relevant meaning; it becomes simply white noise.[10]

Second, this explicitly theological appropriation of rhetoric has certain important implications for the way in which it functions within the relationship between faith and society. Thus rhetoric, although it is still based upon the classical understanding of the art of persuasion – and therefore still finds expression through the manipulation of literary tropes such as metaphor, analogy, simile and so on – has to be expanded to include explicitly behavioural qualities. A theological execution of rhetoric must understand its persuasions in terms not only of language and its various forms but also action, because some of the most important aspects of faith's address to society, and society's re-address to faith, are expressed actively. For example (and as will be discussed below in greater detail), the Christian belief in the power of the Holy Spirit is expressed via a rhetoric of action within society, as social questions are addressed and society is persuaded, by example, to tackle certain questions in explicitly Christian ways (the ideology of this process may be quite manipulative).

[10] Some might argue that this is what social existence is actually like – but if they do, it is difficult to see why they would continue using the term 'rhetoric'. On this question, see Brown 1987, pp. 118–142.

Third, this understanding of rhetoric and its theological appropriation has an important effect upon how theology itself is understood; for if theology can appropriate rhetoric then so in turn can rhetoric appropriate theology, to the extent that one can identify theology with rhetoric. This means that theology is always absorbed within the business of address and persuasion; it is always absorbed within the language and action of faith's symbiotic relationship with society. As I have indicated, this is not always a positive process. Theology as rhetoric can be reduced to the level of an entirely revelatory interpretation of faith's content, with the result that the negative aspects of rhetoric, which can result in sophistry, are ignored by theologians, to their cost. The inverse of revelation is always concealment, and theology's rhetoric must echo this truth in the way in which it relates faith and society together.

This has certain implications for the way in which the various sections of this chapter, which are intended to reflect the different aspects of the relationship between faith and society, are approached. First, the action of Church in the power of the Holy Spirit, if it is rhetorical, must be persuasive towards the socio-political goals outlined in chapters 6 and 7 and which are encountered, consciously or unconsciously, in the Christ event and its representation. Such action as rhetoric is thus emphatically address in terms of pursuit of change, which many would argue is the ultimate (and therefore eschatological) concern of the Christian faith (see Moltmann 1992). Second, the celebration of the Sacrament of the presence of Christ, in so far as it is rhetorical, must also be able to persuade others as to its intelligibility and its applicability to the way in which people live in contemporary society. This, as John Hick has eloquently argued, brings into question the very intelligibility of the incarnation itself; for if the presence of Christ, as rhetoric and therefore as event addressed towards social constructions, is to be an intelligible and acceptable representation of the relationship between time and eternity, then it has to be evaluated in the light of other such representations and social constructions.[11] Third, the doctrines of faith and Church as rhetoric are intimately related to the communication and representation of faith in intelligible, linguistic form, and as such must be open to the normal laws of discourse which operate in society and culture; they must be open to the constructive forces of interpretation, as George Lindbeck (1984) has argued. Fourth, and finally, the interpretation of doctrine, which is always rhetorical and always therefore inherently persuasive (or

[11] I am grateful for conversations on this question with John Hick, who considers this question in his book *The Metaphor of God Incarnate* (1993).

attemptedly so), must always be a two-way street: it must always involve both revelation of the meaning of doctrine, and its concealment by society at large, and indeed manipulation by society. This is the true cost of being rhetorical: theology might lose, albeit in the name of the gospel of Christ (as Paul did on the Areopagus; cf. Acts 17:19–34).

All of this means that if one wishes to speak of theology as rhetoric and subsequently to involve that rhetoric as address in something like a narrative, whereby the story of Christianity is retold again and again for persuasive ends, then it must be a sacramental narrative, i.e. one which speaks, eschatologically, of mystery as both revelation and concealment and, most importantly, makes those qualities or events fundamental to its rhetorical methodology. On one level this means acknowledging the commutative nature of rhetoric, its ability to return questions and addresses back towards their theological origins, with interest; but more importantly it relates the methodological qualities of rhetoric to their origins in the metaphysical claims made in chapter 6, and elaborated there in terms of the representation and interpretation of mystery and the spiritual primacy of immanence. Rhetoric thus occurs for faith against the background of certain claims about reality, named Christologically, and encountered as image and event. Without this understanding theology cannot be genuinely critical, because it cannot mediate fully both the partial nature of Christianity's appropriation of mystery – though it be expressed as a claim upon reality – and the power and ability of society to shape and alter what is said in the name of the Risen Lord.

There is a danger that these points will appear more obscure than they really are; and in many cases, as will be demonstrated in the following pages, the basic arguments, though they be conceptually clarified here, have been rehearsed in Part I in terms of the debates and arguments of modern theology.[12] My point, however, is quite simple: critical theology as rhetoric is inherently practical and therefore governed by the relationship between faith and society; but that rhetoric is itself always shaped and dominated by the constantly changing formations of society and culture which impinge upon faith's self-understanding in history. The result of these pressures and tensions is that theology can mediate a certain understanding of mystery, in terms of the Christ event, only in so far as it abandons any claim to be able to speak authoritatively about revelation. This is the paradox of faith: that seeking understanding, rhetorically, it abandons its own pro-

[12] See, for example, chapter 3 on Rahner and Moltmann, where the question of the rhetorical nature of speech about the presence of Christ is raised (in both good and bad senses of rhetoric).

cesses to the eschatological reality of concealment. This governs the way in which Church actually lives.

In what follows these arguments, and indeed the cumulative weight of the seven preceding chapters, will be brought to bear upon four simple points which, I want to maintain, are the junctures at which faith seeking understanding, and therefore theology, must find some purchase upon the way in which people live socially and culturally, thereby to persuade them in word, image and action that Christianity articulates truth about God as the mystery of the world. If it is successful, then it will be rhetorical in the genuine sense of Aristotle's *On Rhetoric*; if not, then it collapses into sophistry, significant only in so far as it instructs one how not to speak about God.

Witnessing to the presence of Christ

Church's work in the power of the Holy Spirit

The entire process of giving dynamic impetus to the structure of human existence must be undertaken from a specific viewpoint, because structure and dynamic, from any consequent viewpoint, is how human reflection operates, as Kant realized, and as theology must echo in terms of its Christological appropriation of mystery and its rhetorical representation of Christology. All of the questions of chapter 8, consequently – Holy Spirit, Sacrament, doctrine, interpretation – are to be understood in terms of consequent viewpoint: without it, one cannot speak of Church in any practical sense, abandoning it rather to the vicissitudes of essentialism.[13]

Talk of Church, therefore, must occur in terms of talk of specific communities, their relationship with society, and their rhetoric. But how does this actually work? Here it might be worth reflecting on the world of John 3:1–21 and the life of the Johannine community. The emphasis must be upon not so much the general understanding of what it is to be a community *per se*, but rather what it means to be the Johannine community *per accidens*, and therefore in receipt of certain

[13] This, I would argue, is where the ecclesiology of John Milbank (1990) effectively resides; see also Ward 1992a. The problem of course is that their reflections bear absolutely no relation whatsoever to the way in which people worship in community. Moreover, if people like Milbank and Ward are correct, and theology/atheology is simply one discourse among many with no ability to refer to anything and with no right to make truth claims, then the obvious question (which they do not answer) is: 'Why should people listen to you?' Again, one is left to reflect upon the inadequacies of postmodern theologies' treatments of the question of the audience, particularly lay people.

very important gifts. Precisely what those gifts are will become clear as this brief examination develops.

The significant verses in this respect are 3:16–21, because although the preceding passage argues for a vital conviction of the text and presumably therefore the community – that spiritual rebirth is central to being a follower of Christ – it is when the text turns away from the dialogue between Nicodemus and Jesus, and towards the more overtly rhetorical address to the audience, that one sees clearly what John wants to say about the community's way of life. Here John expresses the attitude of belief in divisive and confrontational terms, of judgement and separation, of for and against, of saved and condemned: 'For every one who does evil hates the light, and does not come to the light, lest his deeds should be exposed. But he who does what is true comes to the light, that it may be clearly seen that his deeds have been wrought by God' (John 3:20–1).

One can conjecture about the communal situation which lies behind these words, as scholars have attempted (e.g. Brown 1979 and Painter 1991). What can be said theologically and without conjecture, however, is that the text as it stands seems explicitly to address the community in terms of a dualism between light and darkness, good and evil. Moreover – and as the dialogue between Nicodemus and Jesus made clear – one of the most important questions relating to this dualism is that of knowledge: how does one know who is saved and who condemned? Identifying the religious epistemological grounds upon which this fundamental division is made by the Johannine community will help an understanding of the theological issue at stake here, namely how the community defines itself as Church, and how this self-knowledge affects its relationship with the world at large. Here there are three specific points to consider.

First, by a process of occasionally tortuous logic John seems to want to argue, explicitly in his rhetorical address to the community in 3:16–21, that one can judge people's fate by their conduct, and that their conduct will be determined by their fate. This is the message one receives from vv. 20–1, which would seem to say something about the way in which the Johannine community identified who was within its parameters and who was without. One of the basic religious epistemological grounds by which the Johannine community established its membership was thus by watching what people actually did. 'Being a Christian', consequently, could for this community be reduced to doing the right things, i.e. what is true.

Second, and arguably more importantly, being a Christian in the Johannine community involves something which can fairly be described as a rite of passage; indeed, John 3:1–21 is concerned with an incident which discusses that rite – rebirth in the Spirit – in considerable detail, relating it both to mystery and the Christ event and stating explicitly that participation in the rite itself is entirely involved in the business of knowledge and ignorance which, far from being rational capabilities, are to be understood eschatologically and as determinative for the existence of both the community and those who are without it. In terms of religious epistemology, the Johannine community knows itself and recognizes itself because its membership has gone through this rite. Those who have done so possess eschatological knowledge, which allows them to do what is true and to be seen to be doing what is true. Those who have not done so collapse into eschatological ignorance, which is tantamount to being automatically condemned. Tragically for Christian theology, but seemingly accurately as far as the life of the Johannine community was concerned, this dualism of knowledge and ignorance seems to have involved Christians in a bitter dispute with Jews, as John 3:1–21 and indeed the entire Gospel indicates.

Third, and most importantly, however, the Johannine Christians feel themselves entirely justified in behaving in this fiercely dualistic manner because they believe they possess something which absolutely guarantees them salvation and which other people, by definition if they are not members of the Johannine community, do not possess. Clearly, the Fourth Gospel gives various names to this possession, such as faith (11:25), grace (1:16), peace (14:27), knowledge (3:11) and glory (17:1); but most importantly in this context are the passages in John 16 which speak of the Paraclete or 'Counsellor' (which John 14:26 explicitly identifies with the Holy Spirit). The following verses are central to any understanding of this question and its significance for the Johannine community:

> Nevertheless I tell you the truth: it is to your advantage that I go away, for if I do not go away, the Counsellor will not come to you; but if I go, I will send him to you. And when he comes, he will convince the world of sin and of righteousness and judgement: of sin, because they do not believe in me; of righteousness, because I go to the Father, and you will see me no more; of judgement, because the ruler of this world is judged.
> I have yet many things to say to you, but you cannot bear them now. When the Spirit of truth comes, he will guide you into all the truth; for he will not speak on his own authority, but whatever he hears he will speak, and he will declare to you the things that are to come. He will glorify me for he will take what is mine and declare it to you. All that the Father has is mine; therefore I said that he will take what is mine and declare it to you (John 16:7–15).

These words, though they appear on the lips of Jesus, are integral to the rhetoric of the Johannine community; they articulate as clearly as possible the religious epistemological basis upon which the Fourth Gospel is written, and upon which the Johannine community understands itself and addresses itself to the world in which it lives. It is the community which possesses the Counsellor: and possessing the Counsellor turns everything one says and does into eschatological address, rhetoric rather than sophistry. It is all a matter of judgement, like the Gospel as a whole.

Obviously, the message here – of the presence of the Counsellor or Holy Spirit in the midst of the Johannine community – is fundamental and has been recognized as such by many scholars; but one of the most intriguing elements of the rhetoric in John 16 has gone largely unnoticed. This is the notion of the Holy Spirit as vehicle of continuing revelation: 'I have yet many things to say to you, but you cannot bear them now. When the Spirit of truth comes, he will guide you into all the truth' (16:13; see Segovia 1991). That is, and clearly because of the perceived linear continuity between Father, Son and Holy Spirit, the Third Person will definitely continue the process of education and inculcation of knowledge which was begun by Jesus Christ during his earthly life, but which was not completed before his death, resurrection and ascension. The Johannine community is unique, therefore, because it is still in the process of becoming truly the community of God, not simply (or even) in a socio-cultural sense, but rather gnoseologically and eschatologically: the presence of the Spirit of truth saves because it teaches, and because it teaches the community, according to the Fourth Gospel, it is able to address itself in certain very specific ways towards the world at large. It is not a question of rhetoric simply as persuasion, but rather rhetoric as ever-increasing understanding and knowledge of the community's status before God and the world.

This has profound implications for the way in which the rhetoric of any Christian community understands the presence of the Spirit, because if that presence gives knowledge of salvation from condemnation, and if this dualism becomes central to the community's address to the world – as it does in the Fourth Gospel – then that dualism takes over every aspect of that community's rhetoric. One can see this process occurring in various contemporary denominations, where rigorous certainty, based communally upon the presence and experience of the Holy Spirit, becomes translated rhetorically as an unwillingness to listen to what the world is saying to the community. There is no need to listen, and thereby to enter dialogue, if one knows absolutely the true nature and extent of God's eschatological will to save and whom it embraces.[14] In terms of the scope of Part I of this study, Barth's theology presents such an exclusivist grasping of eschatological knowledge which, though intelligible and even necessary theologically, has dangerous implications for the way in which Church addresses itself to the world.

On the basis of this study as a whole, and of the relationships between mystery, event and rhetoric, one can make the following observations about the Johannine community's self-understanding and address, and the concomitant understanding and address of other communities with a similar mentality. Fundamentally, what is happening when the Johannine community understands itself and the Holy Spirit in this fashion is a collapse of mystery and rhetoric into each other. This process may well, as in the Fourth Gospel, attract Christological labelling, and it may even be clearly related to a knowledge mediated by the eschatological Christ event; but at heart the Christological nature of this collapse does not matter as far as the community's address to the world is concerned. What matters, on the contrary, is that the community's rhetoric is identical with mystery itself, so that what the community says and does, in the power and authority of the Holy Spirit, is mysterious and therefore true. That this truth is named 'Christ' is, therefore, important for the internal act of remembrance of the Johannine community, as the Fourth Gospel makes clear (John 1:14); but as far as its external relations are concerned it has, as Hegel observed wryly in a very different context, about as much significance as the cleaving of a head of cabbage (1977b, p. 476).

The theological threefold division of faith seeking understanding into mystery, event and rhetoric, consequently, has some interesting things to say about the way in which Christian self-understanding operates in the relationship between faith and society. On the one hand, too hasty a shift from mystery to reflection upon the Christ event – Christology – as in Barth's theology, effectively drains mystery of anything mysterious, as well as introducing a Christocentric or even Christomonistic exclusivism into faith's search for understanding. Theology is thereby reduced to retelling God's own story, though inadequately. On the other hand, however, too hasty a collapse of mystery and rhetoric into each other – the opposite of Barth's Christocentricism – has the same exclusivist result: questions of address, though the Christological labels are now more or less inciden-

[14] There is also a question whether one needs Christ or revelation if spiritual knowledge is immediately available – something which charismatic Christianity has never fully recognized (even though Luther condemned it).

tal, really become questions of naming and appropriation, of classifying everything from an absolute eschatological viewpoint. Such a claim kills dialogue as assuredly as does too great an emphasis upon the Christ event as the sole medium of God's revelation.

There would seem to be two obvious responses to this situation, the former of which I want to reject, the latter develop in the remainder of this section. First, one could turn towards complete relativism, as many postmodern theologies desire. One thereby acknowledges the relativity of a community's rhetoric, as well as the relativity of any attempt to mediate the fundamental mystery of the world's existence; but one also relativizes the Christ event even in terms of the metaphysical claims faith wants to make about it, which is entirely unacceptable. Second, by contrast, one can acknowledge the tense relationship between mystery, event and rhetoric, and accept the relativity of any mediation of mystery and any specific communal rhetoric; but one can also assert the absolute significance of the Christ event as the medium by which God and humanity are joined, *for* faith seeking understanding. To achieve this one has to say something about the precise nature of revelation and concealment, and the way in which that nature informs a theological understanding of rhetoric.

The important point here is that rhetoric is dependent not upon mystery directly, but upon the Christ event as the revelation *and concealment* of mystery. Any community's address to the world as consequent viewpoint is thus dependent upon the particular way in which Christian faith and hope believes mystery as the structure of the world is made dynamic by God's action in Jesus Christ. Rhetoric, therefore, cannot circumnavigate Christ, ignoring this element of concealment within revelation, of darkness within light. On the contrary, rhetoric must speak of concealment as it speaks of revelation. In so doing it will say something very important about its own nature, namely that rhetoric is always incomplete and that any community can only address itself to the world on the basis of radical uncertainty. This is why rhetoric involves addressing images to society – because images are also incomplete.

That this uncertainty is integral to the revelation of God in Christ means two things for any Christian community. First, that all communities are fundamentally equal; no one church possesses the Holy Spirit definitively, nor is it capable of doing God's will in any definitive manner. The Holy Spirit witnessed to in the saying that 'where two or three are gathered in my name, there am I in the midst of them' (Matthew 18:20), therefore, is entirely an ecumenical Person: the Holy Spirit brings together all churches and communities and thereby forms the basis of the one Christian address or rhetoric, though it take many different forms. Moreover, because that rhetoric is intimately related to the Christ event which in turn is intimately related to mystery itself, and because the naming of mystery as complete occurs in the appropriation of Spirit language *per se* as a way of answering the ontological question, then one can make an important correlation between mystery as Spirit and the *Holy* Spirit, the Spirit of Jesus Christ. For Christian faith seeking understanding, this consistency witnesses to what believers mean when they confess Christ in faith, hope and love, and use this as the basis of what they have to say to the world in which they live.

Second, the Holy Spirit empowers a community to a viewpoint, or an understanding, of its rhetoric and its relationship to event and mystery; but at no point can this be taken to be *the* meaning or understanding *in toto* of what revelation and grace actually are. Rather, the Holy Spirit empowers a community to a *consequent* viewpoint, both in terms of its socio-cultural context, and its relationship to what is believed to be real about the Christ event's revelation of mystery. Any theological argument which fails to appreciate this point is saying something impermissible about revelation and grace, because they are not to be regarded simply as validations of, or aids to, certain specific, discrete and absolutely true viewpoints.

Far from being the power and influence envisaged in the Fourth Gospel, therefore, which seems to endorse the Johannine community in its certainty and religious imperialism, the Holy Spirit as the Spirit of the Crucified and Risen One is in reality a limiting force – and that is its true power. Paradoxically, what the Holy Spirit gives is the ability to be self-effacing, so that the community's rhetoric, be it in word or action, is really an opening up of dialogue and relationship with the society and culture in which that community exists, rather than the closure that one finds in the Fourth Gospel. This opening up will be established in the acknowledgement that revelation and its interpretation is always simultaneously an acknowledgement of concealment and the greater glory of God's grace, which cannot be encapsulated in one particular expression or institution. As previously stated, Church must be prepared to die for and towards society, in order first to address society (a principle particularly meaningful for the Church of England at present, as it begins to ordain women to the priesthood).

The gift of the Holy Spirit is the gift to a community of the ability to have a consequent viewpoint, namely to be able to understand and interpret the relationship between mystery and event, Christologically, from a specific point of view. That point of view will be socially and culturally conditioned; it will be, methodologically, relative to any other viewpoint (at least those consistent with the Christian nomenclature specified in the appropriation of mystery and event through Jesus Christ); and it will be open to its own extinction, if that is how it can witness to the revelation and concealment of God in Christ. At every stage, however, that consequent viewpoint will *always* be a gift of the Holy Spirit, like the other gifts of the Spirit, and the similar gifts of the Son, such as the Peace. Such gifts demarcate Church and every individual community by affirming Church's tentative grip on its own self-understanding and its own ability, imperfectly, to address itself rhetorically to its socio-cultural context.

Correctly understood, this approach to the first question of Church's self-definition provides three things for theology. First, it makes the expression 'work in the power of the Spirit' into an extremely risky and possibly tendentious claim, because any such work must of its own character be self-effacing. Church only gains its spiritual character by seeming to lose it, which means in modernity going out into the world of secularism in order to witness to secularism in dialogue with faith. Second, it makes it impossible for any one church or denomination, or even religion, to claim the sole definitive right to invoke the Spirit of the Crucified and Risen One, because as Bonhoeffer recognized, it is precisely *this* Spirit of Jesus which is Holy because of its continuation of the abandonment of God to the world. Third, it makes the continuing, eschatological education of Church in the power of the Holy Spirit into an education of its own limitations. Church continues on its pilgrim way, therefore; but that journey is a journey *away* from God, *with* but seemingly *without* God, in order ultimately to be *within* God. That is why this, like every other doctrine of the Christian faith, must be understood in Trinitarian terms.[15]

This paradox, I maintain, is one which is being experienced every day by every church throughout the world. It is named traditionally and Biblically 'losing one's life for Christ', and it is the existential foundation of rebirth in the Holy Spirit. Theologically, identifying the true character of this paradox opens up a way between the Scylla of Christocentric exclusivism, as typified by Barth, and the Charybdis of experiential exclusivism, as typified by various forms of contemporary evangelical fundamentalism. The Holy Spirit is the Person of inclusivism, and as such a personal Spirit articulates, here and now, the powers and grace of the revealed and concealed completeness, incompleteness and potential of divine mystery.

[15] N.B. what I said in chapter 6 about the Trinity being the future of all humanity.

Importantly, Church acknowledges this uncertainty in its address or rhetoric to society and the world, with profound implications for the way in which it understands itself, its doctrines, and their relationship with secular ideas and images. Simultaneously, however, Church must also be a community of hope, and a hope established in an understanding of the historical life, death and resurrection of Jesus of Nazareth. It is not solely the Spirit, therefore, which presents a paradox for the life and rhetoric of Church. It is also the necessity of a sacramental narrative about Jesus Christ which articulates what one might name 'the certainty of hope'. Thus, within a sacramental narrative which articulates in word and action existence in the Holy Spirit and the world of imagination it opens up, there is also a moment of memorial. For Church to be truly Church, this memory must also be a memory of Christ's Sacrament.

The certainty of hope

What does this mean, 'the certainty of hope'? First, one must be clear about what it does not mean. It does not mean 'certainty' in the sense of factual certainty, such as I possess if I assert that 'it is a fact that this chair is mostly made of wood'. Rather, the certainty of hope is the conviction that, when turned inwards, all that Church can truly be certain of is simply *hope*: hope that the narrative begun 2000 years ago, in Jesus of Nazareth, will be ultimately, eschatologically consummated for the world in the return of the Son, and therefore the life eternal of the Trinity. The certainty of hope is the certainty of the necessity to hope, because only in hoping is the community recognizably the community of Christ (something which has important implications for how one understands discipleship).

This hope contains both faith and love within itself, because hoping is believing and living within Church, such as Church demonstrates to the world in its rhetoric and address. This is a statement about the way in which Church orientates itself, both towards the society within which it exists, and the specific religious tradition it inhabits. The primacy of hope is the motor which drives the Church along, and which gives its rhetoric, both inwardly and outwardly, its specifically eschatological character. As Moltmann argued in the 1960s, influenced by Ernst Bloch, it is this character which maintains both an opening to such secular hopes and expectations as socialism, and a hold upon the historical origins of Christianity, namely the proclamation of the kingdom of God as gospel, without which Christian rhetoric simply collapses into ethics or moral discourse.[16]

The close relationship between rhetoric and ethical conduct, which has been recognized and commented upon previously, requires eschatology in order to maintain its status as faith seeking understanding and so as grace in the world. This is why so much Christian rhetoric takes the form of constructing images of Jesus, and why Christian discourse so often becomes fixated upon the question of the historical Jesus; for, as Kant realized and argued in his essay 'The End of All Things', it is the combination of eschatology, ethics, and an image of Jesus, which generally constitutes Christian rhetoric. One does not need to adopt Kant's own understanding of Christian rhetoric, as the proclamation of a liberal religious teacher of morals, to appreciate the methodological strength of his position (although Harnack did adopt it, and Barth opposed it quite explicitly).

In modern theology this emphasis upon ethics and images of Jesus, as it finds expression in an understanding (implicit or otherwise) of Christian rhetoric, generally occurs in one of two ways. Either it surfaces as the personal, spiritual encounter with the individual Jesus, such as one finds in evangelical denominations and, arguably, in Bultmann's theology; or interest in Jesus effectively disappears, leaving in its place an identification of 'Church' and social practice, behind which there may be a latent image of Jesus, but within which it is not particularly apparent. I attempted to avoid the first tendency by emphasizing in the last section the way in which the Holy Spirit operates within and through the community, rather than the individual. This was done to maintain the communal nature of Christianity, and to acknowledge the damage which Christian rhetoric can do if it fails to recognize the way in which society place its own limits – divinely ordained though Christians believe them to be – upon its scope.

The second tendency, however, provides a further challenge. If Church wants rhetorically to offer an image of Jesus to the outside world, and if this image is to be determined by the dual nature of rhetoric and the way it operates within and through language and action, then it follows that the definition of Church as an image of Jesus, sacramentally, involves its own particular difficulties, and also its own particular emphases. For the notion of Church itself as an image of Jesus, as the Sacrament of hope, is not something (whatever the connections with secular eschatology) which society at large can or perhaps wants to understand. On the contrary, it is a discourse

[16] That rhetoric as hopeful discourse has certain ethical implications – the ethos of the kingdom, one might say – is fundamental to the relationship between faith and society; but N.B. that the ethics of rhetoric is a major subject independent of the methodological questions with which I am here concerned, and will have to be considered separately (one day).

and a communication which possesses meaning solely for the community itself. To speak of Church as the image of Jesus, in terms of the Sacrament of hope, is to speak of the way in which Church understands itself. It is to speak liturgically of the Church's self-definition, and what it is to be part of a community which celebrates something which, fundamentally, is still to come. Although the cross and resurrection are believed to be historical events, so that one can, ecclesially, speak of the Crucified and Risen One and His presence in the community, yet the real presence, eschatologically, is still to be fully realized. One awaits it in hope, substantively and existentially; but one truly awaits it.

Admittedly, this is extremely difficult ground, and one must use expressions like 'real presence' with great delicacy and hesitancy; for not every theologian, least of all every denomination, will recognize and allow the degree of flexibility which I want to attribute to them at this point. Moreover, the entire notion of a sacramental image of Jesus, as Church and its celebration of the real presence in the eucharist, is one which although common to all Christian churches is by no means understood always in quite the same eschatological sense that I have outlined here. Such an eschatological emphasis, if it is there at all, is found in relation to pneumatology and social conduct, and thereby to what I discussed above ('Church's work in the power of the Holy Spirit'), rather than in relation to an understanding of the Sacrament, which is overwhelmingly taken to be a memorial or reenactment of something completed and therefore past. In the understanding of many congregations eschatology is thus replaced by something akin to ecclesiology when it comes to self-understanding and self-celebration. Churches regard themselves as communities which come together to define and reenact the rites and celebrations which constitute and establish what it is to be a church.

Because of the way in which rhetoric has been defined in this study, however, at least two of these moves are invalid from the viewpoint of critical theology. First, the domestication of eschatology, whereby it is reduced to the level of personal knowledge of God in the form of an intimate relationship with Jesus, robs rhetoric of its most important motor, because without eschatology, without an acknowledgement of the tension between revelation and concealment and the ultimate resolution of this tension in the kingdom which is yet to come, rhetoric is reduced to sophistry. It becomes persuasive imagery, rather than an argument which can be defended and elaborated rationally and cogently, but which can also be attacked from the viewpoint of society. Without this element of uncertainty Christian rhetoric becomes simply propaganda.

Second, the abandonment of the sacramental image of Jesus, in the form of the eucharist, to the past and therefore to memory overlooks the most important aspect of any memory, namely the imagination and, in this Christian sense, the hope that what occurred nearly 2000 years ago is the eternal present and the ultimate future of all humanity. This dual process, domestication and memorialization, effectively results in the museum-inspired understanding of the liturgy of the eucharist which one sees so often today, and which so easily negates the progressive understanding of rhetoric which one finds in contemporary pneumatologies. Examples of this tendency can be found in the work of Gorringe (1990) and Moltmann (1992), although in different ways and, arguably, to very different degrees.

This means that the rhetoric of the Holy Spirit, which is expressed *from* Church, must be reiterated by a rhetoric of the Sacrament or eucharist, which is for Church's own benefit and which defines it as a community where hope is present in its midst. The connection between these two, the element which identifies both rhetorics as one message, is the eschatological construction of images of Jesus as the valid Christian response to the conviction that the Christ event is a meaningful revelation and concealment of mystery.

Eating the body and drinking the blood of the Crucified and Risen One is an act of hope. It is a rhetorical statement and action, a rhetorical liturgy, in which Church addresses itself (and is implicitly addressed by an incredulous society; see below, 'Interpreting the cross of Jesus') in the presence of Christ's body, very much as it addresses society in the power of the Holy Spirit. The different degrees to which that image is emphasized and, as it were, materialized – by such ideas as transubstantiation, consubstantiation, memorial – are really different ways of looking at that one image, or rather, themselves are different images, which all partake of the same basic colour; for the only important aspect of this particular image, as the World Council of Churches Lima Declaration attested, is that all Christian churches make the same eucharistic confession of hope. Without this it is difficult to see how any church or community can speak in the same breath of the Holy Spirit of unity and the way in which this Person is to be found in the rhetoric of the said community towards its socio-cultural context. Unity in the Holy Spirit requires unity in the body of Christ because they are both, in Trinity, identical as the Christian understanding of the mystery of God, complete, incomplete and potential.

None of this rhetoric actually means very much, however, if such words and expressions as 'hope', 'unity' and 'address' are not given particular content, namely a specific, material sense within the context of the theologian and/or community employing them. For example, 'hope' is a very nice word, one which even functions as itself an image within modern secular society (one think here of its usage by party politicians, particularly in the western world); but in and of itself, and therefore separated from the force-field of a particular ideological current (to use Adorno's terminology again), 'hope' is empty, devoid of any meaningful reference. In this state it functions as empty or emotional persuasion, but is not established in any logical or reasonable understanding of certain specific conditions and certain particular possibilities of change and action. Again, one thinks of the way in which 'hope' often serves in popular slogans, as in: 'The Government hopes that the economy will pick up in the year…'. This is sophistry, pure and simple.

Less pejoratively, words like 'hope' and 'unity' are often found in certain theological and philosophical discourses, and there without any specific meaning or understanding. Certainly, they are being used sophistically; what is really happening, however, is that they are being reduced to the level of essences. On this reading such essences 'exist' or 'act' as pure concepts. They are there to help advance a particular type of discourse, with a very specific pedagogic intent, but in and of themselves they are not established materially. One example in contemporary theology and religious studies would be the later work of John Hick (e.g. 1989), where 'the Really Real' – or the Absolute, *the* transcendent reality which is superior to all masks of religious belief – functions entirely as a pure concept, aiding not one's understanding of a particular religious tradition, but rather shaping one's awareness of something called 'religion' *per se*.

The intent of this approach to theology and religious studies is certainly not to speak of essences or pure concepts, but rather to provide a conceptual framework within which subsequent, more directly material, theologizing can be undertaken. In this sense I would agree with Tracy and Hick, wishing to produce something similar. The difficulty, however, is that when one moves onto the plane of address to particular circumstances, wishing to open it for interpretation and discussion – as I have done, by moving to consider rhetoric in this chapter – then one has to find a very clear avenue via which 'framework construction' can become something within that framework. When one moves from an interpretation of the relationship between structure and dynamic, towards one of the role of consequent viewpoint upon that relationship, then one needs to identify viewpoint's entrance into dynamic and structure. In the more overtly theological terminology I have employed, it is a question of identifying how one moves from rhetoric back into event and mystery. Or, in more overtly Christian terminology, how one moves from talk of action in the Holy Spirit and hoping with Christ in the Sacrament, back into the heart of the Christ event itself, and ultimately into mystery.

This move could obviously occur in a number of different ways, and there are examples in modern theology of different doors through which theologians want to reenter the 'deep structure' of such reflection, having decided to operate on a theoretical level. One thinks, for example, of Moltmann's shift back to the universal level in his books on creation (1985) and the Holy Spirit (1992). My argument, however, is that it is unnecessary to make such *ad hoc* arrangements for philiosophical deep structure, if one has provided for such a move in one's understanding of the Christ event.

Rhetoric, therefore, is definitely reflection from a consequent viewpoint: consequent upon the very specific dimensions of the Christ event, and the way in which that event establishes certain boundaries which are both indexed to the criteria of historicity, eschatology and transforming power, and intentional, because they possess the purposiveness to be realized in a variety of different images of the Christ event. In this respect, any Christian community's rhetoric is part of the ever-continuing process of constructing images of Jesus as the Christ event, which itself is what I named as the moving image of mystery, for Christian faith *the* revelation and concealment of God as the mystery of the world.

The advantages of this way of understanding the relationships between Christian discourse (rhetoric), its basis (the Christ event) and the claimed supernatural reality within which everything is established (mystery) are significant. Not only does it provide a conceptual framework within which one can identify and interpret the operation of structure, dynamic and viewpoint as significantly different stages of reflection within theology. It also establishes anything the community has to say within the identified parameters of the Christ event itself, and therefore faith in Jesus of Nazareth. Thus, whether one wishes to speak of the Christ event simply as the outpouring of the Holy Spirit, or as the hopeful Sacrament of the presence of Christ, or both (or, of course, other derivative images of Christ), the basis upon which one speaks is the Christ event.

As one speaks rhetorically about the Christ event and thereby addresses a specific community, then clearly a certain vocabulary becomes ever more identifiable in what one says. For example, in John 3:1–21 the vocabulary is that of social exclusion and inclusion, of who is within and who without the Johannine community, and how the conditions of possibility of recognizing these different groupings are provided by eschatological knowledge. In Sobrino's theology, the vocabulary is that of revolutionary change, of the need to overcome oppression and poverty materially, thereby moving towards the realization on earth of the kingdom of God. In Moltmann's *The Crucified God*, the vocabulary is provided by an explicitly Christian reflection upon the Jewish holocaust, which again provides a very distinctive rhetoric, and one which should never be forgotten by Christian theology. Finally, McFadyen's *The Call to Personhood* offers a vocabulary of personal change and development drawn from social though and pastoral care, resulting in a moving depiction of the Christian faith, the way Christians live, and the image of Christ created when one evaluates theological questions with these explicit concerns.

Each of these theological models can be accommodated by the conceptual framework I have provided so far in Part II. Moreover, each of these theological models, in so far as they are deliberately productive of new ways of understanding God's relationship with the world, are explicitly required and explained (at least formally) by the conceptual relationships between mystery, event and rhetoric which I have established in this study. One is speaking of interpreting not only the way people live, but also the way people produce models to understand and articulate the way they live and the way they want to live, in Christ. Logically, therefore, the next stage of analysis is to attempt to understand how the process of model production occurs, i.e. how rhetoric functions as language. This is the subject of the next section, which develops the argument away from areas where theology has a limited role – establishing formally what the community should do actively – and towards areas where theology becomes more significant, namely the construction of doctrine and its interpretation in the contemporary world.

On the borderlands of faith and society

The construction and nature of doctrine

One point has to be made very clear here and now. My intention is not to start speaking about the 'rules' or 'laws' within which a denomination organizes the elements of its faith. Rather, by doctrine I mean the effective expression of a community or denomination's faith in recognizable linguistic and/or social form, by means of which that community or denomination models and communicates the way in which it understands the elements of its faith in relation to its socio-cultural context.

Doctrine has been the subject of many attempts at definition, and the above example of this process has been significantly informed by some important work in this area, particularly George Lindbeck's well-known study *The Nature of Doctrine* (1984). Of specific relevance is Lindbeck's emphasis upon the cultural relativity of doctrine and the way in which doctrines are themselves linguistic. This, together with the generally agreed position that doctrines are models attempting to formulate a particular community's understanding of its faith at a certain moment in time, has given rise to the view that doctrines are metaphorical rather than propositional, which has two important implications for an understanding of doctrine. First, it means that a doctrine is part of a developing story or narrative in which a community's self-understanding in relation to the context it inhabits – as well as its historical faith – is conditioned by the manner in which that story or narrative is told. Second, it means that a logic or rationale other than the propositional is required to make intelligible the way in which doctrines operate. The former has become part of the accepted mythology of contemporary theology; Lindbeck attempted to provide the latter in his book.

There are, however, significant problems with this position, which make it necessary to abandon it and develop an alternative view. Primarily, the emphasis here upon metaphor is too narrow, as illustrated by its definition. A metaphor is the application of a name or descriptive term or phrase to an object or action to which it is imaginatively but not literally applicable. As such – and because the role of the imagination here is paramount – one can say that metaphors operate by illustrating and illuminating an idea/action/object through dissimilarity, i.e. the metaphor works because it conveys sense by not being obviously related to the object/action/idea under discussion. An example of this would be the expression 'food for thought', where the metaphor works because it is dissimilar to the process – reflection upon conceptual material – under discussion (see Soskice 1985, p. 15).

On this definition, it is difficult to see how the process of narration, of storytelling – if this is still maintained as a basic understanding of the way in which models operate – can be reduced simply to the level of metaphor: if it were, there would be an awful lot less theology actually done, because people would be too busy thinking up *real* metaphors. Moreover, the emphasis upon metaphor draws attention away from analogy – reasoning from approximately parallel cases – which is, and always has been, more significant for theological methodology. (One has only to think of the work of both Barth and Rahner, and their impressive use of such analogy, to realize the truth of this argument.) Because analogy works by similarity as opposed to dissimilarity, it makes more sense to speak of the primacy of analogical reasoning in theology than metaphorical, postmodernism notwithstanding.[17]

Granted this dualism in the way language works – and metaphor and analogy must be augmented by other tropes – confidence in the positions of so-called 'narrative' or 'metaphorical' theologies begins to break down, a process exacerbated when one realizes that the notion of 'storytelling' in itself is a naive way of understanding the process of self- and social definition which occurs when a community or denomination addresses itself to its context. Moreover – an important objection – the notion of narrative is remarkably unsuited to highlighting the ambivalence of this process of communication, the way in which it can manipulate and deform both faith and society as they are engaged with each other. This failure can be illustrated by reference to contemporary examples, but in general it is sufficient to negate the application of this process to the question of the nature and communication of doctrine.[18]

Instead, the technique/art of rhetoric is advanced in place of narrative, along the lines drawn earlier in this chapter, as the best way of understanding the construction, communication and organization of those models which go by the name of 'doctrine'. Rhetoric – which can include such tropes as metaphor and analogy, as well as others, and which consequently can operate in a 'meta–narrative' fashion – should be regarded as the way of understanding the role and scope of a doctrine within the ongoing process which one names a community's action of self- and social definition. A doctrine is a rhetorical device: it operates on the level not of conceptualization for the sake of formalism and definition, but of pronouncement for the sake of persuasion. In this sense doctrines should be regarded, rightly, as at best word or action models of a position – faith – which some community or group – a church – wants to persuade other people to join or follow. An excellent Bibical example of this process in action would be

[17] Of course, Tracy combines the two in *The Analogical Imagination* (1981).

[18] In McFague's *Metaphorical Theology* (1983) there is no clear reference to the audience, nor any discussion of the ambivalence of communication. See also Stroup 1981, where the same failings are evidenced. Hauerwas 1981 is a better guide here to the potential of narrative theology, mainly because he is always conscious of its necessary, practical quality.

Acts 17:19–34, Paul's speech on the Areopagus, where rhetoric – deploying various literary devices which look suspiciously like putative doctrines – occurs as a means to persuasion. That Paul's attempt failed illustrates the nature of his enterprise: not self-formalization, but in this case persuasion as evangelization.

One can thus make a number of important observations about the way in which a doctrine functions and achieves definition, all of which are governed or conditioned by the understanding of rhetoric adopted in this study. First, a doctrine, though overwhelmingly verbal and thereby linguistic – at least, that is how they are most often encountered – need not occur in this manner. Because rhetoric can function as action or event rather than spoken or written utterance, a doctrine might be a physical expression of religious belief or practice in a context where literally there is only silence.

Granted this culturally relative definition of doctrine, some of the more profound contemporary doctrines are non-verbal. One thinks, for example, of John Tavener's composition for cello and orchestra *The Protecting Veil*, with its musical illustration of Orthodox doctrine, and anti-semitism amongst Polish Roman Catholics during the period 1933–45 (and after), a most physical manifestation of a very real and effective doctrine amongst that community, i.e. that because 'the Jews killed Jesus, therefore their lives are forfeit'. Needless to say, such anti-semitism is entirely abhorrent and cannot, under any circumstances, be regarded as anything other than an evil lie; but that is not the relevant point here. Methodologically, the relevant point is that if doctrines are meant to be socio-culturally conditioned illustrations of what communities actually believe, then such anti-semitism was a central doctrine of the Roman Catholic Church in Poland before, during and after the Hitler years (though of course I do not advance this as an acceptable Christian doctrine; see Siegele-Wenschkewitz 1984).

This illustrates, second, an important and related point: doctrines are not, and cannot be, simply what one might want them to be. Although one undoubtedly chooses what one wants to include in one's rhetoric, so that communication and dialogue between faith and society at least purports to be representative of a specific position, nevertheless other things – other doctrines – can and will be included which one might wish to leave out. This is integral to the process of rhetorical address, and theology cannot argue that it does not occur when the evidence of its reality is so much a part of its twentieth-century experience. One thinks, here, of the various 'doctrines' of Christian superiority – Barth's (the Word made flesh), Rahner's ('anonymous Christianity') or Moltmann's (the Crucified One as answer to the horrors of Auschwitz). Each encapsulates, implicitly, far more of doctrinal significance than the theologian in question intended. That is how rhetoric functions, which is why so much of what sets out to be rhetoric ends up being sophistry: because what is significant is not always what it is saying, but rather what it is *not* saying. (Anyone who doubts this should go away and test the argument against any of the so-called 'narrative' or 'metaphorical' theologies, to understand the double-sided power of rhetoric.)

Third, allied to the fact that doctrines, rhetorically, can be actions rather than verbal constructions and that, rhetorically, doctrines have a shadow side which is always as profoundly important as the side which is presented for understanding, is the argument that doctrines are inherently fluid and flexible and that they can, and must, change constantly. Doctrines thus develop and alter as the situation and context of a community develops and alters. Roman Catholic anti-semitism in Poland, therefore, need not always be a doctrine of that church in that specific context: it can change, it can *be* changed, through a thorough process of education and, yes, rhetorical address and persuasion. Doctrines are models; and models are nothing more than images of something real which somebody, somewhere, wishes to use to communicate a certain understanding of a certain idea or action. Theology is nothing more nor less than model-building, but always for specifically rhetorical purposes. One does not build a model, after all, *solely* for the fun of it; even the imagination and representation employed in model train sets have an important socio-cultural significance which is too often ignored in the most patronizing manner.

Given this, the entire business of constructing and communicating doctrinal models takes on a new significance. No longer is it simply part of the process of 'putting into words' what people actually believe; now it becomes the very basis of faith seeking understanding, of constructing and communicating, rhetorically, with both faith and society in such a way that their inherently commutative relationship is always recognized. A model or doctrine, consequently, says as much if not more about the world in which it exists as about the idea/action/object which it represents. Although to a certain extent hermeneutics has addressed this issue with respect to texts and their interpretation – the way in which reader intent is at least as evident in a reading as is author intent – the present notion has far wider implications, which texts and their derivative, narrative, are simply incapable of exploring. Theology needs to enlarge, almost exponentially, its understanding of what constitutes rhetoric, and what 'doctrines' can be made of, for it to have much to say to and about the way in which communities exist in today's society. The problem is acute: theology's own decline in significance is echoed by the gradual erosion of genuine religiosity amongst the populace of the western world.

The rhetorical character of such address and communication, taken together with the general character of doctrines and the way in which they themselves communicate meaning – analogically, metaphorically and so on – gives a very definite character to theology itself. Critical theology is teaching, and a form of teaching which, unlike dialectic-based disciplines (such as propositional logic or mathematics), is somewhat imprecisely geared towards its subject matter. Thus, critical theology *is* teaching, but teaching in the pedagogic mould, rather than the effective indoctrination of a specific set of data or information. Theology is an applied science, one where its pedagogic intent leads people towards a specific position – some of which is recognizable in the community's rhetoric, some of which lurks beneath the surface – but without the ability, finally, to establish once and for all the precise nature and extent of its subject, God.

This is both theology's strength and weakness: strength, because it enables theology to be flexible and thereby to adapt to different circumstances in different socio–cultural contexts (as in fact is demanded of it by the nature of mystery); weakness, because it is difficult to identify and secure the boundaries of theology in relation to other disciplines. Unlike Thomas Aquinas's time, therefore, when theology was regarded universally as the 'queen of the sciences', theology today, to the extent that it is critical and thereby always engaged in establishing and interpreting doctrine rhetorically in relation to society, is embroiled in a battle for its very survival. For if theology is straightforwardly the business of constructing models (doctrines) and interpreting them in accordance with specific socio-cultural circumstances, then there must be many different ways in which such a discipline can be undertaken; then, logically, one enters that twilight zone where 'theologies of ...' multiply as rapidly as imagination allows, almost to the extent that any new position becomes a new theology. Whilst not in and of itself necessarily a bad thing – after all, if faith is geared towards the future and its revelation of God as Trinity, theology too should be open to the possibility that something new might arise that will be important – this tendency in contemporary reflection – and it has been developing ever since the Second World War – shows alarming signs of relativizing every single attempt to say anything meaningful about the specifically Christian tradition. Granted that there is *one* recognizable such tradition, there needs to be a way of identifying good and bad theological models about it. But how?

First, a statement: it is true that theology can be done by anyone, anywhere, and that it can take on a variety of forms. It can be, for example, linguistic, practical, artistic, musical, physical, because 'statements' about God can be made, rhetorically and persuasively, in terms of a confession of faith, an act of charity, a painting (like Salvador Dali's *Last Supper*), a piece of music (such as John Tavener's *Ikon of the Beloved*), and the birth of a child. To deny this, or even to fail to acknowledge it explicitly, is to return theology to the ivory tower; it is, destructively, to reduce theology to the level where it matters only to the small handful of people who read academic books, or watch academic 'performances' in lecture room and conference hall. Everything I have tried to say in this book, about the way in which people live and understand the mystery of life from within the Christian tradition, militates against such a development.

This leads necessarily to my next, more important point: nevertheless, there is a place for theology and the theologian within the business of rhetoric, though in the Christian tradition, and acknowledging its Jewish origins, it goes by a different name – prophet. The task of the theologian as prophet, therefore, is to think and act and speak rhetorically, to function on the borderlands of faith and society, in MacKinnon's memorable expression, in order to persuade and teach, interpret and apply, the eschatological meaning of the Christian gospel. For the theologian personally this will mean many different things, in many different ways; but in one sense it will be the same for every theologian, everywhere in the world, and at all times. As Part I deomonstrated, being a theologian, being rhetor and prophet, means occupying a specific position on the boundaries of Church and faith. Only from such a position – be it Barth's in Switzerland, or Bonhoeffer's in Tegel, or Sobrino's in El Salvador – can any message *be addressed*.

Accepting this argument has certain implications for many of the books of theology which are written and published today, and which purport to say something meaningful about the relationship between faith and society (though on different levels), without saying anything much at all about what it is to be a theologian and what it is to speak theologically, rhetorically and prophetically. It also, however, has certain quite important implications for the way in which one regards what one might name the 'roots' of doctrinal construction in any age, namely the labels the tradition gives to the recurring elements of mystery, event and rhetoric. Since these names or labels are normative for critical theology (because they conform to the eschatological criteria of mystery as complete, incomplete and potential), they can be elaborated here as a way into the final section of this chapter. There are nine such normative 'roots' for doctrine which need to be recognized at this juncture.

First, there are three roots which name the qualities of mystery, and which must be identified and reflected upon as part of the process of understanding what it is for human existence to be regarded in relation to something which is fundamentally *other*. These three roots are: creation (Spirit), eschatology (the kingdom) and Trinity (God's named being). They are, of course, only roots: one can, for example, have very different doctrines of creation, as illustrated by the theologies of Wolfhart Pannenberg (1991) and Rex Ambler (1990), and the same must be said of eschatology and the Trinity; but the point remains the same. Any Christian reflection upon the nature of mystery worthy of the name, and which seeks to articulate rhetorically a vision of how people live, will discuss in detail these three roots.

Second, there are three roots which name the qualities of the Christ event as complete, incomplete and potential, as past event, present reality and future glory: incarnation, cross and resurrection, the third being ultimately consummated only with the coming of the Son of man on the clouds of heaven (Mark 14:62). Again, there will be widely differing understandings of these three roots, and doctrines of the incarnation, cross and resurrection will be very different in very different circumstances. Nevertheless, reflection upon the Christ event will address these three roots to the community's socio-cultural context, as the necessary elaboration of that event's believed significance for all people.

Third, there are three roots which name the qualities of rhetoric itself: the Holy Spirit, the Sacrament and Church. Here more than anywhere one can perceive and understand the necessary flexibility of doctrine's roots, and yet the equal necessity of establishing once and for all, in continuity with mystery and event, the parameters of what one means by 'rhetoric'. It is not simply a nice name given to metaphor and narrative as they become socially relevant and as people learn to address themselves to society's vagaries. Rhetoric is the very essence of being theological. That is why it is so important to establish rhetoric in belief in the Holy Spirit first and foremost, because it is the Holy Spirit, Christians believe, who makes true rhetoric possible. If one is to avoid sophistry, therefore, one must needs establish one's address – whatever form it takes – in Pentecost and the events which are the climax of Christ's mission and message on earth.

Creation, eschatology, Trinity, incarnation, cross, resurrection, Holy Spirit, Sacrament, Church: these nine roots, I argue, provide every resource that theology, in whatever guise, requires in order to undertake and achieve its rhetorical business. And if I had sufficient space and time, I would now go on to elaborate, in detail, these nine doctrines in relation to the specific socio-cultural context in which I and my denomination (Anglican) find ourselves, addressing these roots rhetorically to the world I live in and to the people I encounter as I live my life.

This, however, is the business of a future project; and because there is insufficient space to achieve this goal satisfactorily here, I must turn now to the final section of this chapter, and indeed this argument, in a more cursory fashion. To conclude, therefore – though solely in a preliminary sense – I want now to take one of these doctrinal roots – the cross of Christ – and interpret it rhetorically. In this way I hope to be able to illustrate what I mean by saying that the theologian operates always on the borderlands of faith and society, and that theology occurs as the construction of models and images of Jesus.

Interpreting the cross of Jesus

I have chosen the cross of Jesus as my test case for two principal reasons. First, because it is so obviously central to the Christian faith, and anything that I say about how to address this cross rhetorically to society will, by extension, be applicable to other doctrinal roots. Second, because paradoxically Christology is relatively neglected in contemporary theology, where writers prefer more topical subjects, like global ecology, or personhood, or ecclesiology. In this sense, what I say here will I hope be significant in its own right, within the ongoing argument, and also provocative of a new line in Christological reflection.

The first thing I want to say is that the classical theory of the antonement – in which through a process of penal substitution Jesus of Nazareth takes the place of fallen humanity, thereby assuming and negating the sins of the world – is, even in its most sophisticated modern form, useless for critical theology.[19] Its difficulty lies in a number of significant areas: in theodicy, where the idea of a vengeful God has never proved satisfactory; in apologetics, where the sacrifice of one

[19] I am thinking here of the eloquent defence of this theory by Fiddes (1988). I say 'theory' rather than 'doctrine' because I want to emphasize that atonement's place in Christian faith seeking understanding can no longer be secure.

individual has never convincingly addressed the problem of evil and its presence in the world; in methodology, where the idea of a necessary sacrifice runs contrary to God's supposed free expression of love (a Christian truth which, as I have demonstrated, has profound methodological implications); and not least in Christology itself, where atonement inevitably becomes reductive of the Christ event's full potential to communicate Christian faith and meaning. For all of these reasons one must look elsewhere for a framework within which to interpret Jesus' cross.

The real difficulty, of course, is that the theory of the atonement is a theory, a way of looking at the cross which seeks, erroneously, to be *the* way of looking at the cross; a tendency towards absolutism which cannot be tolerated either truthfully – because God's sacrifice is irreducible to an intelligible equation – or methodologically – because the principle of pluralism militates against the reification of any one interpretation of any aspect of the Christ event (least of all the cross). Instead of identifying one interpretation of the cross as *the* interpretation, therefore, the task of theology is to advance a way of understanding the cross which will accommodate many different ways of looking at it and thereby many different ways of naming and appropriating it. This is what I have attempted with my understanding of the Christ event, within which the cross becomes one of the fundamental features of any image of Jesus.

The advantages of this approach are readily apparent: not only does it allow the possibility that atonement might be a viable interpretation of the cross in a particular situation, it also preserves a dynamic understanding of the Christ event *in toto*. Instead, therefore, of regarding the cross as a *fait accompli*, achieved by God so that Christians are eternally redeemed simply by acknowledgement of the cross as penal substitution, I want to interpret it as an integral moment within a larger process – a process which is eschatological and thereby simultaneously revealing and concealing of God's will to save creation and all in it. Giving normative status to any theory, such as the atonement, effectively shifts the methodological emphasis in theology away from questions of interpretation, towards ones of cognition and recognition. One cannot 'recognize' Jesus' cross: as I demonstrated, that was the failure of liberal and transcendental theologians, like Harnack and Rahner. Nor can one appropriate it with solely one name: that was Barth's mistake (and the danger confronting contemporary theologians like Moltmann and Sobrino). On the contrary, one can only depict the cross as one sees it, a process which includes questions of perspective and media. [20]

Impressionistically, one can argue that the multiplication of images of the Christ event, and particularly images of the cross, will have an important influence upon the Christian religious consciousness in general (see Rupp 1974, p. 178). That influence, however, will always be compromised so long as there is *in situ* an implicit theological *schema* which militates against genuine methodological pluralism. Here the substantive question is whether or not one thinks it possible to understand the Christ event and its major components definitively. If one does, then one's own truth claims become arbitrary in every context, negating the possibility of genuine communication. If one does not, however, then one must offer a frame of reference within which one can interpret the Christ event in a variety of equally meaningful ways.

This is what I have attempted by asking ontological, epistemological and semantic questions of mystery, by analogy with time, which in turn generated the three qualities of completeness, incompleteness and potential which I subsequently invoked in my interpretation of the Christ event. In the present context it is clear that this framework indicates – one cannot state it any more strongly – that critical theology understands Jesus' cross as *incomplete*; as it is the present confrontation of the individual and community with the death of God incarnate, so it is incomplete in itself as moment of revelation and concealment.

There are two reasons why I make this claim. First, and in terms of the naming process outlined at the end of chapter 6, Jesus' cross is entirely related to his proclamation of the kingdom of God, by which name Christianity understands the present reality of God as the mystery of the world. On this reading, consequently, one understands the cross as the inevitable result of Jesus' mission and message, and therefore as his sacrifice to humanity and society in the name of a vision of what humanity and society could be. The cross is, in this sense, a signpost towards something better, where 'better' is true for Christian faith as the eternal response to the implications of temporality.[21]

[20] Schillebeeckx (1979, p. 64) recognizes this point, though he surprisingly fails to make very much of it. As will become apparent in what I say in the following passages, the substantive issue here for critical theology is how permissive it will be of diverse perspectives and media in the construction of images of Jesus. The possibility – in an era where cinema has been exposed to considerable philosophical reflection (see Deleuze 1986–9) – is that Christology in the 1990s will benefit enormously from the creations of secular authors in a variety of different art forms, thereby generating new interpretations of the scope and effect of theology itself. This is part of critical theology's rhetorical task.

[21] It is thus that one recognizes the strongest links between the doctrines of the cross and incarnation: the cross is a signpost along a road connecting time and eternity which has its origin and goal within the moment of incarnation, thereby making the identity of God and humanity in Jesus inevitable (rather than necessary) as the fullest expression of both beings.

Second, understanding the cross's incompleteness in this way highlights its mediating position between the completeness of Spirit – through which creation occurred – and the potential of the Trinity – within which lies that communion which is the goal of all Christian existence. This interpretation achieves two things. First, it offers a metaphysics within which one can make truth claims about both the creation and destiny of the world in relation to Jesus' cross, so that, expressed straightforwardly, one can speak of the cross being the fulcrum around which the world turns (see Cullmann 3/1962, p. 121). Second, and in terms of Christology rather than theological metaphysics, it identifies the incomplete cross as the inevitable mediation between the completeness of incarnation (as full identity) and the potential of the resurrection (as the universal salvation of all humanity). The cross is incomplete, therefore, as the only way in which the integrity of Christianity's truthfulness can be addressed to the world.[22]

Because the cross is incomplete, it means that it is present reality for humanity; as I demonstrated, this is how people know their lives in the current moment of remembering and imagining the world in which they live. As present reality between Spirit and Trinity, however, the cross also addresses humanity's spirituality, its movement between completeness and potential which can never be understood, only named and appropriated. The most fundamental meaning of the cross, therefore, is that it addresses the spiritual situation of humanity's present reality – its incompleteness, which manifests itself in every misery and distress known and perpetrated in this world. This is what incompleteness means to a humanity limited religiously by its awareness of its spiritual predicament.

Understanding Jesus' cross on this level of spirituality is Christianity's only answer to the problem of evil in the world, because the only way that this particular religion can speak of humanity's current predicament is by articulating the transitory nature of everything it experiences today. Traditionally one would settle this understanding upon the doctrine of the Fall, arguing that since humanity is fallen and therefore sinful it is open to doing sinful things. In an age when such arbitrary descriptions no longer carry persuasive weight, how-

[22] If this is emphasized, then I believe that one of the most difficult stumbling-blocks between Christianity and the other world religions – its insistence upon the exclusive *fait accompli* of salvation in Jesus Christ – can be removed. The incompleteness of the cross means that Christianity cannot appropriate as its principal image a static negation of humanity's ontological limitations. Rather, it must emphasize the dynamic nature of the Christ event, which always – as address – moves faith and community beyond the cross itself. This makes Christian belief into something much more like Judaism or Islam or Buddhism or Hinduism than might otherwise be the case.

ever, theology must articulate the more flexible and sympathetic vocabulary and grammar of spirituality if it is successfully to address the horrors of the world in which we all live.

One of the most significant concepts to arise from this spirituality is that of silence, so often people's first reaction to horror and sin and itself a stage in the transition from incredulity to the realization that humanity is capable of such atrocities.[23] Christologically, the silence of belief as it confronts the world in which it lives can only be echoed by the silence of the cross, in which event the Holy Spirit witnesses silently to the Dead Son (see Balthasar 1990a). Be it national disasters on the scale witnessed in Britain in the 1980s (I am thinking of Zeebrugge, or Piper Alpha, or Hillsborough), or national disasters on the scale of the murder of James Bulger in February 1993, the spiritual silence of Christian response is the silence of the cross, and thereby the silence of God's incompleteness is how God calls humanity to God's communion. In the face of such profoundly evil occurrences, all that faith can do is articulate God's Name, Jesus Christ, as one articulates the names of humanity's victims.

Confronted by the face of evil, faith and therefore theology can only respond spiritually with silence and one Word, Crucified and Risen; and as Jacques Pohier (1985, p. 265) movingly explained, the fact that God is God means that God is not Everything.[24] After the cross, temporally, but within the cross eternally, faith seeking understanding must speak of the fragmentation of God because God has sought to be fragmented, for the sake of humanity. I do not believe that one needs to speak here of 'atonement' as a judicial process, which a God-Man had to undergo in order to redeem all people by appeasing a justly wrathful God. I believe that one must speak here of God seeking 'at-one-ment' with Godself, and that this quality of divine being must inevitably be reconciled with human being by God being torn into pieces on the cross. If one wants to speak of theological ontology, therefore (see

[23] I must thank the congregation of St Thomas of Canterbury's Church in Goring-on-Thames, its priest Father Philip Nixon and its curate Ross Collins for the stimulation of preaching upon this theme on 7 March 1993. In the wake of James Bulger's murder, and the spiritual silence into which it cast most of the nation, the responses of everyone in that congregation helped me to recognize the importance of spirituality in the way theology seeks to understand faith.

[24] Though no doubt many would say it, and I certainly do not wish to isolate my own response as in any way significant, Pohier's *God in Fragments* (1985) has had a profound impact upon my own theological reflection, particularly coming to it from my earlier research upon Bultmann's theology. I think my own theology remains more Christocentric and traditional than Pohier's, but I recognize the power of his reflection upon Easter (pp. 202–12) and its importance for contemporary theology.

Gunton 1983, p. 168), the substantive division one has to consider is not between two different states of being – as if such vocabulary could 'explain' the Christ event – but between completeness and utter fragmentation, a dynamic or power achieved solely upon the cross. There is an important sense in which the true meaning of the Sacrament can only be understood by the symbolism not of a communion wafer, but of an entire loaf ripped apart; though it may seem melodramatic, this aspect of the Sacrament reflects most fully the quality of God's love which theology must address to the world. The rhetorical quality of the eucharistic communion, consequently, has a face to show to society – when it understands the full extent of God's sacrifice on the cross.

Mystery, event and rhetoric

I do not know if this is an adequate message to give to the world. I do not know if the parents confronted by the sudden and brutal murder of their child, or the families of people killed in a disaster wrought by governmental negligence, or the victims of evil in any of its manifestations, find any comfort or solace in the conviction that as their loved ones suffer and die, so God is torn apart and miraculously resurrected as One, and so no one suffers and dies alone. I do not even know if I find these words intellectually satisfying. All I know and can testify is that these words reflect what I understand by Jesus' cross, and what I understand to be the revelation and concealment of God's being Trinity.

It would be easy here to follow Hegel and argue that the negation one witnesses in the world must be reduced speculatively to the level of pure concepts, where one more fully understands the processes at work in such events (see Jüngel 1983, p. 66); and it would be as easy to state as categorically as faith allows that the answer to *any* suffering is to be found in the cross, and that such an ontological understanding of Golgotha solves the problem of evil.[25] I do not believe, however, that such a response is even permitted for the Christian. What is required is not an argument, but a witness, an *address*, in which the silencing of creatures is denounced in the Name of One who could not be silenced (see Sölle 1990, p. 132). Everything else – justice, satisfaction, 'penal substitution', sympathy, reconstruction, even redemp-

[25] I think Frances Young's book *Face to Face: A Narrative Essay in the Theology of Suffering* (1990) addresses as well as any the difficulty with such a facile reduction of this monumental problem for Christian faith.

tion – can be provided by secular society and, arguably, should be provided by society before it is provided by Church (which is why Church must protest as loudly as possible when any government fails in its responsibilities). This is not a complex issue; society must tackle these questions for itself.

What then can Church's address provide, and what part can theology play in this procedure? All that Church can provide is a way towards potential, towards identity with God, articulated in the Word of God's identity with humanity in Jesus of Nazareth. It is not so much a vision to pursue as a vision to address to both faith and society; and the task of critical theology is to stand on the borderlands of these two terrains, in the role of mediator. In that process it will speak of mystery, event and rhetoric.

Are these three things always three? Of course not: the confessed truth of Christian faith is that they are one, indeed One, and that being One they speak meaningfully and truthfully of God in Christ, 2000 years ago and yet simultaneously always. One takes them apart, however – methodologically, by speaking of mystery, event and rhetoric as separate stages of theological reflection – because their ultimate truth is that One is apart, and that the cross is the image of God's sacrifice for the sake of humanity. That Christians believe this to be the truth is fundamental to their religion; but that they cannot simply assert it as *the* truth of the world is fundamental to God's fragmentation in the Name of ultimate union. Caught in a cleft stick, rational sceptics will say; the only character of mystery that human beings are able to articulate as event and rhetoric, critical theology must respond. There is room enough for both.

Conclusion: Revelation, Concealment and the Primacy of the Possible

> *... but these are written that you may believe that Jesus is the Christ, the Son of God, and that believing you may have life in his name (John 20:31)*

> And with one foot on the frontier I declare myself incapable of going further. For one step beyond the point where we have halted – and we should move out of the realm of stupidity, which is even theoretically still full of variety, and into the realm of wisdom, territory which is still bleak and in general shunned (Robert Musil, *On Stupidity*).

What is 'critical theology'? At the end of this book I believe I have a straightforward answer to this question, at least theoretically: critical theology is faith seeking understanding, speaking about mystery, event and rhetoric. What this means in practice, however, is another question, to which I want to turn in this general conclusion.

Many theologians today write books which end, somewhat mystifyingly, with things called 'unconcluding unscientific prescripts' (or words to that effect; see Jasper 1993), the intent being to indicate that no text can achieve closure, least of all a book of theology which must be tested within a context where faith seeks understanding as it lives in society. And some theologians today write of their conclusions being 'doxological statements' (see Cunningham 1991, p. 255 – part of an 'Unconcluding Rhetorical Postscript'), something I find equally mystifying as part of a rational argument. Nevertheless, one must say something by way of closing (opening?) remarks, and I want to preface my own last words with a statement of David Ford's, made during his inaugural lecture as Regius Professor of Divinity in Cambridge: 'Public theology is engaged in a vigil that concerns long traditions of testimony and their present participation in the contingencies of our world' (Ford 1992, p. 27). I want to respond briefly to some of the key words in Ford's statement.

First, I hope that all theologians will agree with Ford that any critical theology rests upon 'long traditions', and that they must be interpreted in relation to 'the contingencies of our world': I take it that this is another way of speaking of faith seeking understanding and that, like it or not, the theologian's task is to undertake this activity as a Christian duty.

Second, I hope equally that all theologians will agree with Ford that theology is about public communication, and that this public communication is intimately related to what theology understands as 'testimony' – witness to what Christianity believes is the graceful truth of its religious belief. I hope that everyone now accepts that theology is about social and political responsibility, rather than the domestication of the Christian message, and that such a responsibility requires the theologian to step out of the Academy and into the street, always willing to have her work tested in any arena selected by her audience. And I hope that theologians everywhere now accept that the process of correction and reconsideration is one of the most creative undertakings that any individual or community can undertake, in humility and responsibility.

Third, however, I am not sure that Ford's usage of the word 'vigil' carries sufficient weight or the most appropriate connotations. Part of the problem here may be the lingering romanticism long associated with inaugural professorial lectures in Cambridge, where Ford's *The Long Rumour of Wisdom: Redescribing Theology* (1992) was preceded by Nicholas Lash's *Theology on Dover Beach* (1979), Henry Chadwick's *Frontiers of Theology* (1981) and Donald MacKinnon's *Borderlands of Theology* (1968).[1] The difficulty with 'vigil', after all – as with the imagery of Arnold's poem, now almost dominant in contemporary English theology – is its fundamental passivity, almost as if the theologian has been transformed into a sentry, guarding the perimeter of the empire as the barbarians congregate upon its frontiers. The tide of Christianity may indeed be receding, though its passing is echoed in every corner of the West; but that is no reason to watch and listen inactively as the sun sets.

Beyond the rhetoric (in the pejorative sense) there is here a substantive point. One person's sunset is another's sunrise, and though the 'tide of Christianity' may indeed appear to be receding to the eyes of academic theologians in the West, elsewhere in the world it is still very much in flow. Are liberation theologians in Latin America involved in

[1] I am of course myself somewhat guilty of the same romanticism – witness my location of critical theology upon 'the borderlands of faith and society'. I can only plead consciousness of my own Cambridge background as an excuse for the continuation of this trend.

a 'vigil' concerning tradition and the world? Is Albert Nolan in South Africa participating in such a vigil? Do progressive theologians anywhere allow themselves the luxury of describing their work as a 'vigil'? Or should 'vigil' be replaced by words more indicative of the urgency and application required of the contemporary theologian – words like 'protest', 'witness', 'prophet' and 'testify'? This is not to denigrate Ford's attempt to redescribe theology, but rather to ask: what is the point of simple redescription without reapplication?

Ultimately, this question is concerned with the more complex one of what it is to be a theologian; what it is to be one who speaks of God from within a specific tradition, embracing certain historical circumstances and addressing a particular audience. One of the reasons why I chose to examine the work of seven theologians in Part I, and why I wrestled with the task of interpreting their positions as part of the process of understanding and communicating what it is that I want to say, is that one must set oneself alongside others who have been given, or who have adopted, the office of theologian, in order to appreciate its responsibilities and potential. Of course, in the process one learns a great deal about things like the structure and dynamic of theology, its character, qualities and peculiarities; but one must not lose sight of the fact that one remains *a* theologian amongst theologians, solely one way of looking at problems which ultimately require practical application.

In this sense being a theologian is to participate in an evolutionary development, particularly in the twentieth century, but more generally in the history of the Christian tradition. I attempted to demonstrate this fact throughout Part I, and I would want to say that contemporary theology understands its office and responsibilities better than earlier generations simply because it stands at a later date within this evolutionary development.[2] Simultaneously, however, I sought to recognize a Christian axiom: that revelation is always simultaneously concealment. To understand the office of the theologian, therefore, is to understand that that of which one seeks to speak is not a fact which can be cognized, verified, classified and displayed for acknowledgement and appropriation, but is rather an event which can only be spoken of tangentially – and even then, solely by analogy. If theology is an inexact and applied science, as I have already argued, I think one must

[2] I make this statement cautiously: all I mean is that today's theologians should be under no illusions about the relativity and inadequacy of their position within Church and society. Of course, evolution here is employed in a literal sense, rather than teleologically: the last thing this book wants to suggest is anything akin to a Whig theory of historical/theological development.

also acknowledge that it is an ironic discipline (see Kierkegaard 1989, p. 247). The theologian speaks of that which he or she believes to be revealed – *because* it is concealed in the world and therefore requires address and interpretation (see Geffré 1987, p. 15 and Gilkey 1991, p. 37).

I think this says something very important indeed about the orientation of contemporary theology. The slide from modernism to postmodernism in critical reflection, particularly as it finds theological relevance in the drift from absolutism towards relativism in methodology, reflects I believe a more fundamental awareness of the impossibility of speaking definitively of God's saving action in Jesus Christ. One must speak, therefore, of what one cannot speak – ironically, analogically, acknowledging the limitations of reason and its tools for the task of communication and address confronting faith. Truth determines method, certainly; but method also determines how one understands and expresses truth. In contemporary theology I recognize an awareness – though not often explicit – of this point, and a willingness to speak deferentially of the mystery of God as creatively and diversely as possible.[3]

There is also the danger in contemporary theology, however, that the structure of argument and communication will be abandoned; that, as Milbank (1991, p. 225) states, the end of modernity means the end of the conviction that ultimate truth is discoverable on the basis of absolute reason. The point here – that there is no foundation for methodological heteronomy – is well taken; but the danger, of course, is that zeal for postmodern humility threatens theology's right and autonomy to communicate rationally and intelligibly what it takes to be *the* truth of faith. This is the bottom line: does theology maintain its status as something critical, desiring to communicate as universally as possible a single message, though in a wide variety of different ways and through a wide variety of different media? Or does theology become postcritical, and thereby something which abandons its obligation to address as completely as possible fundamental metaphysical questions? (see Dulles 1992, p. 15).

I hope that my answer is clear and that, if anything, people will understand my *schema* of mystery, event and rhetoric as pointing towards the expansion of the contemporary understanding of reason, rather than its rejection. Reason which acknowledges that it can speak as meaningfully about what is concealed as about what is revealed;

[3] I think this understanding is implicit in the work of, for example, Green 1989, Geffré 1987, Hauerwas 1988 and McFadyen 1990, though there are of course others in other contexts.

which accepts that it speaks analogically and ironically about what it cannot know; which accepts pluralism not as compromise but as the inevitable implication of its most basic qualities – flexibility, applicability, sensitivity, spirituality (yes, reason is spiritual): this ability mediates everything that humanity believes it understands about its own nature and the presence and absence of its ultimate limit, God. Within this most fundamental human quality critical theology, as a peculiarly Christian discourse, reflects and reflects upon what it is to move between the faith professed by individuals and communities, and the wider society and world in which they live.

Finally, therefore, what I want to speak of is the primacy of the possible: of the primacy of that which lies ahead of humanity and, more specifically named, of Church and the Saviour it professes and addresses to everyone. The time has passed, if it ever were, when theology could simply rest upon what it claimed to be the actual – what it claimed as fact, the powerful data of authority and imperialism. Today critical theology acknowledges entirely its own relativism, because Jesus Christ took upon Himself relativism in the incarnation, and because that relativism expresses the most fundamental truth of the Christian image of God. In the last resort, 'mystery, event and rhetoric' are dispensable terms, as limited in their usefulness as any other theological vocabulary. What *is* important, however, is what lies in between them, namely the acknowledgement that if Christianity is in the business of drawing pictures of God in Christ (method), then it must understand the reasons why its own discourse can only be one amongst many (truth). The Holy Spirit of Church, after all, is always 'the Spirit of the interstices', wherein lies all human spirituality.[4]

In this book I have tried to say something about the way in which people live – generally, religiously, spiritually, but primarily as Christians. I have done this, ultimately, because I accept Paul's beautiful words about faith, hope and love, and because I believe that the fullest implications of what Christianity takes to be the revelation and concealment of God's love for humanity must be elaborated as part of the way in which theology seeks, critically, to address its understanding of faith to the world. It is a spiritual duty, therefore, and one without end, to acknowledge one's own inability to speak comprehensively, and yet to obey the demand that at least one make the attempt. This is why critical theology is about truth *and* method.

How to end, then? I can think of no better way than to appeal to the words of Jon Sobrino, writing of the murder and martydom of the

[4] The expression is that of my good friend Nick Coleman, who used it as the title for his Cambridge PhD thesis (1991).

Salvadorean Jesuits in 1989, believing that my own 'portrait of the theologian as a young man' cannot but be improved by listening to the words of a theologian who daily confronts far greater difficulties than I can imagine, in order to address the Christian faith to an audience desperately in need of the gospel. If they are good enough for Christians in El Salvador, they are certainly good enough for me:

> It is not easy to know how to keep on hoping and we must all answer this question in our own way. It seems that everything is against hope, but for me at least, where I see there has been great love, I see hope being born again. This is not a rational conclusion and perhaps not even theological. It is simply true (Sobrino 1990, p. 57).

Amen.

Bibliography

Addinall P. 1991, *Philosophy and Biblical Interpretation: A Study in Nineteenth-Century Conflict*, Cambridge.
Adorno T. W. 1986, *The Jargon of Authenticity*, London [trans. of *Jargon der Eigentlichkeit*, 1964].
Adorno T. W. 1991, *Negative Dialectics*, London [trans. of *Negative Dialektik*, 1966].
Ambler R. 1990, *Global Theology: The Meaning of Faith in the Present World Crisis*, London.
Aristotle 1991, *On Rhetoric: A Theory of Civic Discourse*, Oxford [written 4th century BCE; trans. G. E. Kennedy].
Ashton J. 1991, *Understanding the Fourth Gospel*, Oxford.
Auerbach E. 1968, *Mimesis: The Representation of Reality in Western Literature*, Princeton, New Jersey [trans. of German text, 1946].
Avis P. 1986, *The Methods of Modern Theology: The Dream of Reason*, London and Basingstoke.
Avis P. (ed.) 1988, *The Threshold of Theology*, London and Basingstoke.
Ayres L. 1992, *Imagining Jesus: An Introduction to the Incarnation*, London.
Badham P. (ed.) 1990, *A John Hick Reader*, London and Basingstoke.
Balthasar H. U. von 1972, *The Theology of Karl Barth*, New York.
Balthasar H. U. von 1990a, *Mysterium Paschale*, Edinburgh.
Balthasar H. U. von 1990b, *Theodrama: Theological Dramatic Theory II: Dramatic Personae: Man in God*, San Francisco.
Balthasar H. U. von 1992, *Theodrama: Theological Dramatic Theory III: Dramatis Personae: Persons in Christ*, San Francisco.
Barash J. A. 1988, *Martin Heidegger and the Problem of Historical Meaning*, The Hague.
Barth K. 1957, Church Dogmatics 2/1: *The Doctrine of God*, Edinburgh [Ger. text in *Kirchliche Dogmatik*, 1932–67].
Barth K. 1968, *The Epistle to the Romans*, London [trans. of *Der Römerbrief*, 2/ 1922; i.e. '*Romans* II'].
Barth K. 2/1975, Church Dogmatics 1/1: *The Doctrine of the Word of God*, Edinburgh [Ger. text in *Kirchliche Dogmatik*, 1932–67].
Barth K. 1982a, *Die Christliche Dogmatik im Entwurf. Erster Band: Die Lehre vom Worte Gottes: Prolegomena zur christlichen Dogmatik*, Zurich [1st edn, 1927].
Barth K. 1982b, *The Theology of Schleiermacher: Lectures at Göttingen, Winter Semester of 1923/24*, Edinburgh [trans. of *Die Theologie Schleiermachers: Vorlesung Göttingen*, 1924].
Barth K. 1985, Der Römerbrief, Zurich [reprint of 1st edn, 1919; i.e. 'Romans I'].
Barth K. 1991. *The Göttingen Dogmatics: Instruction in the Christian Religion I*, Edinburgh [trans. of *Unterricht in der Christlichen Religion: Band I*, 1985].

Baum G. 1987, *Theology and Society*, New York.
Beeck F. J. van 1979, *Christ Proclaimed: Christology as Rhetoric*, New York.
Bell R. H. (ed.) 1988, *The Grammar of the Heart: New Essays in Moral Philosophy and Theology*, San Francisco.
Benjamin W. 1968, *Illuminations*, London [trans. of *Illuminationen*, 1961].
Berger P. and Luckmann T. 1967, *The Social Construction of Reality: A Treatise in the Sociology of Knowledge*, London.
Bernstein R. J. 1979, *The Restructuring of Social and Political Theory*, London.
Bernstein R. J. 1983, *Beyond Objectivism and Relativism: Science, Hermeneutics*, and Praxis, Oxford.
Berry P. and Wenick A. (eds) 1992, *Shadows of Spirit: Postmodernism and Religion*, London.
Bethge E. 1970, *Dietrich Bonhoeffer: Theologian, Christian, Contemporary*, London [trans. of German text, 1967].
Beyer O. 1992, *Leibliches Wort: Reformation und Neuzeit im Konflikt*, Tübingen.
Bloch E. 1986, *The Principle of Hope* (3 volumes), Oxford [trans. of *Das Prinzip Hoffnung*, 1949].
Bloom A. 1987, *The Closing of the American Mind: How Higher Education has Failed Democracy and Impoverished the Souls of Today's Students*, London.
Blumenberg H. 2/1985, *The Legitimacy of the Modern Age,* Cambridge, Mass. [1st ed, 1983].
Bochmuehl K. 1988a, *The Unreal God of Modern Theology: Bultmann, Barth, and the Theology of Atheism: A Call to Recovering the Truth of God's Reality*, Colorado Springs.
Bochmuehl K. 1988b, 'Secularization and Secularism: Some Christian
Considerations', in: Noll M. and Wells D.F. (eds) 1988, *Christian Faith and Practice in the Modern World: Theology from an Evangelical Point of View*, Grand Rapids, Michigan.
Boff L. 1980, *Jesus Christ Liberator: A Critical Christology of our Time*, London [trans. of *Jesus Cristo libertador*, 1972].
Boff L. and Boff C. 1987, *Introducing Liberation Theology*, Tunbridge Wells [trans. of *Como fazer teologia da libertacao*, 1986].
Boff L. 1988, *Trinity and Society,* Maryknoll, New York [trans. of *A Trinidade, a sociedade e a libertacao*, 1986].
Bokwa I. 1990 *Christologie als Anfang und Ende der Anthropologie: Über das gegenseitige Verhältnis zwischen Christologie und Anthropologie bei Karl Rahner*, Frankfurt am Main.
Bonhoeffer D. 1962, *Act and Being*, London [trans.].
Bonhoeffer D. 1966, *Christology*, London [based on lectures of 1933; Ger. text in *Gesammelte Schriften*, III, 1960].
Bonhoeffer D. 3/1967, *Letters and Papers from Prison*, London [trans. of *Widerstand und Ergebung*, ed. E. Bethge, 1951].
Bonhoeffer D. 1973, *True Patriotism: Letters, Lectures, and Notes 1939–45*, London [trans.].
Bonsor J. A. 1987, *Rahner, Heidegger, and Truth: Karl Rahner's Notion of Christian Truth: The Influence of Heidegger*, Lanham, Maryland.
Borg M. J. 1987, *Jesus a New Vision: Culture and the Life of Discipleship*, San Francisco.
Bourgeois P. L. 1990, *Traces of Understanding: A Profile of Heidegger's and Ricoeur's Hermeneutics*, Amsterdam.

Brown C. 1985, *Jesus in European Protestant Thought 1778–1860*, Durham, North Carolina.
Brown R. 1979, *The Community of the Beloved Disciple: A Study of the Gospel and Epistles of John*, New York.
Brown R. H. 1987, *Society as Text: Essays on Rhetoric, Reason, and Reality*, Chicago.
Brümmer V. 1992, *Speaking of a Personal God: An Eassy in Philosophical Theology*, Cambridge.
Bruns G. L. 1989, *Heidegger's Estrangements: Language, Truth, and Poetry in the Later Writings*, New Haven.
Buchdahl G. 1981, 'Reduction-Realization: A Key to the Structure of Kant's Thought', in: *Philosophical Topics*, 12(2), pp. 39–98, Denver, Colorado.
Bultmann R. 1958, *Jesus Christ and Mythology*, New York.
Bultmann R. 1971, *The Gospel, of John: A Commentary*, Oxford.
Busch E. 1976, *Karl Barth: His Life from Letters and Autobiographical Texts*, London.
Callinicos A. 1989, *Against Postmodernism: A Marxist Critique*, Cambridge.
Canetti E. 1979, *The Tongue Set Free*, London [trans. of *Die gerettete Zumge*, 1977].
Canetti E. 1989, *The Torch in my Ear*, Lodon, [trans. of *Die Fackel im Ohr*, 1980].
Canetti E. 1990, *The Play of the Eyes*, London [trans. of *Das Augenspiel*, 1985].
Caputo J. D. 1982, *Heidegger and Aquinas*, New Haven.
Caputo J. D. 1987, *Radical Hermeneutics: Repetition, Deconstruction, and the Hermeneutic Project*, Bloomington, Indiana.
Carnley P. 1987, *The Structure of Resurrection Belief*, Oxford.
Casalis G. 1984, *Correct Ideas Don't Fall from the Skies: Elements for an Inductive Theology*, Maryknoll, New York.
Casey E. S. 1979, *Imagining: A Phenomenological Study*, Bloomington, Indiana.
Casey E. S. 1987, *Remembering: A Phenomenological Study*, Bloomington, Indiana.
Cavell S. 1979, *The Claim of Reason: Wittgenstein, Skepticism, Morality and Tragedy*, Oxford.
Celan P. 1980, *Poems*, Manchester.
Chadwick H. 1981, *Frontiers of Theology*, Cambridge.
Chapman M. D. 1992, 'Apologetics and the Religious *a priori*: The Use and Abuse of Kant in German Theology 1900–20', in: *Journal of Theological Studies*, 43(2), pp. 470–510, Oxford.
Cherwitz R. A. and Hilkins J. W. 1986, *Communication and Knowledge: An Investigation into Rhetorical Epistemology*, Columbia, South Carolina.
Chestnut G. F. 1984, *Images of God: An Introduction to Christology*, Minneapolis.
Clayton J. P. (ed.) 1976, *Ernst Troeltsch and the Future of Theology*, Cambridge.
Coakley S. 1988, *Christ without Absolutes: A Study of the Christology of Ernst Troeltsch*, Oxford.
Cobb J. B. 1975, *Christ in a Pluralistic Age*, Philadelphia.
Collins R. 1984, *Models of Theological Reflection*, Lanham, Maryland.
Congar Y. 1983, *I Believe in the Holy Spirit* (3 volumes), London.
Corcoran P. 1979, *Political Language and Rhetoric*, St Lucia, Queensland.
Coreth E. 1968, *Metaphysics*, New York.
Cox H. 1989, *The Silencing of Leonardo Boff: The Vatican and the Future of World Christianity*, London.

Cragg K. 1986, *The Christ and the Faiths: Theology in Cross-Reference*, London.
Crimmann R. P. 1981, *Karl Barths frühe Publikationen und ihre Rezeption*, Bern.
Crossan J. D. 1991, *The Historical Jesus: The Life of a Mediterranean Jewish Peasant*, Edinburgh.
Cullmann O. 3/1962, *Christ and Time*, Lond [trans. of *Christus und die Zeit*, 1946].
Culpepper R. A. 1983, *Anatomy of the Fourth Gospel: A Study in Literary Design*, Philadelphia.
Cunningham D. 1991, *Faithful Persuasion: In Aid of a Rhetoric of Christian Theology*, Notre Dame, Indiana.
Dalferth I. 1988, *Theology and Philosophy*, Oxford.
Dalferth I. 1989, 'Karl Barth's Eschatological Realism', in: Sykes S. W. (ed.) 1989, *Karl Barth: Centenary Essays*, Cambridge.
D'Costa G. (ed.) 1990, *Christian Uniqueness Reconsidered: The Myth of a Pluralistic Theology of Religions*, Maryknoll, New York.
D'Costa G. 1992, 'The End of Systematic Theology', in: *Theology*, 95 (767), pp. 324–34, London.
Deleuze G. 1986–9, *Cinema* (2 volumes), London [trans. of *Cinema*, 1983].
Dewey J. 1958, *Experience and Nature*, New York.
Döbertin W. 1985, *Adolf von Harnack: Theologe, Pädagoge, Wissenschaftspolitiker*, Bern.
Duke J. O. and Streetman R. F. (eds) 1988, *Barth and Schleiermacher: Beyond the Impasse?*, Philadelphia.
Dulles A. 1992, *The Craft of Theology: From Symbol to System*, Dublin.
Eckardt A. L. and Eckardt A. R. 1988, *Long Night's Journey into Day: A Revised Retrospective on the Holocaust*, Detroit, Michigan.
Edmondson R. 1984, *Rhetoric in Sociology*, London.
Elrod J. W. 1981, *Kierkegaard and Christendom*, Princeton, New Jersey.
Ericksen R. P. 1985, *Theologians under Hitler*, 1985.
Erler R. J. and Marquard R. 1986, *A Karl Barth Reader*, Edinburgh.
Ernst C. 1979, *Multiple Echo: Explorations in Theology*, London.
Fackre G. 1978, *The Christian Story: A Narrative Interpretation of Basic Christian Doctrine,* Grand Rapids, Michigan.
Falck C. 1989, *Myth, Truth, Literature: Towards a True Post-Modernism*, Cambridge.
Feil E. 1985, *The Theology of Dietrich Bonhoeffer*, Philadelphia.
Fekete J. (ed.) 1984, *The Structural Allegory: Reconstructive Encounters with the New French Thought*, Manchester.
Fidde P. 1988, *The Creative Suffering of God,* Oxford.
Findlay J. N. 1970, *Ascent to the Absolute: Metaphysical Papers and Lectures*, London.
Fisher S. 1988, *Revelatory Positivism?: Barth's Earliest Theology and the Marburg School*, Oxford.
Ford D. 1981, *Barth and God's Story: Biblical Narrative and the Theological Method of Karl Barth in the Church Dogmatics*, Frankfurt am Main.
Ford D. (ed.) 1989, *The Modern Theologians: An Introduction to Christian Theology in the Twentieth Century* (2 volumes), Oxford.
Ford D. 1992, *The Long Rumour of Wisdom: Redescribing Theology*, Cambridge.
Forrester D. (ed.) 1990, *Theology and Practice*, London.
Forstman J. 1977, *A Romantic Triangle: Schleiermacher and Early German Romanticism*, Missoula, Missouri.

Frei H. 1992, *Types of Christian Theology*, New Haven.
Freyer T. 1982, *Pneumatologie als Strukturprinzip der Dogmatik: Überlegungen im Anschluss an die Lehre von der 'Geisttaufe' bei Karl Barth*, Paderborn.
Fulkerson M. M. 1991, 'Theological Education and the Problem of Identity', in: *Modern Theology*, 7(5), pp. 465–82, Oxford.
Gadamer H.-G. 2/1979, *Truth and Method*, London [trans. of *Wahrheit und Methode*, 2/1965; 1st edn, 1960].
Gadamer H.-G. 1985, *Philosophical Apprenticeships*, Cambridge, Mass. [trans.].
Geffré C. 1987, *The Risk of Interpretation: On Being Faithful to the Christian Tradition in a Non-Christian Age*, New York.
Geffré C. and Jossua J.-P. (eds.) 1992, *The Debate on Modernity* (Concilium 1992/6), London.
Gerhardsson B. 1982, *The Ethos of the Bible*, London.
Gerrish B.A. 1984, *A Prince of the Church: Schleiermacher and the Beginnings of Modern Theology*, London.
Gibellini R. 1987, *The Liberation Theology Debate*, London.
Gilkey L. 1991, *Through the Tempest: Theological Voyages in a Pluralistic Culture*, Minneapolis.
Gill R. 1980, 'From Sociology to Theology', in: Martin D., Mills J.O. and Pickering W. S. F. (eds) 1980, *Sociology and Theology: Alliance and Conflict*, Brighton.
Gillespie M. A. 1984, *Hegel, Heidegger, and the Ground of History*, Chicago.
Girard R. 2/1977, *Violence and the Sacred*, Baltimore [1st edn, 1972].
Gorringe T. 1990, *Discerning Spirit: A Theology of Revelation*, London.
Goulder M. 1991, 'Nicodemus', in: *Scottish Journal of Theology* 44(2), pp. 153–68, Edinburgh.
Green G. 1989, *Imagining God: Theology and the Religious Imagination*, San Francisco.
Grenz S. J. and Olson R. E. 1992, *20th Century Theology: God and the World in a Transitional Age*, Downers, Grove, Illinois.
Griffin D. R., Beardslee W. A. and Holland J. (eds) 1989, *Varieties of Postmodern Theology*, New York.
Guignon C. B. 1983, *Heidegger and the Problem of Knowledge*, Indianapolis.
Gunn G. 1979, *The Interpretation of Otherness: Literature, Religion, and the American Imagination*, New York.
Gunn G. 1987, *The Culture of Criticism and the Criticism of Culture*, New York.
Gunton C. 1983, *Yesterday and Today: A Study of Continuities in Christology*, London.
Gunton C. 1986, 'The Christian Doctrine of God: Opposition and Convergence', in: Linzey A. and Wexler P. J. (eds) 1986, *Heaven and Earth: Essex Essays in Theology and Ethics*, pp. 11–22, Worthing.
Gunton C. 1991, *The Promise of Trinitarian Theology*, Edinburgh.
Gunton C. 1992, 'Universal and Particular in Atonement Theology', in: *Religious Studies*, 28(4), pp. 453–66, Cambridge.
Gutierrez G. 1991, *The God of Life*, London.
Habermas J. (ed.) 1985, *Observations on 'The Spiritual Situation of the Age'*, Cambridge, Mass. [trans. of *Stichworte 'zur geistigen Situation der Zeit'*, 1984].
Habermas J. 1987, *Knowledge and Human Interests*, Cambridge (trans. of *Erkenntius und luteresse*, 1968).
Habermas J. 1991, *Communication and the Evolution of Society*, Cambridge [trans. of essays from various sources, 1974–6].

Hamilton W. and Altizer T. 1968, *Radical Theology and the Death of God*, London.
Hand S. (ed.) 1989, *The Levinas Reader*, Oxford.
Hanson A. T. 1982, *The Image of the Invisible God*, London.
Harnack A. von 1957, *What is Christianity?*, New York [trans. of Das *Wesen des Christentums*, 1900].
Hartt J. N. 1977, *Theological Method and Imagination*, New York.
Harvey A. E. 1982, *Jesus and the Constraints of History*, London.
Hauerwas S. 1981, *A Community of Character: Toward a Constructive Christian Social Ethic*, Notre Dame, Indiana.
Hauerwas S. 1988, *Christian Existence Today: Essays on Church, World, and Living in Between*, Durham, North Carolina.
Haynes S. R. 1991, *Prospects for Post-Holocaust Theology*, Atlanta, Georgia.
Hegel G. W. F. 1977a, *Faith and Knowledge,* Albany, New York [trans. of *Glaube und Weisheit*, 1802].
Hegel G. W. F. 1977b, *Phenomenology of Spirit*, Oxford [trans. of *Phänomenologie des Geistes*, 1807].
Heidegger M. 1972, *On Time and Being*, New York.
Heidegger M. 1976, *Wegmarken*, Frankfurt am Main.
Hick J. (ed.) 1977, *The Myth of God Incarnate*, London.
Hick J. 1989, *An Interpretation of Religion: Human Responses to the Transcendent*, London and Basingstoke.
Hick J. 1993, *The Metaphor of God Incarnate*, London.
Hines M. E. 1989, 'The Praxis of the Kingdom of God: Ministry', in: Schreiter R. J. and Hilkert M. C. (eds) 1989, *The Praxis of Christian Experience: An Introduction to the Theology of Edward Schillebeeckx*, San Francisco.
Honneth A. and Joas H. (eds) 1991, *Communicative Action: Essays on Jürgen Habermas's 'The Theory of Communicative Action'*, Cambridge.
Hood R. E. 1985, *Contemporary Political Orders and Christ: Karl Barth's Christology and Political Praxis*, Allison Park, Pennsylvania.
Houlden L. 1986, *Connections: The Integration of Theology and Faith*, London.
Hull J. M. 1990, *Touching the Rock: An Experience of Blindness*, London.
Hunsinger G. 1991, *How to Read Karl Barth*, Oxford.
Irving J. 1989, *A Prayer for Owen Meany*, London.
Jameson F. 1981, *The Political Unconscious: Narrative as a Socially Symbolic Act*, London.
Jasper D. 1993, *Rhetoric, Power and Community: An Exercise in Reserve*, London and Basingstoke.
Jaspert B. and Bromiley G. (eds) 1982, *Karl Barth/Rudolf Bultmann: Letters 1922–66*, Edinburgh.
Jeanrond W. 1991, *Theological Hermeneutics: Development and Significance*, London and Basingstoke.
Jenkins D. 1990, *Still Living with Questions*, London.
Jenson R. 1989, 'Karl Barth', in: Ford D. (ed.) 1989, *The Modern Theologians: An Introduction to Christian Theology in the Twentieth Century I*, pp. 23–49, Oxford.
Jones G. 1988, 'The Play of a Delicate Shadow: Bultmann and Hesse in the Magic Theatre', in: *Literature and Theology*, 2(1), pp. 96–111, Oxford.
Jones G. 1989, 'Phenomenology and Theology: A Note on Bultmann and Heidegger', in: *Modern Theology*, 5(2), pp. 161–79, Oxford.

Jones G. 1990a, 'Critical Theology and Education', in: *New Blackfriars*, 71 (838), pp. 237–43, Oxford.
Jones G. 1990b, 'Kritische Theologie: Eine Antworf auf Josef Wohlmuths Beitrag: Zur Bedeutung der 'Geschichtsthesen' Walter Benjamins für die christliche Eschatologie', in: *Evangelische Theologie*, 1(90), pp. 20–26, Munich.
Jones G. 1991, *Bultmann: Towards a Critical Theology*, Cambridge.
Jones G. 1992, 'God's Passionate Embrace: Notes on Sexuality and Theological Ethics', in: *The Journal of Theological Ethics*, 5(2), pp. 32–45, Edinburgh.
Jones L. J. 1988, *German Liberalism and the Dissolution of the Weimar Party System 1918–1933*, Chapel Hill, North Carolina.
Jossua J.-P, 'Changes in Theology and its Future', in: Jossua J.-P. and Metz J. B. 1979, *Doing Theology in New Places*, New York.
Jossua J.-P. 1985, The *Condition of the Witness*, London [trans. of *La Condition du témoin*, 1984].
Jüngel E. 1983, *God as the Mystery of the World: On the Foundation of the Theology of the Crucified One in the Dispute between Theism and Atheism*, Edinburgh [trans. of *Gott als Geheimnis der Welt*, 1977].
Junker M. 1990, *Das Urbild des Gottesbewusstseins: Zur Entwicklung der Religionstheorie und Christologie Schleiermachers von der ersten zur zweiten Aufläge der Glaubenslehre*, Berlin.
Kähler M. 1964, *The So-called Historical Jesus and the Historic, Biblical Christ*, Philadelphia.
Kant I. 1963, 'The End of All Things', in: *On History*, ed. L. W. Beck, New York [trans. of *Das Ende aller Dinge*, 1794].
Käsemann E. 1964, 'The Problem of the Historical Jesus', *Essays on New Testament Themes*, pp. 15–47, London.
Kasper W. 1976, *Jesus the Christ*, London.
Kasper W. 1984, *The God of Jesus Christ*, London.
Kasper W. 1989, *Theology and Church*, London.
Kaufman G. 1981, *The Theological Imagination: Constructing the Concept of God*, Philadelphia.
Kee A. (ed.) 1978, *The Scope of Political Theology*, London.
Kehl M. and Loser W. (eds) 1982, *The von Balthasar Reader*, Edinburgh.
Kerr F. 1979, review of Nicholas Lash's *Doing Theology on Dover Beach*, in: *New Blackfriars*, 60 (708), p. 237, Oxford.
Kerr F. 1986, *Theology after Wittgenstein*, Oxford.
Kierkegaard S. 1985, *Philosophical Fragments/Johannes Climacus*, Princeton, New Jersey [trans. of *Philosophiske Smuler*, 1844].
Kierkegaard S. 1987, *Either/Or*, Princeton, New Jersey [trans. of *Enten-Eller*, 1843].
Kierkegaard S. 1989, *The Concept of Irony*, Princeton, New Jersey [trans. of *Om begrebet ironi*, 1841].
Kinneavy J. L. 1987, *Greek Rhetorical Origins of Christian Faith: An Inquiry*, Oxford.
Kjargaard M. S. 1986, *Metaphor and Parable*, Leiden.
Kooi C. van der 1987, *Anfangliche Theologie: Der Denkweg des jungen Karl Barth (1909 bis 1927)*, Munich.
Küng H. 1964, *Justification: The Doctrine of Karl Barth and a Catholic Reflection*, London [trans. of *Rechtfertigung: Die Lehre Karl Barths und eine Katholische Besinnung*, 1957].
Küng H. 1987, *The Incarnation of God: An Introduction to Hegel's Theological*

Thought as Prolegomena to a Future Christology, Edinburgh [trans.].
Küng H. 1993, *Credo: The Apostles' Creed Explained for Today*, London [trans.].
Kuschel K.-J. 1992, *Born before all Time?: The Dispute over Christ's Origin*, London [trans. of *Geboren vor aller Zeit?: Der Streit um Christs Ursprung*, 1990].
LaCugna C. M. 1991, *God for Us: The Trinity and Christian Life*, San Francisco.
Lakeland P. 1990, *Theology and Critical Theory: The Discourse of the Church*, Nashville, Tennessee.
Lash N. 1979, *Theology on Dover Beach*, London.
Lash N. 1980, 'Up and Down in Christology', in: Sykes S. W. and Holme D. (eds) 1980, *New Studies in Theology I*, pp. 31–46, London.
Lash N. 1986, 'Criticism or Construction?: The Task of the Theologian', in: Lash N. 1986, *Theology on the Way to Emmaus*, pp. 3–17, London.
Lash N. 1988, *Easter in Ordinary: Reflections on Human Experience and the Knowledge of God*, London.
Leeuwen T. M. van 1981, *The Surplus of Meaning: Ontology and Eschatology in the Philosophy of Paul Ricoeur*, Amsterdam.
Leith D. and Myerson G. 1989, *The Power of Address: Exploration in Rhetoric*, London.
Levinas E. 1969, *Totality and Infinity*, Pittsburgh.
Liechty D. 1990, *Theology in Postliberal Perspective*, London.
Lindbeck G. 1984, *The Nature of Doctrine: Religion and Theology in a Postliberal Age*, London.
Linzey A. and Wexler P. J. (eds) 1986, *Heaven and Earth: Essex Essays in Theology and Ethics*, Worthing.
Lombard L. B. 1986, *Events: A Metaphysical Study*, London.
Louth A. 1983, *Discerning the Mystery: An Essay on the Nature of Theology*, Oxford.
Lyotard J.-F. 1984, *The Postmodern Condition: A Report on Knowledge*, Manchester.
Mackey J. 1987, *Modern Theology: A Sense of Direction*, Oxford.
MacKinnon D. 1968, *Borderlands of Theology and Other Essays*, London.
MacKinnon D. 1987, 'The Relation of the Doctrines of the Incarnation and the Trinity', in: *Themes in Theology: The Three-Fold Cord: Essays in Philosophy, Politics, and Theology*, Edinburgh.
Macquarrie J. 1986, *Theology, Church, and Ministry*, London.
Mailloux S. 1989, *Rhetorical Power*, Ithaca.
Malantschuk G. 1971, *Kierkegaard's Thought*, Princeton, New Jersey.
Marion J.-L. 1991, *God without Being*, Chicago.
Marquardt F.-W., 3/1985, *Theologie und Sozialismus: Das Beispiel Karl Barths*, Munich (1st ed, 1972)
Marsh C. 1992a, 'Human Community and Divine Presence: Dietrich Bonhoeffer'sTheological Critique of Hegel', in: *Scottish Journal of Theology*, 45(4), pp. 427–48, Edinburgh.
Marsh C. 1992b, 'Bonhoeffer on Heidegger and Togetherness', in: *Modern Theology*, 8(3), pp. 263–83, Oxford.
Marshall B. 1987, *Christology in Conflict: The Identity of a Saviour in Rahner and Barth*, Oxford.
Marshall B. D. (ed) 1990, *Theology and Dialogue: Essays in Conversation with George Lindbeck*, Notre Dame, Indiana.

Martin D., Mills J. O. and Pickering W. S. F. (eds) 1980, *Sociology and Theology: Alliance and Conflict*, Brighton.
McFadyen A. 1990, *The Call to Personhood*, Cambridge.
McFague S. 1983, *Metaphorical Theology: Models of God in Religious Language*, London.
McGrath A. 1986, *The Making of Modern German Christology: From the Enlightenment to Pannenberg*, Oxford.
McKim D. (ed.) 1986, *How Karl Barth Changed my Mind,* Grand Rapids, Michigan.
Meckenstock G. 1988, *Deterministische Ethik und kritische Theologie: Die Auseinandersetzung des frühen Schleiermacher mit Kant und Spinoza 1789–1794*, Berlin.
Meisel P. 1987, *The Myth of the Modern: A Study in British Literature and Criticism after 1850*, New Haven.
Messori V. 1985, *The Ratzinger Report: An Exclusive Interview on the State of the Church*, Leominister.
Metz J. B. 1980, *Faith in History and Society: Toward a Practical Fundamental Theology*, London [trans. of *Glaube in Geschichte und Gesellschaft*, 1977].
Metz J. B. 1984, 'Facing the Jews: Christian Theology after Auschwitz', in: Tracy D. and Schüssler-Fiorenza E. (eds) 1984, *The Holocaust as Interruption (Concilium)*, pp. 26–33, Edinburgh.
Milbank J. 1986, 'The Second Difference: For a Trinitarianism without Reserve', in: *Modern Theology*, 2(3), pp. 213–34, Oxford.
Milbank J. 1990, *Theology and Social Theory*, Oxford.
Milbank J. 1991, 'Postmodern Critical Augustinianism: A Short Summa in Forty Two Responses to Unasked Questions', in: *Modern Theology*, 7(3), pp. 225–37, Oxford.
Milbank J. 1992, 'The End of Enlightenment: Post-Modern or Post-Secular?', in: Geffré C. and Jossua J.-P. (eds) 1992, *The Debate on Modernity (Concilium 1992/6)*, pp. 39–48, London.
Moltmann J. 1967, *Theology of Hope: On the Ground and the Implications of a Christian Eschatology*, London [trans. of *Theologie der Hoffnung*, 1965].
Moltmann J. 1974, *The Crucified God: The Cross of Christ as the Foundation and Criticism of Christian Theology*, London [trans. of *Der gekreuzigte Gott*, 1973].
Moltmann J. 1977, *The Church in the Power of the Spirit: A Contribution to Messianic Ecclesiology*, London [trans. of *Kirche in der Kraft des Geistes*, 1975].
Moltmann J. 1980, *Experiences of God*, London [trans. of two essays, '*Warum ich Christ bin*' and '*Gotteserfahrungen*', 1979].
Moltmann J. 1981, *The Trinity* and *the Kingdom of God: The Doctrine of God*, London [trans. of *Trinität und Reich Gottes*, 1980].
Moltmann J. 1983, *The Power of the Powerless*, London [trans. of *Ohne Macht machtig*].
Moltmann J. 1984, *On Human Dignity: Political Theology and Ethics*, London [trans.].
Moltmann J. 1985, *God in Creation: An Ecological Doctrine of Creation*, London [trans. of *Gott in der Schöpfung*, 1985].
Moltmann J. 1988, *Theology Today: Two Contributions towards Making Theology Present*, London [trans. of *Was ist heute Theologie*, 1987].
Moltmann J. 1989, *Creating a Just Future: The Politics of Peace and the Ethics of*

Creation in a Threatened World, London [trans. of *Gerechtigkeit schafft Zukunft*, 1988].
Moltmann, J. 1990, *The Way of Jesus Christ: Christology in Messianic Dimensions*, London [trans. *Der Weg Jesu Christi*, 1989].
Moltmann J. 1992, *The Spirit of Life: A Universal Affirmation*, London [trans. of *Der Geist des Lebens*, 1991].
Morgan R. 1976, 'Ernst Troeltsch and the Dialectical Theology', in: J. P. Clayton (ed.) 1976, *Ernst Troeltsch and the Future of Theology*, Cambridge.
Morris C. 1979, *Get Through till Nightfall*, London.
Mulder J. M. (ed.) 1979, *Our Life in God's Light: Essays by Hugh T. Kerr*, Philadelphia.
Mulhall S. 1990, *On Being in the World: Wittgenstein and Heidegger on Seeing Aspects*, London.
Muller G. L. 1979, *Bonhoeffers Theologie der Sakramente*, Frankfurt am Main.
Muller G. L. 1980, *Für Andere Da: Christus-Kirche-Gott in Bonhoeffers Sicht der mundig gewordenen Welt*, Paderborn.
Myers C. 1988, *Binding the Strong Man: A Political Reading of Mark's Story of Jesus*, Maryknoll, New York.
Nash W. 1989, *Rhetoric: The Wit of Persuasion*, Oxford.
Nehamas A. 1985, *Nietzsche: Life as Literature*, Cambridge, Mass.
Newlands G. 1980, *Theology of the Love of God*, London.
Nolan A. 1988, *God in South Africa: The Challenge of the Gospel*, London.
Noll M. and Wells D. F. 1988, *Christian Faith and Practice in the Modern World: Theology from an Evangelical Point of View*, Grand Rapids, Michigan.
Nolte J. 1971, *Dogma in Geschichte: Versuch einer Kritik des Dogmatismus in der Glaubensdarstellung*, Freiburg.
Osborn R. T. 1992, 'From Theology to Religion', in: *Modern Theology* 8 (1), pp. 75–88, Oxford.
Page R. 1985, *Ambiguity and the Presence of God*, London.
Painter J. 1991, *The Quest for the Messiah: The History, Literature and Theology of the Johannine Community*, Edinburgh.
Pannenberg W. 1968, *Jesus God and Man*, London [trans.].
Pannenberg W. 1977, *Faith and Reality*, London [trans.].
Pannenberg W. 1985, *Anthropology in Theological Perspective*, London [trans.].
Pannenberg W. 1991, *Systematic Theology I*, Edinburgh [trans. of *Systematische Theologie Band I*, 1988].
Peck J. (ed.) 1988, *The Chomsky Reader*, London.
Pelikan J. 1985, *Jesus through the Centuries: His Place in the History of Culture*, New Haven.
Peukert H. 1992, 'The Philosophical Critique of Modernity', in: Geffré C. and Jossua J.-P. (eds) 1992, *The Debate on Modernity* (*Concilium 1992/6*), pp. 17–26, London.
Phan P. C. 1988, *Eternity in Time: A Study in Karl Rahner's Eschatology*, Cranbury, New York.
Philips D. Z. 1988, *Faith after Foundationalism*, London.
Phillips D. Z. 1991, *From Fantasy to Faith: The Philosophy of Religion and Twentieth Century Literature*, London and Basingstoke.
Pirsig R. M. 1974, *Zen and the Art of Motorcycle Maintenance*, London.
Placher W. C. 1989, *Unapologetic Theology: A Christian Voice in a Pluralistic Conversation*, Louisville, Kentucky.

Plato 1971, *Gorgias*, London [written 4th century BCE; rev. edn, W. Hamilton].
Podlewski R. 1982, *Rhetorik als pragmatisches System*, Hildesheim.
Pöggeler O 1978, 'Being as Appropriation [Ereignis]', in: Murray M. (ed.) 1978, *Heidegger and Modern Philosophy*, pp. 84–115, New Haven.
Pöggeler O. 1987, *Martin Heidegger's Path of Thinking*, Atlantic Highlands, New Jersey.
Pohier J. 1985, *God – In Fragments*, London [trans. of *Dieu fractures*, 1985].
Polanyi M. 1973, *Personal Knowledge: Towards a Post-Critical Philosophy*, London [1st ed, 1958].
Pugh J. C. 1990, *The Anselmic Shift: Christology and Method in Karl Barth's Theology*, New York.
Rahner K. 1961, 'Current Problems in Christology', *Theological Investigations*, i, pp. 149–200, London [Ger. text in *Schriften zur Theologie*, i, 1954].
Rahner K. 1963, *Hörer des Wortes: Zur Grundlegung einer Religionsphilosophie*, Munich.
Rahner K. 1964, 'Nature and Grace', in: *Nature and Grace: Dilemmas in the Modern Church*, pp. 114–149, New York [trans.]
Rahner K. 1966a, 'On the Theology of the Incarnation', in: *Theological Investigations*, iv, pp. 105–20, London [Ger. text in *Schriften zur Theologie*, iv, 1961].
Rahner K. 1966b, 'Dogmatic Questions on Easter', in: *Theological Investigations* iv, pp. 121–33, London [Ger. text in *Schriften zur Theologie*, iv, 1961].
Rahner K. 1966c, 'Remarks on the Dogmatic Treatise "De Trinitate"', in: *Theological Investigations*, iv, pp. 77–102, London [Ger. text in *Schriften zur Theologie*, iv, 1961].
Rahner K. 1966d, 'The Hermeneutics of Eschatological Assertions', in: *Theological Investigations*, iv, 323–46, London [Ger. text in *Schriften zur Theologie*, iv, 1961].
Rahner K. 1966e, *Christian in the Market Place*, London [trans.]
Rahner K. 1966f, 'The Concept of Mystery in Catholic Theology', in: *Theological Investigations*, iv, pp. 36–73, London [Ger. text in *Schriften zur Theologie*, iv, 1961].
Rahner K. 1967, 'The Eternal Significance of the Humanity of Jesus for our Relationship with God', in: *Theological Investigations*, iii, pp. 35–46, London [Ger. text in *Schriften zur Theologie*, iii, 1956].
Rahner K. 1968, *Spirit in the World*, Lond [trans. of *Geist in Welt*, 1957].
Rahner K. 1972, 'One Mediator and Many Mediations', in: *Theological Investigations*, ix, pp. 169–84, London [Ger. text in *Schriften zur Theologie*, viii, 1968].
Rahner K, 1974, 'The Position of Christology in the Church between Exegesis and Dogmatics', in: *Theological Investigations*, xi, pp. 185–214, London [Ger. text in *Schriften zur Theologie*, ix, 1970].
Rahner K. 1979, 'Anonymous and Explict Faith', in: *Theological Investigations*, xvi, pp. 52–9, London [Ger. text in *Schriften zur Theologie*, xii, 1975].
Rahner K. and Thüsing W. 1980, *A New Christology*, London [trans. of *Christologie: systematisch und exegetisch*, 1972].
Rahner K. 1983, 'The Death of Jesus and the Closure of Revelation', in: *Theological Investigations*, xviii, pp. 132–42, London [Ger. text in *Schriften zur Theologie*, xiii, 1980].
Rahner K. 1986, *Politische Dimensionen des Christentums: Ausgewahlte Texte zur Fragen der Zeit*, Munich.

Ratzinger J. 1988, Eschatology: *Death and Eternal Life*, Washington DC. [trans. of *Eschatologie: Tod und ewiges Leben*, 1977].

Ray S. A. 1987, *The Modern Soul: Michel Foucault and the Theological Discourse of Gordon Kaufman and David Tracy*, Philadelphia.

Reardon B. M. G. 1988, *Kant as Philosophical Theologian*, London and Basingstoke.

Reiner A. J. 1989, *The Emanuel Hirsch and Paul Tillich Debate: A Study in the Political Ramifications of Theology*, Lampeter.

Ricoeur P. 1974, *The Conflict of Interprétations: Essays in Hermeneutics*, Evanston, Illinois [trans. of *Le Conflict des interprétations*, 1969].

Ricoeur P. 1976, *Interpretation Theory: Discourse and the Surplus of Meaning*, Forth Worth [trans.].

Ricoeur P. 1984–8, *Time and Narrative* (3 volumes), Chicago, [trans. of *Temps et récit*, 1983–5].

Ringer F. K. 1969, *The Decline of the German Mandarins: The German Academic Community 1890–1933*, Cambridge, Mass.

Ritschl D. 1986, *The Logic of Theology*, London [trans. of *Zur Logik der Theologie*, 1984].

Roberts J. 1982, *Walter Benjamin*, London and Basingstoke.

Roberts J. 1988, *German Philosophy: An Introduction*, Cambridge.

Roberts R. 1991, *A Theology on its Way?: Essays on Karl Barth*, Edinburgh.

Root R. L. 1987, *The Rhetorics of Popular Culture: Advertising, Advocacy, and Entertainment*, New York.

Rorty R. 1982, *Consequences of Pragmatism (Essays 1972–80)*, Brighton.

Rorty R. 1991, *Essays on Heidegger and Others: Philosophical Papers II*, Cambridge.

Rosato P. J. 1981, *The Spirit as Lord: The Pneumatology of Karl Barth*, Edinburgh.

Rose G. 1992, *The Broken Middle: Out of our Ancient Society*, Oxford.

Ross G. R. 1989, *Common Sense Christianity,* Cortland, New York.

Rowland C. C. 1982, *The Open Heaven: A Study of Apocalyptic in Judaism and Early Christianity*, London.

Rumscheidt M. 1972, *Revelation and Theology: An Analysis of the Barth/Harnack Correspondence of 1923*, London.

Rumscheidt M. 1989, *Adolf von Harnack: Liberal Theology at its Height*, London.

Rupp G. 1974, *Christologies and Cultures: Towards a Typology of Religious Worldviews*, The Hague.

Rupp G. 1977, *Culture-Protestantism: German Liberal Theology at the Turn of the Twentieth Century,* Missoula, Montana.

Sallis J. 1990, *Echoes: After Heidegger,* Bloomington, Indiana.

Sauter G. 1965, *Zukunft und Verheissung: Das Problem der Zukunft in der gegenwärtigen theologischen und philosophischen Diskussion*, Zurich.

Sauter G. 1972, *Erwartung und Erfahrung: Predigten, Vortrage, und Aufsatze*, Munich.

Scharlemann R. P. (ed.) 1985, *Naming God*, New York.

Schillebeeckx E. 1979, *Jesus: An Experiment in Christology*, London [trans. of *Jezus: Het Verhaal van een levende*, 1974].

Schillebeeckx E. 1980, *Christ: The Christian Experience in the Modern World*, London [trans. of *Gerechtigheid en liefde*, 1977].

Schillebeeckx E. 1983, *God among Us: The Gospel Proclaimed*, London [trans. of *Evangelie verhalen*, 1982].

Schillebeeckx E. 1987, *Jesus in our Western Culture: Mysticism, Ethics, and Politics*, London [trans. of *Als politek niet alles is: Jesus in onze westerne cultuur*, 1986].

Schillebeeckx E. 1989, *For the Sake of the Gospel*, London [trans. of *Om het behoud van het evangelie*]

Schillebeeckx E. 1990, *Church: the Human Story of God*, London, [trans. of *Mensen als verhaal van God*]

Schindler H. 1974, *Barth und Overbeck*, Darmstadt.

Schleiermacher F. D. E. 1928, *The Christian Faith, Edinburgh* [trans. of *Die Christliche Glaube*, 2/1830].

Schleiermacher F. D. E. 1988, *On Religion: Speeches to its Cultured Despisers*, Cambridge [trans. of *Über die Religion*, 1799].

Schleiermacher F. D. E. 1990, *Brief Outline of Theology as a Field of Study*, Lampeter.

Scholtz G. 1984, *Die Philosophie Schleiermachers*, Darmstadt.

Schreiter R. J. and Hilkert M. C. (eds) 1989, *The Praxis of Christian Experience: An Introduction to the Theology of Edward Schillebeeckx*, San Francisco.

Schweiker W. 1989, 'From Cultural Synthesis to Communicative Action: The Kingdom of God and Ethical Theology', in: *Modern Theology*, 5(4), pp. 367–87, Oxford.

Schweiker W. 1990, *Mimetic Reflections: A Study in Hermeneutics, Theology, and Ethics*, New York.

Schweitzer A. 1954, *The Quest of the Historical Jesus*, London [trans. of *Von Reimarus zu Wrede*, 1906].

Schwerdtfeger N. 1982, *Gnade und Welt: Zum Grundgefuge von Karl Rahners Theorie der 'anonymen Christen'*, Freiburg.

Scott N. A. 1978, *Mirrors of Man in Existentialism*, New York.

Segal A. F. 1977, *Two Powers in Heaven*, Leiden.

Segovia F. F. 1991, *The Farewell of the Word: The Johannine Call to Abide*, Minneapolis.

Segundo J. L. 1987, *Theology and the Church: A Response to Cardinal Ratzinger and a Warning to the Whole Church*, San Francisco.

Sharratt B. 1982, *Reading Relations: Structures of Literary Production: A Dialectical Text/Book*, Brighton.

Sheehan T. 1987, *Karl Rahner: The Philosophical Foundations*, Athens, Ohio.

Siebert R. 1985, *The Critical Theory of Religion: The Frankfurt School: From Universal Pragmatic to Political Theology*, Berlin.

Siegele-Wenschkewitz L. 1984, 'The Contribution of Church History to a Post-Holocaust Theology: Christian Anti-Judaism as the Root of Anti-Semitism', in: Tracy D. and Schüssler-Fiorenza E. (eds) 1984, *The Holocaust as Interruption* (*Concilium*), pp. 60–4, Edinburgh.

Smart J. D. 1967, *The Divided Mind of Modern Theology: Karl Barth and Rudolf Bultmann 1908–33*, Philadelphia.

Sobrino J. 1978, *Christology at the Crossroads: A Latin American Approach*, London [trans. of *Cristologia desde América latina*, 1976].

Sobrino J. 1985, *The True Church and the Poor*, London [trans. of *Resurrección de la verdadera iglesia*, 1983].

Sobrino J. 1987, *Jesus in Latin America*, Maryknoll, New York [trans. of *Jésus en*

América latina, 1982].
Sobrino J. 1988, *Spirituality of Liberation: Toward Political Holiness*, Maryknoll, New York.
Sobrino J. 1990, *Companions of Jesus: The Murder and Martyrdom of the Salvadorean Jesuits*, London [trans. of *Companeros de Jésus*].
Sölle D. 1978, *Sympathie: Theologisch-politische Traktate*, Stuttgart.
Sölle D. 1985, 'Thou Shalt Have No Other Jeans Before Me', in: Habermas J. (ed.) 1985, *Observations on 'The Spiritual Situation of the Age,'*, pp. 157–68, Cambridge, Mass.
Sölle D. 1990, *Thinking about God: An Introduction to Theology*, London.
Soskice J. M. 1985, *Metaphor and Religious Language*, Oxford.
Steiner G. 1989, *Real Presences: Is There Anything in What We Say?*, London.
Stroup G. 1981, *The Promise of Narrative Theology: Recovering the Gospel in the Church*, Atlanta, Georgia.
Stumme J. R. 1978, *Socialism in Theological Perspective: A Study of Paul Tillich 1918–33*, Missoula, Montana.
Sutphin S. 1987, *Options in Contemporary Theology*, Lanham, Maryland [rev. edn].
Swinburne R. 1991, *The Existence of God*, Oxford [1st edn, 1979].
Sykes S. W. 1979, 'Barth on the Centre of Theology', in: Sykes S. W. (ed.) 1979, Karl Barth: *Studies in his Theological Method*, pp. 17–54, Oxford.
Sykes S. W. and Holme D. (eds) 1980, *New Studies in Theology I*, London.
Sykes S. W. 1984, *The Identity of Christianity: Theologians and the Essence of Christianity from Schleiermacher to Barth*, London.
Szondi P. 1986, *On Textual Understanding and Other Essays*, Manchester.
Tanner K. 1993, 'Respect for Other Religions: A Christian Antidote to Colonialist Discourse', in: *Modern Theology*, 9(1), pp. 1–18, Oxford.
Taylor M. C. 1982, *Deconstructing Theology*, New York.
Taylor M. C. 1987, *Erring: A Post-Modern Atheology*, Chicago.
Thatcher A. 1990, *Truly a Person, Truly God: A Post-Mythical View of Jesus*, London.
Theunissen M. 1984, *The Other: Studies in the Social Ontology of Husserl, Heidegger, Sartr, and Buber*, Cambridge, Mass. [trans. of *Der Andere: Studien zur Sozialontologie der Gegenwart*, 2/1977].
Thiselton A. C. 1980, *The Two Horizons*, Exeter.
Thiselton A. C. 1992, *New Horizons in Hermeneutics*, London.
Thompson J. B. 1981, *Critical Hermeneutics: A Study in the Thought of Paul Ricoeur and Jürgen Habermas*, Cambridge.
Thornhill J. 1992, *Christian Mystery in the Secular Age: The Foundation and Task of Theology*, Westminster, Maryland.
Tracy D. 1975, *Blessed Rage for Order: The New Pluralism in Theology*, New York.
Tracy D., Küng H. and Metz J. B. (eds.) 1978, *Toward Vatican III: The Work that Needs to be Done*, New York.
Tracy D. 1981, *The Analogical Imagination: Christian Theology and the Culture of Pluralism*, London.
Tracy D. and Cobb J. 1983, *Talking about God: Doing Theology in the Context of Modern Pluralism*, New York.
Tracy D. and Schüssler-Fiorenza E. (eds) 1984, *The Holocaust as Interruption* (*Concilium*), Edinburgh.

Tracy D. and Grant R. M. 1984, *A Short History of the Interpretation of the Bible*, London.
Tracy D. 1987, *Plurality and Ambiguity: Hermeneutics, Religion, Hope*, London.
Tracy D. and Küng H. (eds) 1989, *Paradigm Change in Theology: A Symposium for the Future*, Edinburgh.
Tracy D. 1990, *Dialogue with the Other: the Interreligious Dialogue*, Louvain.
Troeltsch E. 1991, *Religion in History*, Edinburgh.
Valdes M. 1991, *A Ricoeur Reader: Reflection and Imagination*, Hemel Hempstead.
Valevicius A. 1988, *From the Other to the Totally Other: The Religious Philosophy of Emmanuel Levinas*, New York.
Vanhoozer K. 1990, *Biblical Narrative in the Philosophy of Paul Ricoeur: A Study in Hermenetics and Theology*, Cambridge.
Velkley R. L. 1989, *Freedom and the End of Reason: On the Moral Foundation of Kant's Critical Philosophy*, Chicago.
Veyne P. 1984, *Writing History: Essay on Epistemology*, Middleton, Connecticut [trans. of *Comment on écrit histoire*, 1971].
Vidales R. 1980, 'Methodological Issues in Liberation Theology', in: Gibellini R. (ed.) 1980, *Frontiers of Theology in Latin America*, pp. 34–57, London.
Wainwright G. 1988, 'Christian Doctrine/Systematic Theology', in: *The Threshold of Theology*, ed. Avis P., London and Basingstoke.
Walker J. 1985, *Kierkegaard: The Descent into God*, Kingston and Montreal.
Ward G. 1992a, 'John Milbank's *Divine Commedia*', in: *New Blackfriars*, 73 (861), pp. 311–8, Oxford.
Ward G. 1992b, 'Why is Derrida Important for Theology?', in: *Theology*, 95 (766), pp. 263–70, London.
Ward K. 1991, *A Vision to Pursue: Beyond the Crisis in Christianity*, London.
Warner M. (ed.) 1990, *The Bible as Rhetoric: Studies in Biblical Persuasion and Credibility*, London.
Webb S. H. 1991, *Re-figuring Theology: The Rhetoric of Karl Barth*, New York.
Wenz G. 1979, *Subjekt und Sein: Die Entwicklung der Theologie Paul Tillichs*, Munich.
Wessels A. 1990, *Images of Jesus: How Jesus is Perceived and Portrayed in Non-European Cultures*, London.
White E. E. (ed.) 1980, *Rhetoric in Transition: Studies in the Nature and Use of Rhetoric*, University Park, Maryland.
White T. H. 1958, *The Once and Future King*, London.
Whiteside K. H. 1988, *Merleau-Ponty and the Foundation of an Existential Politics*, Princeton, New Jersey.
Wiles M. 1982, *Faith and the Mystery of God*, London.
Wiles M. 1992, *Christian Theology and Inter-religious Dialogue*, London.
Williams R. 1979, 'Barth on the Triune God', in: Sykes S. W. (ed.) 1979, *Karl Barth: Studies in his Theological Method*, pp. 147–93, Oxford.
Williams R. 1986a, 'Balthasar and Rahner', in: Riches J. (ed.) 1986, *The Analogy of Beauty*, Edinburgh.
Williams R. 1986b, 'Trinity and Revelation', in: *Modern Theology*, 2(3), pp. 197–212, Oxford.
Williams R. 1988, 'The Suspicion of Suspicion: Wittgenstein and Bonhoeffer', in: Bell H. (ed.) 1988, *The Grammar of the Heart: New Essays in Moral Philospby and Theology*, San Francisco.

Williams R. 1989a, 'The Incarnation as the Basis of Dogma', in: Morgan R. (ed.) 1989, *The Religion of the Incarnation: Anglican Essays in Commemoration of Lux Mundi*, pp. 85–98, Bristol.
Williams R. 1989b, 'Ressurection and Peace', in: *Theology*, 92 (750), pp. 481–90, London.
Williams R. 2/1990, *The Wound of Knowledge: Christian Spirituality from the New Testament to St. John of the Cross*, London [1st edn, 1979].
Williams R. 1991a, 'Theological Integrity', in: *New Blackfriars*, 72 (847), pp. 140–51, Oxford.
Williams R. 1991b, 'The Literal Sense of Scripture', in: *Modern Theology*, 7 (2), pp. 121–34, Oxford.
Winzeler P. 1982, *Widerstehende Theologie: Karl Barth 1920–35*, Stuttgart.
Wisnefske N. 1990, *Our Natural Knowledge of God: A Prospect for Natural Theology after Kant and Barth*, New York.
Wittgenstein L. 3/1967, *Philosophical Investigations*, Oxford [English – German parallel text, 1953].
Wohlmuth J. 1990a, 'Zur Bedeutung der 'Geschichtsthesen' Walter Benjamins für die christliche Eschatologie', iu: *Evangelische Theologie*, 1(90), pp. 2–20, Munich.
Wohlmuth J. (ed.) 1990b, *Katholische Theologie Heute: Eine Einführung*, Würzburg.
Wolff K. H. 1983, *Beyond the Sociology of Knowledge: An Introduction and a Development*, Lanham, Maryland.
Wood R. C. 1988, *The Comedy of Redemption: Christian Faith and Comic Vision in Four American Novelists*, Notre Dame, Indiana.
Young F. 1990a, *The Art of Performance: Towards a Theology of Holy Scripture*, London.
Young F. 1990b, *Face to Face: A Narrative Essay in the Theology of Suffering*, Edinburgh,
Young F. 1991, *The Making of the Creeds*, London.
Yovel Y. 1980, *Kant and the Philosophy of History*, Princeton, New Jersey.
Zahn-Harnack A. 1951, *Adolf von Harnack*, Berlin.
Zizioulas J. D. 1985, *Being as Communion: Studies in Personhood and Church*, New York.

Index